GOLDA:
The Uncrowned Queen of Israel

GOLDA:
The Uncrowned Queen of Israel

A Pictorial Biography

by
ROBERT SLATER
author of RABIN OF ISRAEL

jD | JONATHAN DAVID PUBLISHERS, INC.
MIDDLE VILLAGE, NEW YORK 11379

GOLDA:
The Uncrowned Queen of Israel

JONATHAN DAVID PUBLISHERS, INC.
68-22 Eliot Avenue
Middle Village, NY 11379

10 9 8 7 6 5 4 3 2

Library of Congress Cataloging in Publication Data

Slater, Robert, 1943-
    Golda, the uncrowned queen of Israel.

    Includes index.
    1. Meir, Golda, 1898-1978 2. Prime ministers—
Israel—Biography.   3. Israel—Politics and government. I. Title.
DS126.6.M42S58   956.94'053'0924 [B] 81-1005
ISBN 0-8246-0244-7   AACR2

Printed in the United States of America

Table of Contents

CONTENTS *(continued)*

Acknowledgments

The author wishes to thank the following for reprint permission: *Foreign Policy* magazine, for permission to quote from its spring, 1976 edition; Herzl Press, for permission to quote from *The Plough Woman: Memoirs of the Pioneer Women of Palestine*, edited by Rachel Katznelson Shazar (Rubashow); *The Observer*, for permission to quote from a series of interviews by Kenneth Harris with Golda Meir in 1971; G.P. Putnam's Sons, for permission to quote from *My Life*, by Golda Meir; and Yaacov Sharett, for permission to quote from his father's *Personal Diary*, published by Maariv Books.

Thanks also to the *Time-Life* Jerusalem Bureau and the *Time-Life* headquarters in New York City; the Zionist Archives of the Jewish Agency in Jerusalem; and the State of Israel Archives, where official documents of the State of Israel from the 1947-48 period, released by the State Archives for the first time in 1979, were perused.

The following partial listing comprises those books which were of special importance in the research for this book: Moshe Dayan, *Story of My Life*, Jerusalem: Steimatzky's, 1976; Jacques Derogy and Hesi Carmel, *The Untold History of Israel*, New York: Grove Press, 1979; Abba Eban, *An Autobiography*, Jerusalem: Steimatzky's, 1977; Julie Nixon Eisenhower, *Special People*, New York: Simon and Schuster, 1977; Chaim Herzog, *The War of Atonement, October, 1973*, Boston: Little, Brown, 1975; Henry Kissinger, *The White House Years*, Boston: Little, Brown, 1979; Sheyna Korngold, *Zichronot (Memories)*, Tel Aviv: Idpress, 1968; Dan Kurzman, *Genesis 1948*, New York: Doubleday, 1970; Peggy Mann, *Golda*, New York: Washington Square Press, 1973; Golda Meir, *My Life*, New York: G.P. Putnam's Sons, 1975; Richard Nixon, *Memoirs*, New York: Grosset and Dunlap, 1978; Yitzhak Rabin, *The Rabin Memoirs*, Jerusalem: Steimatzky's, 1979; Marie Syrkin, *Golda Meir, Woman With a Cause*, New York: G.P. Putnam's Sons, 1963; Marie Syrkin (editor), *Golda Meir Speaks Out*, London: Weidenfeld and Nicolson, 1973.

In addition, I conducted roughly 100 interviews with people who either were close acquaintances of Golda Meir or who were directly involved in the events surrounding her life. Some individuals were interviewed three or four times. Among those interviewed are Mahmud Abu-Zuluf, Chan Shapiro Albert, Yigal Allon, Shulamit Aloni, Moshe Bar-Am, Uzi Bar-Am, Walworth Barbour, Zvi Bar-Niv, Judy Bauman, Haim Bar-Lev, Yitzhak Ben-Aharon, Zvi Berenson, Moshe Bitan, Danny Bloch, Zalman Chen, Chaim Cama, Yonah Cama, Simcha Dinitz,

Abba Eban, Yitzhak Elam, Aryeh Eliav, Hanan Eynor, Walter Eytan, Elias Freij, Israel Galili, Mordechai Gazit, Menachem Gelehrter, Nahum Goldmann, David Golomb, Judy Gottlieb, Isser Harel, Micha Harish, Abraham Harman, David Harman, Lesly Hazelton, Chaim Herzog, Lou Kaddar, David Kalderon, Aryeh Lapide, Haim Laskov, Naftali Lavie, Aryeh Levavi, Israel Lior, Netanel Lorch, Regina Medzini, Menachem Meir, Emile Najar, Shlomo Nakdimon, Yitzhak Navon, Shimon Peres, Yitzhak Rabin, Ben Rabinovitz, Masha Rabinovitz, Sarah Rehabi, Rinna Samuels, Yossi Sarid, Ze'ev Sharef, Aziz Shehadeh, Ya'acov Shimshon Shapira, Rebecca Shulman, Clara Stern, Shmuel Toledano, Ya'acov Tzur, Channa Weinberg, Yigael Yadin, Haim Yahil, Aharon Yariv, Zvi Yaron, Hannah Zemer, Gabi Zifroni, Nomi Zuckerman, and others who wished not to be identified.

Photo Credits: Archives of the Prime Minister; Carole Gootter, Israel Defense Forces Archives; Israel Government Press Office; Keren Kayemet; private collections of family and friends; James Sanders; Neil Tepper.

Foreword

Toward the end of Golda Meir's career she was the subject of an authorized biography and was the central character of a Broadway play. Earlier she had written her memoirs, *My Life*.

GOLDA: The Uncrowned Queen of Israel differs from the other books about Golda in that it treats some of the lesser known details of her life. It focuses on the later years of this remarkable woman, the period when she wielded enormous influence over people and events. But Golda Meir's early years are not ignored, for it was then that the personality of the woman was formed.

Of the many colleagues and relatives of Golda who agreed to be interviewed for this book, I would particularly like to thank Lou Kaddar, Golda's longtime confidante and personal secretary. She welcomed me into her home for so many talks about Golda that I believe we both stopped counting. She remained gracious throughout.

A project of this scope inevitably involves many helping hands, and to mention all those who were of assistance would be impossible. Debbi Baker, with whom I have worked before, proved again to be a very efficient, hard-working colleague, translating scores of articles and transcribing numerous taped interviews. Walter Eytan and Reuven Rosenfelder, who carefully read the manuscript and offered constructive criticisms, were also extremely helpful. Needless to say, as the author I take full responsibility for the contents of this book.

Special thanks are due the *Time-Life* Jerusalem Bureau, where I have worked for several years, for allowing me access to its files, and to the *Time-Life* New York Headquarters, where I encountered a very helpful group of archivists.

Some of Golda's relatives and close friends—Judy Bauman, Judy Gottlieb, Lou Kaddar, Regina Medzini, and Channa Weinberg—were extremely kind in making available to me some wonderful photographs, including some thus far unpublished. To them I express my gratitude.

I also wish to thank my publisher, Rabbi Alfred J. Kolatch, for his continuing support and patience as this book went through its various stages. It is he who deserves much credit for the book's final shape.

A final personal word. An enterprise of this sort, which consumed much of my time for the good part of a year, also demanded much of my immediate family. At all times they—my wife and three children—exhibited patience, understanding, and tolerance. My wife, Elinor, was an active participant in this book, collecting photographs, reading chapter drafts, coming up with scores of useful suggestions. I thank her.

Robert Slater

Jerusalem, Israel
April, 1981

Prologue

Tuesday. December 12, 1978.

A great lady was dead!

The rains fell and friendly female soldiers from Israel's Defense Forces supplied umbrellas to mourners standing in a circle around the grave of Israel's beloved leader. Golda had captured the heart of the world. She had presided over the State of Israel with dignity. And now Israel and the world had come to pay its respects.

It was difficult to identify all the famous faces. Their heads were bowed; their eyes were fixed on the cold, wet ground. Occasionally a grieving face showed itself. Henry Kissinger, Moshe Dayan, Cyrus Vance, Abba Eban, Harold Wilson, Yitzhak Rabin, Lillian Carter, Shimon Peres. Their faces were etched with a special sadness.

Golda Meir had been front-page news in every part of the world during her lifetime, and she was front-page news in death. The New York *Daily News* ran a full front-page photograph of her. In Paris, the conservative *Le Figaro* paid tribute to her as "Israel's uncrowned queen." One Belgian newspaper screamed: "Israel's Intrepid Granny, Golda Meir, Is Dead," while a second described her as "Israel's Strongman."

Tributes of love and adoration poured in from all over. One of the most touching was the very personal note written in the communal dining room at Kibbutz Revivim, where Golda had visited her daughter, Sarah, regularly over the years. The message read, "Our Golda is no longer with us."

The rain continued to fall as the military chaplain intoned the ancient Hebrew burial prayers. Occasionally a mourner would raise a hand to brush the rainwater off a cheek.

In the crowd, leading the mourners, was Israel's new prime minister, Menachem Begin, the man who had won all the acclaim for which Golda had hungered during her years of public service. How she would have loved to have been in Oslo to receive the Nobel Peace Prize!

Instead, during the Oslo ceremonies Golda lay in a Jerusalem hospital, suffering her last painful hours of life. Prime Minister Begin, en route to Norway on Friday, December 9, called Hadassah Hospital to check on her condition. "She is in her last hours," he was told. He knew he would have to hurry home.

She, too, knew the end was near. She asked that only her family and closest friends be granted visitation rights. To Shimon Peres, now the head of the opposition Labor Party, she acknowledged that her time was running out: "They say I'm made of steel, but even steel is weakened sometimes."

Begin spoke with Jerusalem again later that Friday, and this time he received

Memorial to Golda. Mourners at the memorial service for Golda (just before the burial). Front row, left to right: Zechariya Rehabi, Golda's son-in-law, Sarah's husband; Sarah, Golda's daughter; Menachem, Golda's son; and Clara, Golda's sister.

the news that Gold Meir had died. At age eighty, after a fifteen-year battle of which few were aware, her life had been claimed by cancer.

Begin remained in Oslo only long enough to attend the ceremony that Anwar Sadat, president of Egypt, co-recipient of the prize, had decided to skip. Sadat thought the award had been prematurely offered.

Golda Meir had no taste for frills; she instructed that her funeral be simple. No eulogies. Some of her closest associates were unhappy with the request, but they honored it. She had asked, too, that there be no memorials to her after death. This request, too, would be honored.

But there was no way to prevent the nation over which Golda had presided as prime minister for five and a half years from expressing its sorrow. The morning of the funeral Israelis queued up in front of the modern Knesset building, Israel's parliament, anxious to walk past her coffin. Nearly 100,000 people formed a snakelike line stretching all the way to the Israel Museum, a half-mile away.

A brief ceremony was held at the Knesset. Golda's son, Menachem, recited the Jewish prayer for the dead, the *Kaddish*. Orna Porat, a German-born actress who had converted to Judaism, read portions from Golda's memoirs, *My Life*. She then read a speech Golda had given while prime minister in 1970. In the speech Golda had promised to do whatever possible to achieve peace.

Six colonels from the Israel Defense Forces carried Golda Meir's coffin to an army command car. Only 300 of the mourners were permitted to attend the graveside service, for space was limited. Simcha Dinitz, Golda's longtime adviser, knew that Golda would not have liked the restriction. Everyone should have been welcome.

The funeral motorcade wound its way up Herzl Boulevard toward Mount Herzl. Golda was to be buried in a plot reserved for Israel's "great figures." To the right of her grave was the grave of Levi Eshkol, the man who had preceded her as prime minister; the grave to the left of Golda's was empty. Heavy clouds rolled in over the Judean Hills as the congregation gathered. The pine trees behind the gravesite rustled gently. Then the downpour began.

The United States sent the largest contingent to the funeral: forty-two members, headed by Lillian Carter, President Jimmy Carter's eighty-year-old mother. There had been a report that the Egyptians might send a representative, but they did not. Some argued that it was still too early for a gesture of that kind.

At the funeral. **A host of dignitaries attended Golda's funeral (December 12, 1978). Here, former British Prime Minister Harold Wilson (third from right) stands next to Moshe Dayan (fourth from right). Wilson had always been a close friend of Golda's and of Israel's.**

Saying goodbye to Golda. The funeral. Mt. Herzl. December 12, 1978. Front row, center to right: Mrs. Hubert H. Humphrey, Senator Jacob Javits, Yigael Yadin (Israeli deputy prime minister), former Israeli President Ephraim Katzir, U.S. Secretary of State Cyrus Vance and Mrs. Vance. Harold Wilson is fifth from left in row above umbrellas. Senator Daniel Moynihan is fourth from right, third row from top. Golda's funeral literally brought the Camp David peace process to a momentary halt as world leaders, including some actively participating in the Camp David negotiation, paid their final respects to the deceased leader.

The Africans were also not represented, despite Golda's having been like a queen to them in her days as foreign minister. Africa had loved Golda. But the Africans, like so many others, now embraced the Arabs. Although they would have liked to pay their personal respects, they thought it best to keep their distance.

Many paid tribute to Golda Meir, speaking to the legend, ignoring the battles they had fought with her, choosing instead to remember her as a heroine. "The miracle of Golda Meir," a *New York Times* editorial began, "was how one person could perfectly embody the spirit of so many." Walter Cronkite of CBS television told the American nation that "she lived a life under pressure that we in this country would find impossible to understand. She is the strongest woman to head a government in our time and for a very long time past."

The statesmen with whom Golda had dealt personally were most effusive in their encomiums. "If it had not been for Golda," said Henry Kissinger to the Israeli people, "Israel would not have come out of the Yom Kippur War the way it did. If it had not been for Golda, you would not have overcome."

The skies open. Foreign leaders, Israeli government officials, and diplomats shielded themselves from the heavy rains on the day of the funeral. Here, they wait for the funeral procession to arrive. Identifiable in the front row are Yigael Yadin, deputy prime minister of Israel; Cyrus Vance, American secretary of state; Harold Wilson, former British prime minister; Moshe Dayan, Israel's foreign minister; Henry Kissinger, former American secretary of state.

Exchanging a word. **As the rains fall, Henry Kissinger speaks with Israeli Foreign Minister Moshe Dayan's wife, Rachel. Also in the photograph are Yitzhak Rabin, former Israeli prime minister (far left) and Moshe Dayan (third from left).**

Anwar Sadat described her as a "first-class political leader" and an "honest foe." In a personal letter to Golda's children Sadat wrote:

> I must record for history that she had been a noble foe during the phase of confrontation between us, which we all hope has ended forever. While we are working to achieve a total and a permanent peace for the people of the area, I must mention she had an undeniable role in starting this peace process when she signed with us the first disengagement agreement.

> She has always proved that she was a political leader of the first category, worthy of occupying her place in your history and worthy of the place she occupied in your leadership. I repeat my condolences to you.

Golda, the woman of steel; Golda, the first-class competitor, was a remarkable woman, perhaps the most remarkable of our time. Her world was filled with drama and violence, yet she appeared at home in it. She rose to the heights of political power in her country when politics was a male domain.

GOLDA: The Uncrowned Queen of Israel is the story of this woman's captivating personality, of the men and women she favored and despised, of her passionate devotion to the Jewish people and of her contempt for anyone less devoted.

A last goodbye. Senior army and police officers salute Golda Meir's simple wooden coffin as it is lowered into the ground a few steps from the grave of her predecessor, Levi Eshkol. The burial was at Mt. Herzl in Jerusalem.

U.S. representative. Lillian Carter, President Jimmy Carter's mother, pays her last respects to Golda. She led the American delegation to the funeral. Escorting her are President and Mrs. Navon of Israel.

It is also the story of an "image." By the time Golda Meir became prime minister of the State of Israel in 1969, every political leader of consequence had learned how to package himself for the vast world television audiences. Politicians left no stone unturned in their attempt to make themselves known and liked. Golda, on the other hand, had achieved international fame and recognition without following the familiar pattern. For the better part of her career she had no media adviser; she had no liaison between herself and the press. In fact, as prime minister she rarely held press conferences. She thought little of them.

Nonetheless, the press—both in Israel and abroad—made Golda a legend. Its adoration, its benevolence came in large part because to nearly everyone Golda Meir was the genuine article. And she was appreciated for that by both her supporters and detractors.

This is the story of a woman who achieved the kind of success few women have known. It is the story of a woman who ranked as one of the world's most admired women, at times outdistancing even royalty and first ladies.

The name Golda Meir was magic.

1

The Early Years

She was lucky to be alive.

In the nine years between her older sister Sheyna's birth and hers, Golda's mother had given birth to four sons and a daughter. None had survived infancy.

The arrival of Golda Mabovitch was especially significant for the Mabovitch family. After so many hopes dashed, so much love unspent, the Mabovitches understandably showered unbounded attention on the new baby. "She is my joy!" Blume Mabovitch shouted ecstatically as she played with her new daughter.

Growing Up in Russia

Golda was born in Kiev, Russia, on May 3, 1898. Her father, a carpenter by trade, had moved there with his family to find employment. Kiev was part of the Pale of Settlement, a ghetto-like area first established in 1794 to discourage Jews from mixing freely with Christians. The Jews of the Pale lived uneasy lives.

Golda's first eight years were not happy ones. Being a Jew in Russia meant living a bleak life filled with terror and uncertainty. It meant being ever on guard, watching for the Czar's soldiers, who enjoyed rampaging through Jewish communities, spreading destruction and death. It was not the kind of atmosphere conducive to normal child's play.

In the Mabovitch family there were many strong-willed figures who, despite the harassment of the non-Jewish world, clung proudly to their Jewish heritage. Significantly, it was the women who manifested most of the resilience, the men being more prone to a certain innocence and an unfounded optimism toward life. Towering over the family was Golda's namesake, her great-grandmother, Bobbe Golda—a woman of such commanding stature and such unfailing common sense that even outsiders turned to her for counsel. From her, Golda inherited a sense of realism: one should expect more tragedy than joy in life.

Golda's parents were fundamentally good people who showed their naiveté by allowing unfounded hope to be their only shield against the Czar's oppressive rule. Though Golda spoke lovingly of them for preserving Judaism, she bridled at what she considered their simplistic, passive approach to life. Etched in her memory was the scene she observed at the age of four: her father dutifully nailing boards across the doors and windows of their home in anticipation of a dreaded pogrom. Golda could not understand submission as an answer to oppression. For Jews, there had to be a better defense than to retreat into hiding.

Golda's rebelliousness in later years was undoubtedly rooted in her early experience as a Russian Jew.

Despite their submission to the outside world, in their home Moshe Mabovitch and his wife, Blume, were strict disciplinarians. He was tall, slender, strong; she was short and stocky, with red hair and a fiery temper to match. Moshe was particularly stern and dogmatic. His fiat became household doctrine. But from two of his daughters, Sheyna and Golda, his approach earned not respect but outright rebellion.

His attitude did not mellow with time. At a later date, when the sisters argued that they wanted to pursue their studies, their father's answer was: "Young women should seek husbands, not education." The narrowmindedness of the Mabovitch household propelled Sheyna and Golda into the outside world at a relatively young age; and they soon became independent, highly motivated, iron-willed young women.

Reunited. **Golda, her mother, and two sisters had remained behind in Russia while Moshe Mabovitch worked in the United States to support the family. After a three-year separation the Mabovitch family was reunited. Here, they pose for a family portrait sometime after 1906. Left to right are Golda, Moshe, elder sister Sheyna, Mother Blume, and younger sister Clara (called Zipke within the family circle). Sheyna, the fiery revolutionary of the family, exhibits some of that zeal here, still wearing the Russian revolutionary style of dress.**

Supporting a family in that time and place was difficult, and so, like many husbands and fathers before him, Moshe Mabovitch decided to journey to the United States, spend a year or two earning money, then return to Russia. In the meantime Golda and the rest of the family moved from Kiev to Pinsk, where they awaited Moshe's return. When three years had passed and Moshe had not returned, Blume packed up her family and, in 1906, left for Milwaukee, Wisconsin, where Moshe had managed to find work as a carpenter.

Childhood in Milwaukee

When Golda saw her father for the first time in three years, she barely recognized him. She was disappointed. The role-model she expected was not there, nor did she find it in her mother. She turned to other members of the family and found Sheyna.

Teen-aged Sheyna had been attracted to the world of the revolutionaries. Clandestinely, she met often with her Socialist-Zionist friends to lay plans for the overthrow of the Czar. The searing passion with which she and her friends played out their fantasies left an indelible mark on the young, impressionable Golda.

Compared to Sheyna, the self-confident family rebel, Golda was an arch conservative. She was totally conventional and unobtrusive. For quite a time it seemed as if Golda was part of an audience watching a play, with Sheyna as the main character.

Searching for her own identity, Golda turned to books. A natural inquisitiveness began to reveal itself. She wanted to learn more and more; and twice a week, with her friend Regina Hamburger, she would visit the Milwaukee Public Library.

Since Yiddish was spoken at home, to Golda the English studied at school was a foreign language. Judging from letters to Sheyna, who had journeyed to Denver in search of a cure for her tuberculosis, mastery of the language was not simple. But Golda persevered, and she emerged as the brightest student in her graduating class at Milwaukee's Fourth Street Elementary School. In fact, she was selected as valedictorian despite the fact that some of her teachers thought her a chatterbox. (Later, the school was renamed the Golda Meir School for Gifted and Talented Children.)

By age 14 a quiet obsessiveness had taken hold of Golda, a commitment to books and learning that branded her as yet another teen-aged rebel in the Mabovitch household. In the fall of 1912 she entered North Side High School in Milwaukee, an extraordinary accomplishment, for poor Jewish families could not as a rule afford to send their daughters to high school.

Golda now decided on a career in teaching, a vocation that she considered "intellectually and socially useful." But her father was not happy with her concentration on education. "It doesn't pay to be too clever," Moshe once advised Golda. "Men don't like smart girls."

Moshe believed in marriage as the insurance policy all girls needed. When the Milwaukee public school system announced that married women would not be hired to teach in its schools, Blume and Moshe Mabovitch feared that Golda might refuse to marry. They were desperate; they would try to impose their will on their daughter at any cost.

The Denver Experience

In the winter of 1912 Golda decided to run away from home. She would travel

Young Zionist. In Milwaukee in the early days, Zionism meant outings and get-togethers, not packing bags for Palestine. Here, we see Golda (top, second from right) at one of her first Zionist picnics in Milwaukee. At this juncture in the family's Zionist adventure, Golda and her family appear as equals in their ideological zeal. In time, however, Golda would surpass them all and become a renowned Zionist leader. Sheyna stands second from left; Golda's mother is next to Sheyna, and Sheyna's daughter, Judith Corngold Bauman, is second from left in the foreground.

to Denver, where she would move in with Sheyna. She concocted a plan with Regina Hamburger, but the scheme almost fell apart before Golda had even left Milwaukee.

Determined conspirators, Golda and Regina made up in boldness what they lacked in shrewdness. Neither Golda nor her parents were familiar with railroad schedules, and because of their shared ignorance a comical situation occurred: a letter from Golda confessing to her plan lay in her parents' hands for hours while the young girl was still waiting for the train at the Milwaukee railroad station. Had the Mabovitches thought of checking at the station, they would have had plenty of time to catch up with their daughter.

Golda arrived in Denver. In a letter to Golda in March 1913, Regina wrote about the reaction to her disappearance: "Everybody thought you had eloped with an Italian."

Golda was developing into a handsome teen-ager, although Sheyna thought that her sister's prominent nose didn't seem to match the rest of her face. But she saw in the curvature of Golda's mouth the most positive physical feature: it reflected "willpower and independent judgment." She spoke also of Golda's "intelligent face."

In Denver Golda came under Sheyna's direct influence for the first time. The bond that developed was not only one between sisters, but between mentor and pupil, ideologue and protégé. Red-haired Sheyna had a fiery temper. Individualistic and revolutionary in her thinking, she radiated the strength of one willing to give everything for her convictions.

Golda recalled vividly how her sister had attended secret meetings with fellow revolutionaries in Russia. Now, in America, she was awestruck by the free-wheeling parlor discussions in which Sheyna participated with Jewish intellectuals. How fascinating was the life of Sheyna, how exciting the plans of the young revolutionaries!

Golda had gone to Denver to pursue her studies, but with the influence of Sheyna so strong, her personal goals began to change. School no longer seemed so desirable now that she had been exposed to Sheyna's ideas and lifestyle.

While a patient at the Jewish Hospital for Consumptives in Denver, Sheyna had come into contact with other young people seeking the same cure. She quickly discovered, however, that they had more than a disease in common. All were Jews who had grown up in intense poverty. They shared a sense of rage at the despotism of the pre-World War I world. These were angry young intellectuals eager to latch on to panaceas. Frequently, in conversations at Sheyna's home, they evaluated and reevaluated a whole galaxy of philosophies and ideologies: Socialism, Marxism, Zionism, and more.

At first Golda sat quietly and listened, teetering between awe and confusion. All those long names and fancy ideologies: why so many? And which deserved more attention? She could not conceal her excitement. She clung to the words she heard as though the fate of mankind hung in the balance.

In time Golda began to see her sister's friends in a different light. She began to feel contempt for these armchair philosophers. She had wanted to ask, "Why use the parlor room and not the battlefield?" But she kept silent, a teen-ager deferring to the more mature, wise people in their twenties.

Golda's own political consciousness was inchoate, developing more slowly than her older sister's. Yet, coming from a family that had endured its share of suffering, Golda found it natural to champion the cause of the poor. When injustice appeared, she became enraged, but more important, she yearned to take action. Golda's mother had a favorite phrase for her, a *kochloffel,* the Yiddish word for stirring spoon: she constantly seemed to be stirring things up.

In 1908, when Golda was only ten, she had organized the rather pretentious-sounding American Young Sisters' Society. Its aim was to raise money so the poor children of Milwaukee might have the necessary textbooks for school. Six years later Golda busied herself with relief work to help Jewish refugees, victims of mass deportations early in World War I. She recoiled when anyone suggested later that she had become interested in the needy because she was simply a philanthropist. "It was because I was indignant," she protested.

Golda, not Sheyna, emerged as the real activist. Although Sheyna was capable of great bursts of rage and outrage, she had none of the speaking or organizational talents of her younger sister. Sheyna was not fit for the give and take of politics.

The intellectual atmosphere in Denver had stimulated Golda, and she began to doubt that she could pursue a teaching career, which would require being confined to the classroom. The heady air of Sheyna's parlor had distracted her. Increasingly, Sheyna disapproved of Golda's attitude. She castigated her for losing interest in school. Growing more independent, Golda moved away from Sheyna and found work first in a laundry, then in a department store. But soon her time was taken up with a new interest.

Golda Meets Morris

Golda found that young men gravitated towards her. Her mind, still open to a wide variety of ideas, was like a bright searchlight. Slowly, it began to focus on the best that the world had to offer. She felt a strong urge to explore as much of its ideas and culture as she could. And she felt the need to share her thoughts and observations with a good friend. Morris Meyerson seemed the ideal companion.

Timing was all-important in Golda's romance with Morris, one of the young Russian Jewish immigrants who had drifted into Sheyna's Denver living room. Had Golda met him later, she might well have rejected Morris as unsuitable. But, in Denver, still sifting through new ideas, Golda had no reason to reject Morris on ideological or any other grounds. She was not looking for a romance with someone in the Zionist movement; she herself had at that stage made no commitment to leave the United States to settle in Palestine. She simply wanted someone with whom to communicate freely.

Morris, whom everyone, including Golda, called by his last name, dreamed of becoming an engineer, but he was poor, and his widowed mother and his three sisters looked to him for financial support. When he found work, it was usually as a sign painter. He had no time to pursue advanced studies, but being intellectually inclined, Morris spent much of his leisure in the public library and in lecture halls. With Golda he relaxed, as they discussed literature and music.

Probably because of her embarrassment at having a romance at such an early age, Golda remained secretive about Morris. Those friends that knew of the relationship teased her; they referred to Morris as "Mr. Somebody."

Golda was in love. In writing about Morris to her close friend Regina, Golda confessed: "He isn't very handsome, but he has a beautiful soul."

Her discussions with Morris directed her attention to a world of new ideas and personalities. As a result, she again began to consider a teaching career, but she was unable to make a firm choice.

In 1914, when Golda's parents discovered that she was working in a Denver department store, they were infuriated. No self-respecting Jewish girl should do that kind of work. They induced her to return home, promising that she could attend high school in Milwaukee. Having finally decided that she would definitely pursue a career in teaching, Milwaukee seemed to be the best place to achieve this goal.

Growing into womanhood. Golda is back in Milwaukee, having returned from her adventure in Denver. Now in high school, she was planning a career as a schoolteacher. The year is 1914.

Return to Milwaukee

Golda's return to Milwaukee at age sixteen gave her life new direction. She spent the next two years completing her high school education and wound up as class vice-president. She then entered the Milwaukee Normal School for Teachers. The year was 1916. But now again, as in Denver, she had become diverted, this time by the swirl of activity in her parents' home.

Friends from the Milwaukee days. Golda, in 1915, with Peretz Hirshein, a writer, and Regina Hamburger Medzini.

During World War I the Mabovitch home became a kind of way station for Jewish Legion volunteers. These were young Jewish men who had organized themselves into an exclusively Jewish unit within the British Army; their aim was to free Palestine of its Turkish rulers. Whereas in Denver Golda had been exposed to a plethora of theories and ideologies, here, in her parents' home, the accent was heavily on Zionism.

Moshe and Blume made it clear to Golda that the establishment of a Jewish homeland in Palestine—Eretz Yisrael—was ennobling, but they refrained from encouraging her to take its message literally, that is, to settle there.

Zionism, for Golda, was all romance. She saw it through the lives of special folk heroes like A.D. Gordon and Rachel Bluwstein, pioneers who had conquered the harsh soil though they had little skill in farming; they were poets more than farmers. She learned even more from such Palestinian emissaries as Nahum Syrkin, Shmaryahu Levin, and Yitzhak Ben-Zvi. When they visited Milwaukee, they brought with them exciting tales of heroism, always accompanied by a persuasive appeal to American Jews to come settle on the land.

The emissaries' talk of blending Zionism and Socialism into a new amalgam that would heal the wounds of the Jewish people appealed to Golda. She became more and more convinced that Zionism would end anti-Semitism. But her idealism demanded action, and upon learning about the Jewish Legion, she tried to join. She was terribly disappointed to learn that the Legion was an all-male unit, and her hopes were dashed.

As the war progressed, the Jewish condition grew steadily worse, and Golda searched for avenues to express her deeply-held Zionist beliefs. The most obvious organization to join was Hadassah, the major Zionist woman's organization of the day. But Golda wanted to be connected with an organization that blended Zionism with Socialism.

In 1915 she became infatuated with Poale Zion, the Workers of Zion, a small, largely Yiddish-speaking branch of the Labor Zionist movement. Poale Zion members believed that Jews could build a nation by the sweat of their brow. Although Golda was technically too young to join, the members of her local branch were impressed by her, and Golda was accepted as a member.

When one joined Poale Zion, he or she was actually making a commitment to settle in Palestine. And such was Golda's intention. But World War I was raging, and such a journey was unthinkable. To salve her conscience, Golda assured herself that she was different from the run-of-the-mill American Zionist—the ones who attended all the right rallies, read the right magazines (*Young Maccabean* or *New Judea*), and solicited funds with Jewish National Fund collection boxes on street corners. They would remain in the United States, but she, one day, would live in Eretz Yisrael!

As Golda became increasingly drawn to Zionism, a gap developed between her and Morris. He did not share her enthusiasm for Palestine. Golda, however, was not yet ready to abandon romance, and she reluctantly repressed her infatuation with Palestine and Zionism, hoping that before long Morris would see things her way.

Foreign Office,
November 2nd, 1917.

Dear Lord Rothschild,

I have much pleasure in conveying to you, on behalf of His Majesty's Government, the following declaration of sympathy with Jewish Zionist aspirations which has been submitted to, and approved by, the Cabinet

"His Majesty's Government view with favour the establishment in Palestine of a national home for the Jewish people, and will use their best endeavours to facilitate the achievement of this object, it being clearly understood that nothing shall be done which may prejudice the civil and religious rights of existing non-Jewish communities in Palestine, or the rights and political status enjoyed by Jews in any other country"

I should be grateful if you would bring this declaration to the knowledge of the Zionist Federation.

Balfour Declaration. British Foreign Minister Arthur Balfour's statement promising a Jewish homeland in Palestine became the focal point of Jewish hopes for a renewal of a peaceful, independent life in Eretz Yisrael. The promise expressed in the letter, written to Lord Rothschild on November 2, 1917, was eventually broken by British backtracking in the 1920s and 1930s.

Morris did not consider Zionism to be the solution to the Jewish problem. "The idea of Palestine or any other territory for Jews is to me ridiculous," he argued. "Racial persecution does not exist because some nations have no territories, but because nations exist at all." Morris favored internationalism—a world in which nations per se would not exist.

Golda thought the idea absurd. "Internationalism," she believed, "doesn't mean the end of individual nations any more than orchestras mean the end of violins."

But withal, Morris was still dear to her. She appreciated his beautiful soul, and she would let nothing damage the romance.

While still enrolled in the Milwaukee Normal School for Teachers, Golda taught Yiddish in a *Folkschule* located in the Jewish Center of Milwaukee. Three days a week she exposed the Jewish children of the city to her favorite language; she taught them to read it and write it and appreciate its literature. She believed that Yiddish along with Hebrew were important aspects of Jewish culture.

Although extremely busy studying and teaching, Golda still found time to work for Poale Zion. She became an effective speaker and organizer. Her talents did not go unnoticed.

In 1916, two of the founders of the Midwest branch of Poale Zion, Baruch Zuckerman and B.J. Shapiro, made the trip from Chicago to Milwaukee to urge Golda to move to Chicago, where her talents could be put to better use. Finding Zionist work much more attractive than courses in pedagogy and the history of education, she gladly accepted the offer.

But leaving Milwaukee meant leaving Morris. It was not an easy decision, and it was with a feeling of guilt that Golda left for Chicago to move in with the B.J. Shapiro family. B.J.'s wife, Raziel, became one of Golda's closest friends.

To make extra money and to leave her with enough time for the many evening meetings of Poale Zion, Golda found a part-time job, working afternoons as a librarian in the Chicago Public Library. This would enable her to do organization work late into the evenings and to sleep late in the mornings. She relished these years as a time of growth and preparation for life in Palestine.

Surrounded by the love of B.J. Shapiro and Raziel and the adoration of Chana and Judy, the Shapiro children, Golda was very happy. She played with them and sang to them, and they called her their "good fairy." They loved the wonderful stories and fairy tales Golda told them at bedtime, and especially the Yiddish folksongs with which Golda lulled them to sleep.

Golda remained in Chicago only a short time. She returned to Milwaukee when Morris finally was more agreeable to the idea of the two of them settling in Palestine.

The Decision to Marry

Upon her return to Milwaukee Golda and Morris debated the pros and cons of marriage and of settling in Palestine. Both were strong-willed people, but the stronger of the two won out. And although Golda did not threaten or deliver

Golda and Morris. **Taken at the time of their marriage in 1917, this is one of the first photographs showing Golda and Morris. Golda struggled over whether to marry Morris, conscious of how little he shared her Zionist dreams. In the end she let romance dictate her course: she married Morris and took him with her to Palestine.**

ultimatums, she let it be known very gently but in no uncertain terms that with or without Morris she planned to live the remainder of her life in Palestine.

On December 24, 1917 Golda and Morris Meyerson were married in the Mabovitch home. Being good Socialists, they had planned a simple civil ceremony to be conducted at Milwaukee's City Hall, but Blume Mabovitch insisted on a religious ceremony, and in deference to her the couple became man and wife in the presence of a rabbi.

Family visit. Golda during a visit to her sister Sheyna in Denver in 1918. Sheyna is seated next to her husband, Sam Corngold. Their small daughter, Judith, is between them.

"This is the life for me." Golda's first real encounter with the organized Zionist movement gave her a spiritual lift. She attended the first American Jewish Congress, in Philadephia in December, 1918, and during its proceedings this photograph was taken. The Congress inspired her to write enthusiastic letters to Morris, proclaiming her jubilation at taking part in the Zionist enterprise.

Age twenty. A young woman with a clear purpose, Golda's heart was set on reaching Palestine. In this photograph, she was simply biding time, awaiting the appropriate moment to take leave of the United States.

Pupil and mentor. Golda and Sheyna had far more than an ordinary sister relationship. As the ideologue in the family, Sheyna encouraged in her younger sister an interest in higher purposes, which was not present elsewhere in the Mabovitch household. Here, the sisters appear sometime after World War One, probably 1919 or 1920, just before embarking upon their dramatic journey to Palestine.

Golda's enthusiasm for Zionist work won her many friends. Even Golda's father, long a skeptic about her abilities, was eventually won over by her enthusiasm and dedication. After listening to her hold forth one day, Moshe relented in his opposition to her street-corner speeches, an activity in which he had believed no respectable Jewish girl should engage. He discovered that his daughter was, indeed, a rare talent. "What a tongue, what a spirit," he bragged.

Expecting to make the trip to Palestine soon, Golda intensified her Zionist work. The conflict between her and Morris about settling in Palestine had subsided, and Golda pursued her obsession with intensified vigor.

Then. Golda, Raziel Shapiro (standing), and Regina Medzini in Chicago in 1918.

Now. The same threesome fifty-three years later in the prime minister's garden.

In December 1918, while attending a meeting of the American Jewish Congress in Philadelphia, Golda sent this enthusiastic note to Morris: "I tell you that some moments reached such heights that after them one could have died happy." That particular convention, the first ever held by that organization, was highlighted by the resolution calling for the establishment of a Jewish homeland in Palestine. Golda was so ecstatic that she didn't miss a single session.

For Golda Mabovitch Meyerson this was real living!

2

Palestine-bound

Among the group of twenty-two American immigrants that set sail from New York aboard the S.S. *Pocahontas* on May 23, 1921 were Golda, Morris, Sheyna, and Sheyna's two small children, Judith, aged 10, and Chaim, 3. Accompanying them was Golda's friend Regina Hamburger.

For Golda, the decision to journey to Palestine was the most important one she had ever made. And now, as she stood on the deck of the *Pocahontas* and studied the rolling waves of the Atlantic, she knew she would have to make a second fateful decision, for she could not live with one foot planted in the United States and the other in Palestine. She would have to make a choice. When the ship made its stopover in Naples, Italy, Golda made the decisive move. She surrendered her American passport.

In Italy, Golda and her group switched from the *Pocahontas* to a second ship, which took them to Alexandria, Egypt. From there all Palestine-bound passengers took a train to Tel Aviv.

On July 14, 1921, as the train pulled into the small, shabby railroad station planted in the sands of Tel Aviv, Golda wondered whether she and the others might not be too fragile for the rigors of pioneer life. The sun scorched the earth. The sand was like hot coals. Not a blade of green grass was in sight. As the small group walked to the marketplace, they were disturbed by what they saw. Flies hovered over the food that humans would soon be eating. In general, the hygienic conditions were shocking.

Golda and entourage had come to Tel Aviv with little money, and the first order of business was to find living quarters and employment.

Golda desperately wanted to work the land, but that would mean joining a kibbutz. (The kibbutz was a collective settlement which not only served to defend the Yishuv [Jewish community] against Arab attacks, but also attempted to create a new lifestyle based on social justice.) And joining a kibbutz was no easy matter, for there were few kibbutzim, and candidates were carefully scrutinized.

Golda and Morris first found lodging in Tel Aviv, and Golda, without difficulty, obtained work giving private English lessons. Soon after, she was offered a permanent position teaching high school English. This left her dissatisfied: "I've come to Eretz Yisrael to work, not to teach English," she said.

Pioneers together. Among the men and women who emigrated with Golda on the S.S. *Pocahontas* was Raziel Shapiro, wife of B.J. Shapiro, an early Zionist leader from Chicago. Golda and Raziel remained friends for the next half century.

The New Immigrants

As for any new immigrant to Israel, the first few years were difficult. Adjusting to a whole new way of life, a new language, new values and standards required determination and fortitude. But Golda, in letters addressed to family and friends in the United States during the summer of 1921, let it be known that the discomfort of the new life did not faze her: not the minor ones—the flies and

Childhood co-conspirator. Regina Hamburger Medzini, shown here with Golda, helped Golda plot her secret departure from Milwaukee at age fourteen. Regina and Golda were first-grade classmates in Milwaukee's Fourth Street Elementary School, and in 1921 they were shipmates on the *Pocahontas*. They became lifelong friends.

poor hygiene; not the major ones—the oppressive heat, the rampant poverty, the disease.

"The surprising thing, Sam," she wrote in a buoyant letter to Sheyna's husband on August 24, 1921, "is that only the new immigrants who only recently arrived are talking about leaving the country, whereas the older workers are still full of excitement. In my opinion, as long as they are here, those who with their own hands created even this little bit, I must not leave the land and you must immigrate."

Golda's parents drew strength from her letters. By 1926, they too joined Golda and Sheyna in Palestine. And Sam joined Sheyna soon thereafter.

For Golda, immigration to Palestine and joining a kibbutz were part of the same dream. It was as if the entire Yishuv were reflected through the prism of the kibbutz. While others might rationalize that a clerk in Jerusalem or a grocer in Tel Aviv was as essential to the Yishuv as the kibbutznik, Golda fervently believed that only through the kibbutz could the Zionist dream be realized.

The kibbutz in which Golda sought membership was Merhavia, in northern Palestine. A friend from Milwaukee was a member, but for Golda and Morris joining Merhavia proved no small feat. They had planned to start their new life on the kibbutz within a few weeks after arriving in Palestine. They had been informed, however, that their applications had been denied on the grounds that married couples (and spoiled Americans) were not solid candidates for kibbutz life. Persisting, Golda asked Merhavia members to give her and Morris a firsthand look at the kibbutz, a tactic that worked well. The kibbutzniks got to know them better, and Golda and Morris were soon granted membership.

Merhavia's forty members consisted of a large group of American boys who had come over to Palestine with the Jewish Legion in World War I and had stayed on, and also of American girls who had come before the war. When Golda first met the female kibbutzniks and learned that some of them had been in Palestine for as long as eight years, she was in awe. That, she thought, was a veritable lifetime.

Despite her Socialist ideals, Golda could not abandon her American standards easily. She was 23 years old and still completely American in her tastes and needs. While others could enjoy a herring that had merely been washed, Golda insisted that it be carefully skinned as well. Others saw little wrong in leaving uncleaned tables after a *kumsitz* (get-together), but Golda argued that the men ought to be responsible for washing them. When Golda was on duty, kitchen tables were covered with oilcloth; babies carrying infectious diseases were bathed in water to which alcohol had been added (then considered by the kibbutz a great luxury). Five babies of the kibbutz, in fact, were later humorously nicknamed "Golda's Brandy Babies."

With fellow kibbutzniks peering over her shoulder to see if the spoiled American would make it, Golda vowed silently that she would not surrender to fear or weakness. She had no knowledge of poultry farming, but she accepted her responsibilities with unrestrained enthusiasm. Until then she had feared so much as approaching a chicken, but now her chickens were a source of personal pride, for she was able to supply her fellow kibbutzniks with eggs, and occasionally with chickens, to be served at mealtime.

Gradually, Golda found kibbutz life satisfying. The members of Merhavia began to treat her with respect, and she enjoyed the sociability. She loved dancing the hora on Friday nights, late into the night. The recriminations against her bourgeois, non-Zionist past had begun to fade.

All in all, Golda spent only three years at Merhavia (including six months in 1925 when she and Menachem, her infant son, lived there), and when she left it was almost entirely on account of her husband. Morris insisted that if he and

Golda were to become parents, their children must be born away from the kibbutz. Although distraught over leaving Merhavia, Golda had little choice.

Returning to a kibbutz was forever on Golda's mind. In 1934 she went to Kibbutz Ein Harod to apply for membership, but there was insufficient housing, and her application was denied. One of the regrets of her life, she often said, was that she was forced to give up the kibbutz routine: "That's the failure of my life. Had I stayed on a kibbutz, I would have been at one with myself all my life."

Life on the kibbutz. Golda adored the ways of the kibbutz, and repeatedly she told friends of how happy she would have been to spend her life on one. Husband Morris felt differently, and eventually Golda was forced to give up communal life. Here, Golda is shown working with the chickens at Kibbutz Merhavia shortly after she and Morris immigrated to Palestine in 1921.

Marital Problems on the Kibbutz

Personal problems were not unknown to Golda, but she was always able to resolve them without excessive emotional cost. But the conflict that arose in the 1920s was considerably more complex.

At its core was Morris. Because he accompanied her to Palestine physically but not in spirit, he was a constant thorn in Golda's side. Had she not loved him so much, the problem could have been resolved easily. But her love for him was deep.

Morris and Golda felt differently about kibbutz life, but this never led Golda to conclude that their marriage was in jeopardy. She was unable to detach herself from her husband emotionally even when it had become painfully clear to both that the marriage was destined to fail. It all seemed so strange, so at odds with her otherwise logical mind.

There was never much hope that Morris would grow to love the kibbutz. This quiet, gentle man clashed with the rough, gregarious kibbutz types. He required his private moments and despised the communal existence. He disagreed violently with the childrearing methods collectively followed by the kibbutz parents.

If he had little love for kibbutz ideology, Morris had even less affection for the backbreaking work that was demanded. Still worse, he had contracted malaria and had developed kidney trouble, which added to his unhappiness. In a letter to a friend in the States, written from Merhavia in 1923, he expressed his bitterness: "Ah, Palestine, Palestine, you beggarly little land, what will become of you? How ironic sound the fine words at Poale Zion meetings about a free workers' Palestine."

Kibbutz life was also intellectually and culturally stifling for Morris Meyerson. This man who loved music and art found himself living among sober, hard-working kibbutzniks whom he considered insensitive and humorless. To Morris the kibbutz was a wasteland, yet he could not leave it because he could not leave Golda.

Morris was often characterized by his peers as an unrepentant non-Zionist, which is not borne out in actual fact. Nor is the contention that his attitude toward Zionism negatively affected his marriage.

If Morris was not an ardent Zionist when he first reached Palestine, he underwent a dramatic transformation later on. For one accused of being a non-Zionist, Morris did some rather "Zionistic" things. Unlike Sheyna's husband, Sam, who in the 1920s and 1930s divided his time between Palestine and the United States, Morris remained in Palestine without interruption and with little protest. He developed a strong love for the land, as demonstrated by the guided tours he conducted with pride for family and friends. He took his guests to all of Jerusalem's historic sites and never failed to fascinate them with his narration.

In 1923 Golda and Morris began discussing starting a family. Golda was most anxious, but Morris was ambivalent: he was appalled at the prospect of turning his own child over to the collective embrace of the kibbutz. To him, childrearing was the prerogative of parents, not an activity to be taken over by a commune.

The idea that all kibbutzniks should become surrogate parents began as a practical necessity. With limited time available and much work to do in the fields, the kibbutzniks could not allow themselves the luxury of foregoing work and devoting their time to the raising of children. Therefore, from infancy on children were raised in "children's houses," and parents visited them regularly during visiting hours.

Morris would have no part of this system. If Golda wanted a child, they would have to leave the kibbutz and settle in the city. There, Morris insisted, a baby could be raised normally. Golda finally yielded, although not without bitterness: "He had to follow me to Palestine to have a wife. I had to follow him to Tel Aviv to have a child."

In November of 1924, Morris and Golda's first child, Menachem, was born [their only child, a daughter named Sarah, would be born in May, 1926]. Soon after, in 1925, they moved to Tel Aviv.

Struggle in the City

Golda spent the four years between 1924 and 1928 experimenting with ways to salvage a marriage that was clearly faltering. She often looked back on those years as the most miserable of her life. She felt cheated. She had come to Palestine to help build a country, and now she was no longer being true to herself. Moreover, city life, with its burden of poverty, made the struggle to preserve the marriage all the more difficult.

In Tel Aviv, Golda found work as a cashier in the Histadrut's Public Works and Building Office (later called Solel Boneh, the powerful construction cooperative). Morris was without employment; he was still recuperating from disabilities suffered while on the kibbutz, including the residual effects of malaria.

Making ends meet was difficult, and the young couple led a spartan existence. On one occasion Golda passed a shop window in which she spotted a red wool shirt selling for 35 piasters (then the equivalent of $1.75): "I wrestled with myself. I deliberated and finally I bought the shirt. For weeks afterward, I ate myself up. How did you let yourself waste such a large amount of money on a shirt?"

Before long Golda was offered the opportunity to transfer to the Jerusalem office of Solel Boneh, and with it came an offer for Morris to be employed as bookkeeper. The Meyersons seized the opportunity.

Morris did not believe in frugality. He favored buying a bouquet of flowers for Golda over depositing money in the bank. Consequently, the couple's financial situation was precarious, and as an extra source of income Golda was forced to do the laundry at their child's school.

The year 1928 was a turning point in Golda's life. She was 30 years old and she had achieved one goal: she had settled in Eretz Yisrael. But now, seven years later, she knew that her life lacked direction; her deep sense of purpose had all but left her. And she was disturbed about it.

Golda felt strongly that had it not been for Morris she might have already accomplished more. By May of 1925 it was clear that she had been toying with the idea of leaving her husband, for it was then that she took six-month-old baby Menachem and returned to Merhavia, this time without Morris. After three years on the kibbutz, Golda considered a permanent separation inevitable.

First Taste of Public Life

Golda's first real experience in public life came in 1922 when she was chosen to represent Merhavia at a convention of kibbutz movements. On this, as on other occasions, Golda delivered her speech in Yiddish; her Hebrew was not yet fluent. Immigrants who had resided in the country for two years almost always lectured in Hebrew, but Golda found mastery of the language difficult, and her superiors granted her permission to speak in a more comfortable tongue. At times audiences taunted the woman for not addressing them in Hebrew, and Golda often broke into tears.

Despite the language barrier, Golda's message was understood and accepted. Addressing the convention in 1922, she created a storm when she scolded the women present for considering kitchen work disgraceful. The prevailing belief had been that women of the kibbutzim should not be relegated to the kitchen, that they should assume their place alongside the men in the fields.

Golda's sincerity and dedication was rewarded: she was selected the kibbutz delegate to the prestigious Council of the Histadrut. Over the next few years her ability was recognized, and gradually she gained the respect of the labor movement.

In 1928 Golda was offered and accepted the post of secretary of the Moetzet Hapoalot, the Women's Labor Council. She knew that the position would require her moving back to Tel Aviv and that overseas travel, principally to the United States, would be extensive, for she would serve as the Palestine delegate to the Pioneer Women, the American counterpart of Moetzet Hapoalot.

The next six years were, in a sense, a training period for Golda's future in politics. She traveled widely, speaking before numerous audiences, always bringing a message from the Jewish community in Palestine. In 1932 she was chosen to spend two years in the United States with the Pioneer Women. Her two children, Menachem and Sarah, joined her.

Golda's mission to the United States was successful. With her midwestern American accent and flawless English, she won friends easily. The people of the United States could identify with her. Because other Yishuv leaders could not equal her command of the English language—her calling card and her most valuable resource—Golda was able to reach the Jewish and non-Jewish communities of America better than anyone else. She became the labor movements' apostle to America, bringing the Yishuv's message of pioneering and heroism to all who would listen.

A Figure from the Past

In 1930 Golda was presented with a major opportunity by a man she had appeared to snub during her Milwaukee days. In 1915, together with Yitzhak Ben-Zvi, who would be the second president of the State of Israel, David Ben-Gurion had arrived in the United States to interest American Jews in Palestine. Both men had recently been banished from Palestine by the Turks.

Ben-Gurion had been scheduled to speak in Milwaukee one Saturday evening. Tired of attending Zionist meetings simply to please Golda, Morris insisted that instead they go to a concert being given by the Chicago Symphony Orchestra. Golda reluctantly agreed.

The next day, when a decision was being made as to where Ben-Gurion should

Public servant. Golda appears here on board the ship *Esperea* en route to the United States. The early 1930s marked a major turning point in her public career: for the first time she took on an overseas assignment as a representative of the Yishuv. She served as the Palestine delegate to the Pioneer Women, the United States counterpart of the Moetzet Hapoalot, the women's labor council. Golda remained in the United States from 1932 to 1934 while Morris stayed behind in Palestine.

have lunch, Golda graciously volunteered her home. She was turned down with a hostile explanation: "A *havera* [member] who does not attend Ben-Gurion's meeting does not deserve to have him for lunch."

Ironically, fifteen years later Ben-Gurion would become one of the first of the Yishuv leaders to appreciate Golda's speaking talents. Writing from a workers' convention in London to the newspaper *Ha'aretz* in Palestine, he noted: "After Kantridge Golda spoke, and I trembled at her daring words. Her speech shook the convention. She spoke with genius, assertively, bitterly, with hurt, and sensibly. Although I had heard of her success in the women's convention and other gatherings arranged for her by the labor movement in different places, her speech was a great surprise to me."

Ben-Gurion and Golda, in time, would part company over some serious political issues, but he would never lose his personal admiration for that talented lady from Milwaukee.

Golda Joins Histadrut Leadership

In 1934 Golda moved into the leadership ranks of the Histadrut. Founded in 1920, the Histadrut was more than a trade union. Besides conducting the usual activities of a trade union, it provided employment through its fully- or partly-owned corporations. It also provided schooling, a health service, labor exchanges, and banking and insurance services. The Histadrut acted as a shadow government for the Yishuv. On its executive committee were the men who one day would furnish the leadership of the new Jewish state: Ben-Gurion and Moshe Sharett,

Struggle for immigration. Jews of the Yishuv discovered to their regret that the British had no intention of implementing the Balfour Declaration. Here, in 1934 in Haifa, Jews hold a rally in protest against British restrictions on Jewish immigration to Palestine. The Hebrew slogan above the dais reads in part: "The strength of the Yishuv lies in unrestricted immigration. Curtailing immigration destroys the Hebrew economy."

future prime ministers, and Zalman Shazar, a future president. Within a week after she returned from her two years in the United States, Golda was asked to join the Va'ad Ha'poel—the Workers' Committee—the Histadrut's Executive. The year was 1934.

As a member of the Workers' Committee, Golda was given the rather unimportant task of running the Histadrut's tourist department, essentially a public relations job involving escorting visiting dignitaries through a kibbutz or through the Histadrut's consumer cooperative, Tnuva.

A year later, in 1935, Golda was elected to the secretariat of the Va'ad Ha'poel. She thereby became a member of the Yishuv's ruling circle. In 1936 she was assigned management of the Histadrut's mutual-aid programs. Eventually, she became Chairman of the Board of Kupat Holim, Histadrut's sick fund—a program for universal medical coverage.

Labor Leader

Acting as a labor leader was clearly not easy for Golda Meyerson. Intellectually, she rejected the idea of class struggle. She felt that as valid as were the claims of the labor force, encouraging its members to take to the barricades was no more than a call for violence. She preferred to settle conflicts peaceably, yet the realities confronting the Yishuv workers demanded more than passivity. Jewish laborers went unemployed while Jewish entrepreneurs hired cheap Egyptian and Sudanese labor. The starving Jewish pioneers nearly persuaded Golda to abandon her moderate stance, but she vacillated, and she ultimately resolved that confrontation was best avoided.

Before joining the ranks of labor, Golda had had a rather starry-eyed vision of Socialism. It was a doctrine towards which only decent people gravitated, the kind incapable of telling a lie. The indecent Socialist, if he existed at all, Golda contended, was not welcome in the Palestine of the 1930s: "Gangsters, police, drunks, thieves, and tramps are not known or wanted in Palestine. This is a land ruled by agricultural workers."

Palestine was, of course, not ruled by the workers but by the top echelon of the Histadrut. Had the rank-and-file truly been in command, they would have looked after their wages wholeheartedly and paid precious little attention to such low-priority, non-Socialist concerns as immigration and statehood. Here, Golda quarreled with the workers, arguing that by increasing immigration and by striving for a Jewish state the rank-and-file would attain the security necessary to build a solid economic base. For such notions, she was criticized as being antilabor, yet she was most decidedly not.

Problems of a Working Mother

No one among the Yishuv's leadership experienced as much inner turmoil as did Golda. Although the men among the ruling elite spent as much time away from their families as she, few felt the guilt Golda did. She was constantly trying to establish a balance between her family life and her public work, and while in later years she played down the conflict between family and career, in 1930 Golda wrote about it in poignant terms:

"... There is a type of woman who cannot remain at home ... In spite of the place which the children and the family as a whole take up in her life, her nature and being demand something more, she cannot divorce herself from the larger social life. She cannot let her children narrow her horizon. And for such a woman there is no rest."

Family portrait. The Meyerson family poses for a portrait in the late 1930s. From left to right: Sarah, Golda, Morris, and Menachem. The photograph shows a family serenity, which was not actually prevailing at the time. Golda and Morris had already drifted apart.

Golda understood the subtleties involved: outside the home the mother continues to develop, and she may indeed be able to offer her children more by being active in the world, by becoming a more interesting person with wider interests. But, noted Golda, "... one look of reproach from the little one when the mother goes away and leaves it with the stranger is enough to throw down the whole structure of vindication. That look, that plea to the mother to stay can be withstood only by an almost superhuman effort of the will."

Golda's own son, Menachem, had given her that look more than once, and on occasion she had found it nearly impossible to leave him. Most of the time, however, despite her son's pleas, she went off to attend to her outside activities.

Writing once to Sheyna as she made her way to yet another labor conference (in London in 1928), Golda observed that "my social activities are not an accidental thing: they are an absolute necessity for me. I am hurt when Morris and others say that this is all superficial, that I am trying to be modern. It is silly. Do I have to justify myself?"

Golda took issue with Sheyna's comment that she, Golda, was just another wild-eyed idealist. "Believe me," wrote Golda, "I know I will not bring the Messiah, but I think that we must miss no opportunity to explain what we want and what we are to influential people."

To compensate for her long absences, Golda tried to shower her children with extra attention when she was at home. She made a special point of doing all the housework—from the serving of meals, to the washing of dishes, to the cleaning of the house. For Menachem and Sarah, she bought presents and imposed discipline—both to remind them that they had a mother. But the guilt remained. She knew that her children had suffered much because of her absences.

Menachem was especially affected by his mother's lifestyle. When asked long afterwards to recall his life in the 1930s and 1940s, he did so with reluctance; it seemed to conjure up a series of unpleasant memories. He would speak about his father with ease, a lilt rising in his voice. And he took pride in telling others that he thought he resembled his father in philosophy and temperament. But he could recall Golda only as a woman on the run. Her life was an unending schedule. Menachem and his sister often had to make an appointment with their mother to go to an afternoon movie. He and Sarah would arrive fifteen minutes early and would then debate how late their mother would be. Golda always appeared, usually just as the movie was about to begin.

Menachem's poor school grades saddened his mother. From her own past Golda knew the importance of education. But Menachem wanted to play the cello. This was his passion. During his high school years, he finally transferred to night school so he could practice the instrument during the day.

Less sensitive about her mother's absences, Sarah was nonetheless affected as well. She was a sickly child but a superior student. When Sarah was called upon to fill out school questionnaires requiring that the child indicate the occupation of the mother, Sarah tried too minimize the importance of Golda's work. The child stated simply that her mother worked for the Histadrut.

Morris Leaves Golda

It was Morris who actually walked out on Golda.

In 1928 Morris left home and rented his own apartment. Plagued by the frightening prospect of actually losing her husband, Golda rushed to his side in an attempt to woo him back. She succeeded, and a shaky status quo remained in force for much of the 1930s. Morris was tender and loving, but usually he received only coolness from Golda. He discovered that she had become involved with other men, and he was deeply hurt. Yet Morris loved her. He never considered divorce.

Golda made no secret of her extramarital relationships. Indeed, virtually every one of her close friends knew precisely the identity of her intimate male friends.

Morris Meyerson in 1937.

Few spoke openly about them. One acquaintance put it this way: "Golda was a healthy female whose relationship with her husband went to pot, thoroughly and finally, when she was 30 years old. Why should it be assumed that she lived in celibacy?"

David Remez, an early leader of the labor movement was one of Golda's intimate friends. He took an instant liking to her, and as a consequence he did much to promote her through the ranks of the Histadrut. In fact, it was he who suggested that Solel Boneh transfer her from the Tel Aviv office to Jerusalem. Golda's detractors accused her of using unfair tactics to achieve power within the Histadrut.

Golda was attracted to Remez for his charm and his sincere devotion to Zionism. She admired his commitment to the labor movement and his mastery of Hebrew. In turn, Remez showed a special interest in Golda. He praised her efforts to improve her Hebrew language skills, and the two often conversed at length about the important issues of the day. It was obvious that Golda had far more in common with Remez than with Morris.

In her memoirs, Golda handled the relationship with Remez with predictable discretion: "We saw a great deal of each other, and we had much in common in terms of our approach to things. Remez was one of the very few of my comrades with whom I ever discussed any personal, nonpolitical matters." Indeed, Golda Meyerson and David Remez shared a great deal.

3

The Struggle for Statehood

From her earliest days in Palestine, Golda had considered statehood for the Jewish people a remote dream. For nearly 2,000 years the Jews had been wanderers, and the possibility of establishing a Jewish state in the near future seemed fanciful. The Yishuv, with its 80,000 residents, was too small, too weak. Even more important, the governing authority over Palestine was British, and the British were in no hurry to relinquish their mandate.

Few Jewish leaders considered the Arabs living in Palestine a potential threat. Yet, the bloody riots initiated by them in 1921, 1929, and again in 1936 provided a portent of how stiff a price the Yishuv would have to pay for the realization of its dream. Golda never dared expect that she would live to see Jews living in a sovereign state. She was thankful for the happiness she found in working *toward* the day when "one million" Jews would live in Palestine.

The Peel Commission

Yet, talk of statehood persisted, receiving its greatest impetus in July, 1937, when the British Peel Commission concluded, after five months of study, that Palestine should be partitioned into two states: one Arab, one Jewish. The Jewish state would comprise a relatively small area: the coastal plain and Galilee.

Some Zionist leaders, notably Chaim Weizmann, were so overjoyed that the British had gone on record in favor of Jewish statehood that they closed their eyes to the problem of survival in the tiny area that had been allocated to them. Ben-Gurion, then chairman of the Jewish Agency's Palestine Executive (in effect "prime minister" of the Yishuv), was also ecstatic. He believed that establishing a Jewish state, regardless of size, would induce the Arabs to live in peace with Jews and that at a later point they would be amenable to adjusting the borders in a manner more acceptable to Jews.

Golda Opposes Peel Commission

Golda was shocked. Ben-Gurion, she felt, was reasoning poorly. "Some day," she argued at a party meeting during the debates about the Peel Commission report, "my son will ask me by what right I gave up most of the country, and I won't know how to answer him."

Early defense efforts. Arab resistance to the presence of the Yishuv in Palestine grew during the 1920s and 1930s. Bloody riots were staged in 1929 and 1936. Inevitably, given the passive nature of the British towards the Arabs, Jews took up their own self-defense despite British rules against bearing arms. Here, in December, 1938, proud Jewish soldiers take time out from training.

Seeking solutions. Lord Peel, glove in hand, with members of the Peel Commission in November, 1936, at the Mt. Scopus military cemetery in Jerusalem. After five months of study, Peel and his group concluded that Palestine should be partitioned into two states, one Arab and one Jewish. The Arabs rejected the package out of hand.

She attacked Ben-Gurion for arguing that acceptance of the Peel plan would bring an end to Arab riots and for declaring that a Jewish state would be in a position to change its borders after its establishment. "That happens," she noted sarcastically, "normally in wartime." She encouraged the Yishuv leaders to oppose the Peel proposals on grounds that the Jewish state would be too small and too crowded to be viable.

Golda's attitude toward statehood soon underwent a radical change, and she eventually became convinced that half a loaf was better than none. The change came as she grew to realize how little was Jewish influence in the world at large.

Golda apologized for her earlier views, admitting that Ben-Gurion was right, that she was wrong, that a small state was better than no state. But the whole debate proved academic: the Arabs rejected the entire proposal out of hand. They would countenance no scheme that would create a Jewish state.

The Battle to Save Europe's Jews

The event that triggered Golda's change of mind came at the international conference on refugees called by Franklin D. Roosevelt, held in Evian-les-Bains, France, in July, 1938. Golda attended as the "Jewish observer from Palestine," a rather undistinguished title. She had pinned great hopes on this conference.

In private talks, the "observer" from Palestine urged the other delegates to express sympathy for the desperate plight of Jewish refugees in Europe, which was growing worse daily. After listening politely to Golda, the delegates perfunctorily explained that while they wished to help, their hands were tied. As the conference was concluding, the chairman grudgingly called upon Golda to address the audience.

As she walked to the podium, members of the audience were struck by the appearance of the handsome woman from the kibbutz. She got right to the point: if other nations would not absorb Jewish refugees, the Yishuv was prepared to do so. "We have very little bread," she said, "however, we will share the crumbs of that bread with them."

The audience was moved—either by the force of the speaker's words or by a sense of guilt. Whatever the reason, it led to an astonishing scene. First, the American representative leaped from his seat and bolted for the exit. He was followed by the British delegate and then the French one. Like mischievous children ordered to leave by a stern schoolteacher, they fled, closing their ears to Golda's rising voice as she continued to plead: "We want them. We'll share whatever we have with them. Please let us only have them."

The plea fell on deaf ears. By 1939 only 60,000 German and Austrian Jews had reached Palestine, a miniscule number compared to those waiting to leave Europe.

In frustration, Golda wrote an article for Histadrut's *Dvar Hapoelet* (May 3, 1939). It was a plea to the Yishuv leadership to take more interest in the plight of European Jews: "Every day brings forth new edicts which engulf more hundreds of thousands of people; and we know that Jewish mothers are asking for only one thing: take our children away, take them to any place you choose, only save them from this hell!" She implored her readers to help bring these children to Palestine: "Here they'll be safe: safe for their mothers and safe for the Jewish people."

The British White Paper

Four days later the British Government issued the White Paper with its infuriating message: Jewish immigration to Palestine would be limited to 10,000 refugees per year for each of the next five years, plus 25,000 additional over the next five years (that is, a total of 75,000 within the five-year period). After the five-year period all Jewish immigration would cease. For Golda and her colleagues this document amounted to a renunciation of the Balfour Declaration, which had raised so many hopes in 1917. The British had then promised their support for a Jewish homeland in Palestine. Now they were reneging.

Illegal entry. A group of Jewish immigrants fight British restrictions against Jewish immigration to Palestine. Newly arrived by ship, they walk across desert-like sand dunes near the Mediterranean coast on their way to new homes in the Yishuv.

Anger in the streets. Jews, marching in the burning Tel Aviv sun on May 18, 1939, rise up against the White Paper. Issued eleven days earlier, the White Paper called for an end to Jewish immigration to Palestine after five years. The Hebrew sign carried by protestors reads, "The Bible is our mandate and the English can't put an end to that."

More fury against the White Paper. A mass demonstration in the Tel Aviv Stadium on May 18, 1939, in protest against the British restrictions on immigration.

The Holocaust

The next five years—1940 to 1945—were the most frustrating of Golda's entire life. She and the other Yishuv leaders sat in Palestine while a tragedy of incredible proportions was being played out in Europe. Jews were the victims, and they were helpless. The Yishuv did its best to make contact with the European Jews, to aid them in resistance, to encourage them. But in truth, little was accomplished.

Millions of Jews were marched off to gas chambers, and Golda, as well as the others, could do nothing but agonize over what was transpiring: "I have sometimes wondered how we got through those years without going to pieces."

World War II is a shadowy part of Golda's life. Acquaintances have few vivid recollections of her at the time. It is almost as if she and those around her had consciously erased that period from memory.

Her frustration is best illustrated by an episode that took place in April, 1943, when resistance fighters of the Warsaw Ghetto turned to the Yishuv for counsel. Should they make a stand against the Nazis?

DP camp. The central thoroughfare of Camp Bejt Bialik, just outside Salzburg, Austria, where 2,000 Jewish DPs lived. A former Nazi concentration camp, it was renamed after liberation in honor of Chaim Bialik, famous Hebrew poet.

Golda Meyerson and the other members of the Va'ad Ha'poel sat around the table in Tel Aviv, debating how to advise them. In principle they favored resistance. But to encourage the Jews of Warsaw to fight the enemy while they, the Jews of the Yishuv, remained in the comfort of their homes seemed gratuitous. "How could we in Tel Aviv tell them to die?" Golda asked. And as the Yishuv leaders were debating, news flashed over the radio that the Warsaw Ghetto uprising had begun. The Jews of Warsaw had made their own decision.

Golda's World War II Assignments

Some of the tasks Golda performed during the war were rather routine. She was appointed by the Mandatory Government to the War Economic Advisory Council. Palestine was on a war economy, and the Council's task was to serve as a liaison between the British Mandatory authorities and the public. Golda was most involved in improving production and distribution. She also spent months negotiating with the British in an attempt to improve the wages of the Yishuv's civilian force.

The Yishuv vs. the British

In her free time Golda worked to strengthen the Yishuv. Early in the war debate erupted over whether Jews of the Yishuv ought to enlist in the British Army. Arguing that "the idea of waiting to fight Hitler until the Germans approached the borders of Palestine was absurd," Golda advocated enlistment.

Her Tel Aviv apartment, located near the Mediterranean, was an ideal center for the illegal immigration work that was to be carried on. It was a safe place: the British wouldn't dare investigate a Yishuv official. And for her personal protection Golda adopted an underground name, Pazit, from the Hebrew word *paz,* meaning "gold."

Golda's daughter, Sarah, wanting to do her share, expressed an interest in joining a kibbutz, a prospect which troubled her mother. Suspecting an ulterior motive, Golda worried that Sarah might have become enamored of the kibbutz "idea" as part of her search for a way of dropping out of school. But Sarah was persuasive, and in 1944 she went to live at Kibbutz Revivim, south of Beersheba.

Helping fellow Jews in the Yishuv establish the right to handle their own defense was no easy matter, for the British wanted Jewish efforts against the Nazis channeled through the British Army. Few articulated this right of Jewish self-defense better than Golda; few possessed her emotional force or ability to reprove with stinging words.

Golda's testimony at the September, 1943 trial of two Palestinian Jews, Sirkin and Richlin, is a case in point. These two men were accused of stealing weapons from the British Army for the Haganah, the Yishuv's fighting arm. The prosecutor alleged that the Jewish youths had volunteered for the British Army with ulterior motives, and during the trial he turned his full wrath on Golda Meyerson.

"You are a nice, peaceful, law-abiding lady, are you not?" he asked sarcastically.

"I think I am," Golda retorted with equal sarcasm.

The audience rustled to attention. What was it this Jewish woman had said? Her tone sounded defiant, out of place. *Who was this woman anyway?* some wondered to themselves. The prosecutor was about to resume the questioning.

"And you have always been so?"

"I have never been accused of anything."

Again the tone of arrogance. Jews were supposed to be more respectful in a British court. Attention was now riveted on Golda. Except for the tangy dialogue between prosecutor and witness, there was absolute silence.

With great persistence the prosecutor tried to bring Golda to acknowledge that Jewish volunteers had acted deceitfully. But she would say only that Jews intended to defend themselves, and if that was a crime, so be it.

Favoring enlistment. On July 13, 1940, Jewish volunteers march on Allenby Street in Tel Aviv in favor of enlistment into the British Army.

Preparing to fight. **Jewish residents of the Yishuv read British mobilization orders in March, 1941. In the Yishuv debates were held over whether to join the British in the fight against the Nazis. The Jews chose to side with the British, but after World War Two they again undertook the struggle to oust the British from Palestine.**

Golda by now knew she had embarrassed the prosecutor, and she was enjoying it. Her voice grew stronger. "If a Jew or Jewess who uses firearms to defend himself against firearms is a criminal," she observed tartly, "then many new prisons will be needed."

Suddenly the prosecutor thought he spotted a chance to score a point. "Do you mean to say that there are many firearms?"

Golda would not be trapped. She responded to the question she had wanted to answer: "There are many who are ready to defend themselves."

It was a performance of the first rank, and after her testimony Golda acquired new respect and recognition from the Yishuv leadership. By not allowing the prosecutor to entrap her, and by not revealing Haganah secrets, she had proven her loyalty and skill under the most trying circumstances. More than any other event, the trial marked the beginning of Golda's political career. She soon became a chief spokesman for the Yishuv.

Jewish soldiers at war. Jewish infantry units in the British Army are shown resting between maneuvers somewhere in Palestine in March, 1941.

Keren Kayemet Archives

Holocaust Aftermath

The lesson of the Holocaust, the loss of six million Jewish lives, was shattering to Golda. It taught her that Jews could depend only upon themselves for survival. And the rescue of the remaining Jewish refugees became for her the *raison d'être* for a Jewish state. She now understood the meaning and importance of sovereignty. "If there had been a tiny state during the days of the Holocaust, we would have saved many Jews," she insisted.

Religion vs. Socialism

Some Jews believed in the formation of a Jewish state as a religious duty. Golda did not. Though she came from a traditional Jewish home, she regarded herself as a member of a race or culture, not of a religion. In her adult years she was not observant in her home nor did she attend synagogue regularly. Basically, it was Socialist instinct rather than religious zeal that motivated her in her efforts on behalf of Jewish statehood.

War's over! Victory celebration in Tel Aviv on May 8, 1945. World War Two had just ended.

Keren Kayemet Archives

Scars of war. A group of Jewish youngsters with death camp numbers tattooed on their arms aboard a refugee ship in Haifa port on July 15, 1945. Very few of these immigrant ships were permitted to enter Palestine ports, and of the sixty-three which attempted to between 1945 and 1948, all but five were turned back by the British.

Certainly here was a paradox in Golda Meyerson's life. Though she would work tirelessly for the Jewish people, she exhibited almost no interest in Jewish religion. (This was common to the Founding Fathers of the State of Israel. Most had come from deeply religious homes in Russia and Europe, and they had deliberately turned their backs on religion to become one hundred percent Socialist.) Golda often said that had she lived in the Soviet Union for most of her life, she might have become an Orthodox Jew, for there the synagogue was the only place to express one's Judaism. But having left Russia at an early age, her interest in religion quickly waned, and when she recalled the Orthodox men in her family, she did so with no great reverence. They seemed strangely alien to her.

Golda's true religious beliefs were hard to discern, for if she believed in an all-powerful divinity, she concealed it well. Rather than place God at the center of her universe, she argued that the Jewish people was the focus. Thus, she took the central axiom of Jewish faith—that God chose the Jews— and turned it on its head: "The Jews were the first people that chose God, the first people in history to have done something truly revolutionary, and it was this choice that made them unique."

Those who were close to Golda often wondered whether she believed in God at all. At times she confessed that the tragedies that had befallen Jews in her lifetime, particularly the Holocaust, were enough to call into question God's existence. For how, if He were truly omnipotent, could He allow such catastrophes to occur?

Post-World War II Yishuv Activity

After World War II the Jews of the Yishuv turned their full attention to the British nemesis. The Nazi dragon had been slain, and now the time had come for Jews to intensify the struggle—the *ma'avak*, as it was called in Hebrew—against their British landlords. Tens of thousands of Jewish refugees were waiting impatiently to flee Europe so that they might leave the miserable experience behind them. But despite Jewish pleas to open the gates of Palestine, the British clung to the spirit of the White Paper.

In March, 1946, the Anglo-American Committee of Inquiry recommended the immediate admission into Palestine of 100,000 refugees a month, a major departure from the stringent quotas of the 1939 White Paper. But the British would have nothing to do with the proposal.

The Mission to Rescue Holocaust Survivors

To Golda, the need for a Jewish state had become self-evident. To the 22nd Zionist Congress in Basel, Switzerland, meeting in December, 1946, she explained that statehood was now essential in order to insure that never again would the Yishuv find itself powerless to rescue fellow Jews: "We must become the masters of our undertaking. Only then will we be able to accomplish whatever is vital to the life of the Jewish people without begging the indulgence of others, and as we deem fit."

Fighting the British

With the European Jewish refugees in desperate straits, a vast "illegal" rescue mission was undertaken by Yishuv operatives to help those distressed souls reach Palestine. By the beginning of 1946, one thousand of those "illegal" immigrants were making their way to Palestine. In the spring of that year, however, the situation took a turn for the worse. The British had intensified their blockade around Palestinian shores.

Hunger Strike at La Spezia

In April, 1946, the British had captured two illegal ships, the *Fede* and the *Eliahu Golomb*, with its 1,014 refugees aboard, before they had even left the port of La Spezia, Italy. Rather than capitulate to the British, the refugees refused to disembark. They called a hunger strike—they would eat only when the ship set sail for Palestine.

The Yishuv had little military hardware with which to fight the British, but one effective weapon was to attract worldwide publicity. The La Spezia hunger strike seemed ideal. Golda proposed to Yishuv leaders that a select number of *them* begin a hunger strike in sympathy with the La Spezia refugees. The attendant publicity would surely do wonders for the cause. The leaders readily agreed.

It was decided that only those with a doctor's certificate attesting to their good health would be permitted to join the hunger strike, because many of the leaders were advanced in age, and their health might be affected by such an ordeal.

Golda had just been released from the hospital, but she insisted on participating. Before beginning her fast, however, she met with the British chief secretary, who asked her if she actually thought a hunger strike by the Yishuv leaders would alter British policy. "No," she replied frankly. "I have no such illusions. If the death of six million didn't change government policy, I don't expect that my not eating will do so. But it will at least be a mark of solidarity."

The hunger strike of the Yishuv leadership was more circus than solemn occasion. The thirteen leaders—Golda included—sat on chairs in the courtyard of the Jewish Agency compound in Jerusalem, chatting with delegations, meeting reporters, accepting the well-wishes of passersby. Nomi Zuckerman, the daughter of Golda's American Zionist mentor, Baruch Zuckerman, stopped by one day, as did Sarah, Golda's daughter, who had come all the way from Revivim. Sarah was worried about her mother's health.

Golda was elated about the strike. To ease Sarah's concern, Golda entertained her daughter with jokes. One was about Zalman Shazar, who had wanted so badly to join the strike that he approached a gynecologist to grant him the necessary certificate. Golda thought the story hysterically funny. Shazar, seated nearby, listened in stony silence.

Golda and the others drank tea but ate no solid food. As Golda grew weak from hunger, a cot was made available, which she used more and more frequently. The third day of the hunger strike fell on the Jewish holiday of Passover, when Jews are commanded by law to eat matza. In compliance, each of the thirteen leaders ate a tiny piece of the unleavened bread and then quickly resumed their hunger strike.

Campaign against the British. The leaders of the Yishuv stage a hunger strike to protest the British preventing the ship *Fede*, teaming with Holocaust survivors, from leaving La Spezia, Italy, for Palestine. The strike was held in front of the Jewish Agency building in Jerusalem in 1946.

Hunger strike leader. Golda is shown during the fast on behalf of the *Fede* refugees.

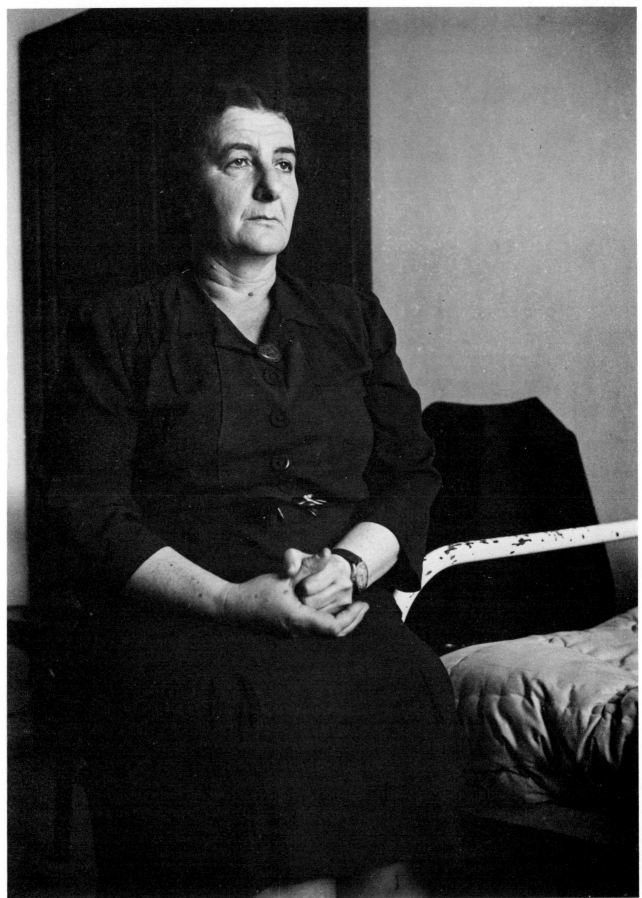

The *Fede* fast of Passover, 1946.

Breaking the fast for that brief moment proved important, for news of how the hunger strikers had celebrated Passover was reported around the world!

Meanwhile, the refugees aboard the two La Spezia ships had vowed that each day ten men and women would kill themselves in order to convince the British of their seriousness. The threat worked, for on May 8 the British permitted the ships to sail. Golda's fast ended after 104 hours.

(The two ships were among the very few to actually reach Palestine between 1945 and 1948. Of the sixty-three that had set sail in that period, all but five were intercepted by the British.)

Keren Hayesod

Worthwhile wait. **Golda and Mrs. Ada Fishman await the arrival of Jewish refugees in 1947.**

Jewish Resistance to British Rule Stiffens

On June 29, 1946 the British began to respond to Jewish resistance. They swept through the Yishuv, arresting its leaders and incarcerating them in Latrun. Conspicuously absent among those seized was Golda Meyerson. Reports circulated that the British had not detained her because she was a woman, but no one was certain whether this was out of regard to the fair sex or because the prison could accommodate only male prisoners. Golda was furious. It would have been an honor to be among those arrested. Adding insult to injury, there were a series of annoying phone calls from David Ben-Gurion's wife, Paula, who repeatedly inquired of Golda as to whether she had been arrested *yet*. Ben-Gurion himself was in Paris at the time—in virtual exile. He knew that if he were to return to Palestine, he would be arrested immediately.

Golda Heads Jewish Agency Political Department

With Moshe Shertok, the director of the Jewish Agency's political department, imprisoned in Latrun, a temporary replacement had to be found. The replacement was to be chosen by Shertok, David Remez, and the other incarcerated leaders. Their choice was Nahum Goldmann, the German-born Jewish Agency member from the United States.

Using friendly British officers at Latrun, the incarcerated Jewish leaders sent a

Jewish Agency leadership. Nahum Goldmann, the German Zionist leader who led the reparations negotiations with postwar Germany; David Remez, Golda's close confidant and sometime mentor; and Golda at a Jewish Agency meeting in 1947. Goldman and Remez played key roles in Golda's becoming acting director of the Jewish Agency's Political Department following the arrest of the Yishuv leaders on "Black Saturday," June, 1946.

Central Zionist Archives

Jewish Agency

The Old Man. **David Ben-Gurion and Golda appear at a meeting of the Jewish Agency Executive in 1947.**

message to the Agency in Jerusalem. They asked Goldmann to leave New York for Palestine at once to take charge of the political department. Explaining that he had much to accomplish in New York, Goldmann turned down the offer.

Whom would they choose? Remez recommended Golda, arguing that her experience in international conferences and in negotiating with the British over the past seventeen years had made her a suitable candidate. In addition, he argued, her command of the English language would be an asset. But the others were distressed over the possibility of her appointment: never before had a woman reached so high a position in the Agency. Withal, Remez won out, and Golda became acting director of the political department.

In her new position, Golda became the top representative of the Yishuv in its dealings with the British. Later, when Shertok was freed, and he left for New York to handle the campaign for the United Nations Partition Resolution, Golda remained in her post as acting head of the department.

4

Inching Toward Statehood

The Jewish Agency had its share of hawks and doves in post-World War II days. Hawks favored an activist policy, their goal being to make life for the British in Palestine as uncomfortable as possible. Doves favored moderation. Golda was manifestly an activist.

On July 1, 1946, in her first meeting as acting director of the Agency's political department, she called on the British High Commissioner, Sir Alan Cunningham. The British were demanding that Golda and other Yishuv leaders cooperate by turning over to them the membership lists of the two extremist Jewish underground organizations: the Irgun, headed by Menachem Begin, and the Lehi.

Recalling the hostile actions of the British of only a few days earlier—June 29—when they swept through the Yishuv looking for leaders and arms, Golda's reply to Cunningham was swift and direct: "Absolutely no."

To the Jewish Agency Executive, meeting in Paris that August, she recounted her visit to Yagur, a settlement near Haifa, shortly after the British had been there: "I never saw a pogrom in my life. But I have heard and read a great deal about them. I believe that what happened in Palestine on the 29th of June was what I imagined a pogrom to be."

The political future of the Yishuv came up at that Paris meeting as well. The British had recently proposed the Morrison-Grady Plan, a scheme of federalization under which provinces or cantons would be established in Palestine, one of which would be Jewish. A few members of the Agency Executive, eager to achieve some kind of autonomy, wanted to grab at it. Golda, too, was eager, but she realized that this plan had nothing to do with the statehood she and others had been talking about.

"We must state clearly," she told the Executive, "that the proposal of a province in Palestine cannot be a basis for negotiations, but that Jews are ready to negotiate if the proposal is for a Jewish state in Palestine. In that case, we shall discuss everything: boundaries, immigration, economics, etc. The question is: what is our starting point?"

She chastised Eliezer Kaplan of the Agency for backing the British proposal. "Kaplan really wants a state, but he starts asking for a province. There is a danger that everything in his proposals might be accepted except this last cardinal point."

In rejecting the plan, the Agency passed an unpublicized resolution favoring the establishment of a Jewish state in a *part* of Palestine.

Passing incident or Putsch attempt? That question remains unresolved to this day. The *Altalena*, an Irgun vessel which had set sail from southern France, arrived near the Palestine shore carrying a cargo of 5,000 rifles and 250 light machine guns. A cease-fire having been declared, the Israeli provisional government ordered the *Altalena* to turn over its cargo to the government. Under the direction of the Irgun leader Menachem Begin, the *Altalena* refused, and a battle ensued between the Irgun men aboard ship and the Haganah forces on shore. Some fourteen Irgunists died, and the others on the ship eventually surrendered. Some Israelis feared that the Irgunists' resistance was the start of a broader attempt to replace the existing Israeli government.

The Vote for Partition and Statehood

One year later, in November, 1947, the United Nations, meeting in New York, assembled to debate and vote on a proposal similar to the one approved by the Jewish Agency at the Paris meeting: the partition of Palestine into two states, one Jewish and one Arab.

As the voting began, Golda sat in the parlor of her home, a note pad on her lap, ready to tote up the figures as the vote was announced over the radio. She chose to be alone on that historic evening. When the final tally was entered, a new era in Jewish history had begun: the United Nations had sanctioned a Jewish state!

Golda wept, as did Jews the world over.

She left her quarters and hurried to the Jewish Agency compound in Jerusalem. With Ben-Gurion in Tel Aviv and Shertok in New York, the task of addressing the thousands of people gathered in the courtyard fell to her. She appeared on the balcony as spotlights beamed in on her and then shifted to the flag with its light blue Star of David.

A roar went up from the crowd, then Golda spoke: "For two thousand years we have waited for our deliverance. Now that it is here, it is so great and wonderful that it surpasses words."

Her voice broke for a moment, but then she recovered and shouted: *"Mazel tov*—Congratulations!"

The joy of the moment was drowned almost immediately by the flood of Arab hatred. Arab assaults on Jewish targets accelerated, and it became clear that a Jewish state in Palestine would have to be paid for dearly with the blood of its Jewish citizens.

Home free. The Haganah ship *Exodus,* **made famous by the movie of the same name, is shown here in Haifa on March 22, 1947.**

The Jerusalem-Tel Aviv Road

Keeping the Jerusalem-Tel Aviv road open was of paramount importance. Arab snipers held their fire when the British used the road, but they turned on Jewish convoys with full force. On behalf of the Agency, Golda had demanded that the British assign police escorts for Jewish travelers. A compromise was reached: the British would provide escorts if the Agency would agree to have all convoys searched for smuggled arms.

The Jewish leadership considered the British policy one-sided. The Arabs, Golda argued, weren't searched, and she demanded that the British act fairly toward the Jews.

Keren Hayesod

First U.S. ambassador. James G. McDonald, who became the first U.S. ambassador to Israel on March 29, 1949, having tea with Golda in 1947.

In a conversation with Sir Alan Cunningham on December 17, 1947 in Jerusalem, she made this point quite directly. When Cunningham asked her if she was proposing that the British search both Jews and Arabs, Golda replied in the negative. He then explained that British policy was to arrest *all* armed men during attacks.

"But," declared a deeply distressed Golda, "government forces arrive after the incident and search only the Jews."

"I didn't say we would search," Cunningham stated, "but I will arrest Arabs if I find them [armed] during an attack."

"That's your function?" inquired Golda. "Not to prevent an attack? There are weapons in Gaza and Beersheba being prepared for strikes against Jews."

"To search for weapons only among the Arabs, that's your proposal?" Cunningham countered.

"Precisely," said Golda. "When Jews will attack Arabs, search them."

Eleven days later, on December 28, Golda planned to travel on the Jerusalem-Tel Aviv road. One of her colleagues in the political department, Eliahu Sasson, had advised against the trip. "Can you imagine what it would mean for the enemy if you were struck by a bullet?" Golda assured him she had no intention of being a

"My favorite photo." Golda loved this photograph. She appears at a dedication of a forest named in memory of Orde Wingate, a British officer who helped organize Haganah raids on Arab guerrilla hideouts in 1938. The photo was taken in 1947.

Divided city. It is December, 1948, and Jerusalem stands divided. Under the 1947 partition scheme devised by the U.N. Jerusalem was to be internationalized. The Arab decision to make war against the Jews effectively nullified that portion of the partition plan. With the end of the 1948 war, Israelis held the western sector of the city, and the Arabs, the east, including the Old City. Jerusalem was to remain divided until the Six Day War of June, 1967, when Israel captured the eastern sector.

heroine, nor did she want to be killed: "I do not travel up and down the road just so maybe a bullet will hit me."

As the convoy was about to leave, Golda was asked whether she had room in her car for two more people, a man and a woman. She agreed readily. The woman joined her, but the man, Hans Beyth, acting director of the Agency's youth and immigration department, did not. Armed with a pistol, he did not want to use it while riding in a car filled with passengers. Traveling instead by bus, Beyth was later shot by Arab snipers. Beyth died and Golda harbored guilt over his loss for a long time. Had she been more insistent, Beyth might have traveled in her car and would still be alive.

The next day Golda met with Sir Henry Gurney, the British chief secretary. The subject was arms searches of Jews. Gurney tried to argue that searches were necessary because Arabs were coming under attack.

"Very interesting," Golda replied. "If a Jew attacks a Jew, there is a difference between an attacker and the one attacked. If an Arab attacks an Arab, there is a similar difference. But if an Arab attacks a Jew, another law prevails." She closed the conversation by promising that given no choice, "we will defend ourselves." Gurney understood and promised to curtail the searches.

A few days later Golda discovered that Gurney's promise was an empty one. Traveling by bus from Jerusalem to Tel Aviv, she watched as a British major halted Jews and began searching for weapons. Golda demanded the officer's card, which she received without comment, but the search continued. The major decided to permit the bus to go on its way, but he took prisoner a girl who had been seated in the Haganah escort car.

"In that case," Golda said with finality, addressing the major, "I'm going with you."

"You can't do that," explained the unnerved officer. "I'll have to arrest you."

"That, young man," said Golda sonorously, "is precisely what I want you to do." She then sat down next to the girl in the car.

The major had planned to take his "prisoners" to a British police station deep in Arab territory, but Golda prevailed and the two were taken to one in a Jewish region. When Golda told the desk sergeant her name, he lifted both hands to his head and cried, "Oh, my God!"

Soon, a higher ranking officer arrived. He offered Golda a drink and safe passage in his armored car to Tel Aviv. She accepted. When he dropped her off near Tel Aviv, she remarked, "It is you who are in danger now." Then, aware that it was nearing the holiday, she called after him, "Happy New Year."

Golda's confidential messages to Moshe Shertok in New York at this time attest to her concern over an early British pullout. Without the British, the Arabs would be free to mount an all-out attack against the Jews.

On December 22, 1947 Golda cabled Shertok:

RELIABLY INFORMED OPINION PREVAILING AMONG BRITISH OFFICIALS WITH-
DRAWAL TO BE CARRIED OUT SUDDENLY, MUCH EARLIER THAN ANNOUNCED.

Four days later, again she cabled:

INFORMED BY SERIOUS SOURCE ADMINISTRATION TO CEASE BY FEBRUARY
15TH. ARABS THEN TO START THEIR ATTACK. HAVE MANAGED LEAKAGE HER-
ALD TRIBUNE.

By the following month Golda seemed more concerned that the British might take action against the Yishuv. On January 13, 1948, she cabled Shertok:

SAW CHIEF SECRETARY YESTERDAY EVENING RE ROUTINE MATTERS. DURING
CONVERSATION HE RAISED QUESTION EXPLOSIVES U.S.A., ACCUSED JEWISH
AGENCY POLICY OF LIES, DECEPTION, SUSPICION, CHAUVINISM. I PROTESTED
STRONGLY, WHEREUPON HE BLAMED US FOR DISSIDENT ACTIVITIES, INSISTED
THAT WE SHALL SEE THAT THERE IS CONNECTION. I AM CONVINCED GOVERN-
MENT PREPARING SOMETHING AGAINST HAGANAH AND PROBABLY AGAINST
JEWISH AGENCY.

Burma Road. **When it became impossible to use the regular Jerusalem-Tel Aviv Highway because of the presence of Arab fighters, frustration grew in the ranks of the Haganah. A plan was devised to build a new road that was beyond the reach of the Arab Legion. Eventually this Burma Road, as it came to be called, proved useful for bringing supplies to the besieged Jerusalem residents.**

Keren Kayemet Archives

Breaking the siege. Jerusalem residents are ecstatic as a food convoy brings much-needed supplies to the city in June, 1948. Heavy fighting marked the way along the supply route, with Jewish units suffering heavy casualties. In time the siege was lifted.

Money was needed to execute the war against the Arabs. Eliezer Kaplan, treasurer of the Jewish Agency had returned from a visit to the United States in January of 1948 and reported that all the Yishuv could expect in the few critical months ahead was five million dollars. If the Arabs mobilized their armies against the Yishuv, they would be throwing into the fray tanks, artillery, and aircraft. Ben-Gurion suggested that not five million but five or six times that much would be needed, and that "to make the Americans realize how serious the situation is," he and Kaplan would have to leave for the United States immediately.

Listening to Ben-Gurion, Golda sensed that he was talking from heart more than head. "What you are doing here," she interjected quietly, "I cannot do. However, what you propose to do in the United States I *can* do."

Then in a most uncharacteristic reversal of roles, she put the following idea into Ben-Gurion's head: "You stay here and let me go to the States to raise the money." Undoubtedly what impelled her was the fact that Eliezer Kaplan was an ineffective public speaker. Sending him as a spokesman would never yield the large amount of money needed by the Yishuv.

Ben-Gurion was offended at Golda's temerity, and again he insisted that he and Kaplan make the trip. But Ben-Gurion did not prevail. The other Agency members backed Golda, and she was assigned the nearly impossible mission.

Raising Funds in the United States

Golda was warned not to disclose to American Jews how ill-prepared the Yishuv was. Jews, she was told, were not likely to respond to anyone telling them such unpleasant truths. They would think they were throwing good money after bad.

The voice of the Yishuv. **Fundraising with United States leaders in January, 1948, Golda issued a blunt appeal to American Jews to help the Yishuv survive the threatened Arab attacks. Although she doubted that American Jews would respond, she was shocked to find how generous they would be. On a national tour, Golda raised 50 million dollars for Israeli arms, a sum never before raised in that amount of time.**

But Golda would not, could not fabricate or tell half-truths. It was simply not part of her makeup. She had won over audiences in the past with her direct, honest approach, and she could do it again.

Golda's first audience in the United States was carefully selected. Rather than launching the appeal by addressing a small, purely Zionist group, she chose a non-Zionist forum, the Council of Jewish Federations, meeting in Chicago on January 21. She telephoned Henry Montor, the director of the United Jewish Appeal, in Chicago, who informed her that the list of speakers had already been drawn up. She said she was coming anyway. Before she arrived, she purchased a warm coat for the cold Chicago winter.

The audience had indeed expected to hear that the Yishuv could handle the Arabs without much difficulty. Golda told them a different story. "You cannot decide whether we should fight or not. We will. No white flag of the Jewish community in Palestine will be raised for the Mufti. That decision is taken. Nobody can change that. You can only decide one thing: whether we shall be victorious in this fight or whether the Mufti will be victorious in this fight." When the speech was over, a strange, frightening silence fell over the audience. Golda worried that her message had fallen on deaf ears.

But the audience had been deeply affected. First there was ear-shattering applause. Then people rushed to the stage with pledges. A million dollars was raised within minutes. Men began calling their bankers to secure loans. Later that day Golda cabled Ben-Gurion with the incredible prediction that she would be able to raise 25 "Stephens"—their code name—25 million dollars. "Stephen" was the name of the American Zionist leader Stephen S. Wise.

Flushed with her triumph, Golda happily agreed to take her message around the country in the company of Franklin D. Roosevelt's former secretary of the treasury, Henry Morgenthau, Jr. She spoke several times a day, and from each city she reported to Ben-Gurion how many "Stephens" had been pledged that day. On February 10, Gideon Ruffer (later Rafael), of the Yishuv's U.N. delegation, wrote Ze'ev Sharef, a staff member of the Agency's political department in Palestine: "Golda goes from strength to strength and million to million." When her tour ended, she had raised $50 million, a sum beyond anyone's wildest imagination.

Ben-Gurion waited at Lod Airport near Tel Aviv to greet Golda upon her return to Israel. He was clearly moved by her feat: "The day when history will be written, it will be said that there was a Jewish woman who got the money which made the state possible."

The key to Golda's success in Chicago and elsewhere had been her great talent as a speaker. Ironically, she was not a true orator. Her speeches rarely contained memorable rhetoric. Instead, she used simple, hard-hitting sentences. Often they were ungrammatical. Later, when as foreign minister and prime minister she hadn't the time to write her own speeches, if a writer injected a highflown word into a speech prepared for her, she would often stumble over it.

Golda knew how to convey a message through the power of her voice, the strength and authenticity of her emotions, the simplicity of her thoughts. Her messages, which clearly described the plight of the Jewish people, needed no embellishments. She could reach an audience better than any of her peers. Having experienced both cultures at firsthand, Golda was a bridge between the American Jewish community and the Jews of the Yishuv.

Secret Negotiations with Arabs

Golda felt at home in her role as public speaker, but this would not be true for every role assigned her.

In the fall of 1947 Golda was called upon to conduct secret talks with Arabs on issues of peace and war. She was well aware that the Arabs disparaged women who sought involvement in politics. In their eyes, a woman was useful for procreation but little else, certainly not for negotiating a resolution to the Jewish-Arab conflict. Nonetheless, as the acting head of the Jewish Agency's political department, Golda was selected for this delicate task.

The Yishuv leaders had long believed that Abdullah, king of Transjordan, was different from the other Arab rulers, more amenable to living in peace with the Jews. They also believed that if Abdullah could be won over, other Arabs might think twice about launching a full-scale attack on the Yishuv. Golda presented this view to the Jewish Agency Executive on October 19, 1947, asking that it be kept secret.

Meeting with Abdullah

On November 17, 1947—twelve days prior to the United Nations vote on partition—Golda secretly met with Abdullah. The meeting had been arranged by Abraham Daskel, director of the hydroelectric center in the Jordan River village of Naharayim. They met in Daskel's villa near the bridge that joined Palestine with Transjordan. Accompanying Golda were her advisor, Ezra Danin, an Iraqi Jew who enjoyed close relations with the king, and Eliahu Sasson, who acted as interpreter.

Seeing a woman seated before him, the king was visibly shaken. "But Ezra," he said quietly, "I thought Mr. Shertok would be leading your delegation."

"Don't worry, Your Majesty," Danin replied, "Mrs. Meyerson is replacing Mr. Shertok and has full authority from the Jewish Agency to talk with you."

The king began speaking in Arabic. He began with a series of compliments to the Yishuv: "During the last thirty years, you have grown and strengthened yourselves. Your achievements are many. We cannot disregard you and we must compromise with you. There is no quarrel between you and the Arabs. The quarrel is between the Arabs and the British, who brought you to Palestine; and between you and the British, who have not kept their promises to you."

The king then made his proposals. He was prepared to agree to the partition of Palestine if it would not discredit him in the eyes of his fellow Arabs. One way for him to save face with the Arabs would be for the Jews to agree to the establishment of a Hebrew Republic within Transjordan. Under such an arrangement, military and legislative power would be divided equally between Arab and Jew, but Abdullah would be sovereign of the new federation.

Golda's face showed consternation. "Your Majesty," she began firmly, "our cause is being discussed at present at the United Nations and we are hoping for a

On the road to freedom. **At the United Nations the Yishuv won the promise of partition. Here, on November 30, 1947, in front of the Jewish Agency building in Jerusalem, Jews gathered to mark the momentous occasion of the international community's having sanctioned the establishment of a Jewish state alongside an Arab one.**

resolution that would establish two states—Arab and Hebrew. We wish to speak with you only about an agreement based on such a resolution."

The king and Golda found common ground in Abdullah's hope that Transjordan would take control of the Arab part of Palestine, but the king was emphatic that the Arab portion must not become a state. "I want to ride, not to be ridden," he stressed. If the Jews were to help him annex the Arab portion of Palestine, he added, he would be prepared to sign an agreement with them.

Golda and the king agreed to meet sometime after the United Nations vote, Abdullah suggesting that "some day" she might be his guest in his palace in Amman, the capital of his kingdom. The conversation ended amicably. Golda was satisfied that the king had peaceful intentions.

Sir Alec Kirkbride, the British high commissioner in Amman, appeared to sense, when he heard about the secret encounter, that Golda had been speaking to Abdullah at a distinct disadvantage: "When I was told of this interview, I thought that the Israelis had made a mistake by being represented by a woman. Although he respected the opposite sex, King Abdullah was a conservative. "In his eyes," continued Kirkbridge, "women could not be the equal of men, particularly in politics. Arguing politics with a woman made him uncomfortable. In addition, Golda had had little experience in negotiating with the Arabs. It is regrettable that this mission was not entrusted to someone like Sharett, who knew the Arab language and the Arab mentality."

Maintaining the contact with Abdullah had not proven easy. He had hoped that the Jews might accept his compromise offer, and thus the other Arab rulers would view him as the only one on the Arab side who could make partition work. But when it became clear to the king that the Jews would reject his concessions, he turned against them. He sent Golda a message stating that he was a man of his word, and a promise made to a woman would not be broken. But Golda knew that Abdullah was gradually drifting over to the side of the more belligerent Arabs.

Trip to Amman

On March 30, 1948 the National Council of the Yishuv, which by this time had replaced the Jewish Agency, asked Golda to attempt to meet with the king again. It took until May for the monarch to grant her request. In the early part of that month, reports began to circulate that the king was about to join the fighting against the Yishuv.

Daskel had received word that Abdullah was prepared to see Golda on May 11, but only in Amman. To come to Naharayim was too dangerous. Upon hearing the news, Golda took the first plane out of Jerusalem. During a stopover in Haifa she asked a dressmaker to make a simple black Arab dress for her, which she would wear as a disguise.

Abdullah provided Golda with a car and driver at the border; he insisted that she don the Arab garb immediately to lessen the risk. Wearing a black veil over her face, and the dress that had been sewn for her in Haifa, Golda sat in the rear seat of the car next to her "husband"—actually Ezra Danin—dressed in a Bedouin *keffiah*.

The three-hour drive from the border to Amman was tense. The driver was Abdullah's trusted servant, and as the car reached each of the ten checkpoints, he called out his own name. Each time the car was permitted through without anyone addressing a word to the woman and gentleman in the back seat.

Finally the vehicle arrived at a stone house above the road to the airport. The guests were escorted into a circular salon, painted green, with a large fireplace tiled in black. Tea was served until the king appeared. When Abdullah entered, his tone and attitude were noticeably different from what Golda had remembered from their first meeting. His fellow Arabs now had him in their control, and unless the Jews would make generous concessions, war was all but inevitable.

The king proposed that the Jews cancel their plans to establish a Jewish state and accept, instead, autonomy for one year. After that Transjordan would annex all of Palestine. A joint parliament, half Jewish, and a joint Cabinet, also half Jewish, would be set up. The alternative was simple: war!

Golda was shaken by the king's ultimatum. Recalling his pledge of November, she said to him sternly, "Have you broken your promise to me, after all?"

The new army. Golda with soldiers of the newly-formed Israel Defense Forces in 1948.

"I am not allowed to keep my promises," he answered. "Last year I was alone; I had complete freedom of action. Today I am merely one chief of state among five others."

Abdullah then pressed for a compromise: "Put off your declaration of independence, suspend immigration for a few years. Why are you in such a hurry? I have no choice: either you agree to my new proposal, or it will mean war—whatever the cost to me. However, I will always be glad to talk to you and to sit down with you around a table in order to achieve peace."

Golda could only reply, "A people that has waited two thousand years can hardly be described as being in a hurry." And addressing the king's proposals, she said curtly, "Do you think we did all that just to be represented in a foreign parliament? Not even ten Jews with any influence would accept your proposals. We can give you the answer here and now. If Your Majesty has turned his back on our original understanding and wants war instead, there will be war. Despite our handicaps, we believe that we will win. Perhaps we shall meet again after the war, when there will be a Jewish state."

Realizing that further discussion was pointless, the king said sadly, "I am sorry. I deplore the coming bloodshed and destruction. Let us hope we shall meet again and not sever our relations."

During the entire trip home Golda was depressed over the gloomy message she was carrying with her. Moreover, she was concerned about her safety, as well as Danin's. The Arab driver taking them to Naharayim was petrified each time they stopped at a checkpoint. There was complete darkness all around, and Iraqi troops were not far away. Golda, too, was frightened. Eventually a Haganah guard from Naharayim spotted the two and ushered them home safely.

In Tel Aviv, at a meeting, Golda caught up with Ben-Gurion, the leader of the Yishuv. She passed him a note: "It didn't work. There will be war."

On May 13 Moshe Shertok cabled to Nahum Goldmann, president of the World Zionist Organization, the following summary of Golda's encounter with the king: "THE KING LOOKED WORRIED, HARASSED; CONVERSATION STRENGTHENED GOLDA'S IMPRESSION THAT THE KING'S ULTIMATE BEHAVIOR DEPENDS ON GREAT BRITAIN."

Nearly one year later, in March, 1949, Walter Eytan, the director-general of the new Israeli foreign ministry, was one of a delegation holding talks with Abdullah. "And how is Mrs. Golda Meyerson?" the king asked.

"Mrs. Meyerson is now Israel's minister to Moscow," was Eytan's reply.

Abdullah's face broke into a smile. "Good," he said, "leave her there."

Early in 1951 the same Abdullah noted to another Jewish emissary that in his view Golda Meyerson was largely responsible for the 1948 war—because she had turned down his offer of peace.

Golda herself never felt guilt over the failure of her secret meetings with Abdullah. Before entering those sessions, she had little hope for a peaceful resolution of the problem.

Golda never met Abdullah again, for in 1951, while attending prayers in Jerusalem, the king was assassinated.

The capability of a new Jewish state to defend itself against the Arabs was in grave doubt. Even optimists thought the chances for success were no better than 50-50. In a meeting with Sir Alan Cunningham, just as British forces were pulling out in May, 1948, the British official suggested that Golda remove her daughter, Sarah, from the Negev desert kibbutz, Revivim. "There will be war," he said gravely, "and they stand no chance in those settlements. The Egyptians will move through them no matter how hard they [the kibbutzniks] fight. Why not bring her home to Jerusalem?"

Golda eyed Cunningham coldly. "Thank you. But all the boys and girls in those settlements have mothers. If all of them take their children home, then who will stop the Egyptians?"

The Establishment of the State

Despite such dark thoughts, plans were being made for the dramatic announcement of May 14, 1948. Had things gone as planned, Golda would not have been present at the Tel Aviv ceremony on that historic Friday afternoon, when the establishment of the new State of Israel was proclaimed. A few days earlier Ben-

The greatest moment of all. **David Ben-Gurion, the new prime minister and father of his country, reads the declaration of Israeli independence during moving ceremonies in the Tel Aviv Museum, May 14, 1948. With the announcement of Israeli statehood, Arab armies mounted an all-out effort to wipe out the new state. Thus, even as Ben-Gurion read the fateful words, there was full realization that a great, bloody struggle would have to take place before independence would be truly assured.**

Gurion had ordered her to return to Jerusalem and to remain there indefinitely. Flying to Jerusalem in a two-seater, Golda and the pilot went through a terrifying experience after engine trouble developed. Despairing of finding a landing site, the pilot considered setting down in an Arab village, but finally was able to bring the aircraft safely back to Tel Aviv. Golda would attend the ceremony after all.

For security reasons, the rather unpretentious Tel Aviv Museum was chosen as the site for the ceremony where the Declaration of Independence would be issued. Because of its small size, the building could be easily guarded. Only about 200 people had been invited, and each was sworn to secrecy about the time and

מדינת ישראל תהא פתוחה לעליה יהודית ולקיבוץ גלויות
תשקוד על פיתוח הארץ לטובת כל תושביה, תהא משתתת על
יסודות החירות, הצדק והשלום לאור חזונם של נביאי ישראל, תקיים
שויון זכויות חברתי ומדיני גמור לכל אזרחיה בלי הבדל דת, גזע ומין,
תבטיח חופש דת, מצפון, לשון, חינוך ותרבות, תשמר על המקומות
הקדושים של כל הדתות, ותהיה נאמנה לעקרונותיה של מגילת
האומות המאוחדות.

מדינת ישראל תהא מוכנה לשתף פעולה עם המוסדות והנציגים
של האומות המאוחדות בהגשמת החלטת העצרת מיום 29 בנובמבר
1947 ותפעל להקמת האחדות הכלכלית של ארץ־ישראל בשלמותה.

אנו קוראים לאומות המאוחדות לתת יד לעם היהודי בבנין
מדינתו ולקבל את מדינת ישראל לתוך משפחת העמים.

אנו קוראים – גם בתוך התקפת־הדמים הנערכת עלינו זה
חדשים – לבני העם הערבי תושבי מדינת ישראל לשמור על השלום
וליטול חלקם בבנין המדינה על יסוד אזרחות מלאה ושוה ועל יסוד
נציגות מתאמה בכל מוסדותיה, הזמניים והקבועים.

אנו מושיטים יד שלום ושכנות טובה לכל המדינות השכנות
ועמיהן, וקוראים להם לשיתוף פעולה ועזרה הדדית עם העם העברי
העצמאי בארצו. מדינת ישראל מוכנה לתרום חלקה במאמץ משותף
לקידמת המזרח התיכון כולו.

אנו קוראים אל העם היהודי בכל התפוצות להתלכד סביב
הישוב בעליה ובבנין ולעמוד לימינו במערכה הגדולה על הגשמת
שאיפת הדורות לגאולת ישראל.

מתוך בטחון בצור ישראל הננו חותמים בחתימת ידינו
לעדות על הכרזה זו, במושב מועצת המדינה הזמנית
על אדמת המולדת, בעיר תל־אביב, היום הזה, ערב שבת
ה' אייר תש"ח, 14 במאי 1948.

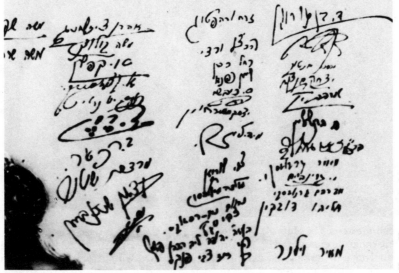

Historic document. The final section of the Declaration of Independence, with
signatures at the bottom. The tenth signature in the middle column is that of
Golda Meyerson.

place of the event. Golda, one of the two women (the other was Rachel Kagan) invited to sign the document proclaiming the establishment of the State of Israel, wore her best black dress for the occasion. The thirty-seven signers approached the document in alphabetical order. Moshe Shertok held the paper down so each could affix his or her signature. As Golda lifted pen in hand to write her name, tears welled up in her eyes.

War commences. On May 14, 1948, members of the new Israeli Army occupy a building recently evacuated by the British forces. The British left on the very day the new State of Israel was established. With the British Mandate over and British forces en route home, a vacuum was created, with no third force to stand between rival Jewish and Arab military units.

Keren Kayemet Archives

Siege. **Jerusalem was a focal point of the struggle for independence in 1948. Arab gunmen managed to hold the city under siege for months at a time, stepping up their campaign after the state was declared. Here, Jews in Jerusalem prepare for further siege by taking small amounts of water under the rationing scheme imposed on all residents.**

"Why do you weep so much, Golda?" asked David Zvi Pincus, a member of the religious Mizrachi Party. "Because," she replied emotionally, "it breaks my heart to think of all those who should have been here today and are not."

The event had a surrealistic quality for Golda. She recalled studying American history and reading about the signers of the American Declaration of Independence: "I couldn't imagine that these were real people doing something real. It was like a fairy tale almost. I couldn't imagine them to be real men, and there I was sitting and signing a declaration of independence."

5

Golda as Diplomat

Although Golda felt she deserved an appointment to the Cabinet in Israel's first government, Prime Minister David Ben-Gurion had other ideas. Foreign Minister Moshe Sharett, acting in concert with Ben-Gurion, suggested that Golda be appointed as Israel's first minister to the Soviet Union. The position was not insignificant. To Israelis, good relations with Russia were essential, since Russia was one of the first nations to recognize the new state.

Being appointed minister to a country as important as the Soviet Union was not as prestigious as an appointment to Israel's first Cabinet. Golda was singularly unimpressed when rumors began to circulate about her probable appointment. "Well," she said to Sharett, eager to find an excuse to escape the contemplated assignment, "thank God you can't offer it to me. My Russian is almost nonexistent."

When Sharett dismissed this shortcoming as trivial, Golda realized that the die was cast. Meanwhile, she went off to the United States on a fund-raising tour, putting the thought of an assignment to Moscow out of her mind.

But "Moscow" would not go away. During her travels Golda received a telegram from Sharett formally asking her to accept the assignment. To friends she raged bitterly at the unfairness of the offer, a mission that would keep her out of Israel in its formative years. She was also apprehensive about having to enter a whole new world—a world of diplomacy of which she knew nothing.

But Golda had no choice. Personal likes and dislikes were not more important than the welfare of the state. "One's duty is one's duty," she often said, "and it has nothing to do with justice." This was the standard Golda had set for herself, and by this standard she always judged others.

A Broken Leg in Brooklyn

Golda's sense of duty to the new state sent her on a round of farewells in the United States, after which she returned to Israel to prepare for her new task.

It was the first week of June, and the announcement that she would be going to Moscow as Israel's first minister had just been made public. Golda was en route to Brooklyn, via taxicab, where she planned to take her leave of old friends Fanny and Jacob Goodman. Suddenly, the taxi in which she rode collided with another. Golda was thrown to the floor. Her screams caught the attention of passersby, and a

Israel's first foreign minister. Golda appears here with Moshe Sharett in August, 1948. Sharett was then the nation's first foreign minister. Later, Prime Minister David Ben-Gurion would make the decision to replace him, and Golda would be given the job.

Keren Hayesod

The three sisters. Of the Mabovitch sisters, only Sheyna (center) and Golda (right) immigrated to Israel. Clara remained in the United States. Here, the two Israelis pose with their American sister at the Essex House in New York.

private ambulance was called. Golda, in severe pain, was taken to Bellevue Hospital, where she had to wait in dirty surroundings for several hours before being examined. The diagnosis: a fracture of the leg. Eventually Golda was transferred to the Hospital for Joint Diseases, where a member of the staff asked if she wanted any help. "I'm fine," Golda responded, "but I'm concerned about those poor devils in Bellevue."

Although proof of the newly appointed minister's injuries could easily have been established with X-rays, the Soviets characterized the entire episode as a mere diplomatic illness. Israel, they insisted, was seeking an excuse to delay the exchange of representatives between Moscow and Tel Aviv. The Russian representative to Tel Aviv could not present his credentials until his Israeli counterpart did so in Moscow. The Russians believed that the Israelis were stalling so that the Russian representative would be delayed in arriving in Tel Aviv, thus enabling the American representative to Israel to arrive before his Soviet counterpart. In this manner, the American would become doyen of the diplomatic corps.

The Israeli foreign ministry felt pressed to send a reasonably healthy Golda Meyerson to Moscow, but telegrams inquiring about the state of her health and expected date of departure met with a chilly response from the ailing minister-designate. The Soviets may consider it all a snub, her doctors advised, but leaving the hospital too soon could result in further complications. Her leg had improved, but phlebitis had set in and several blood clots had developed.

Again, impelled by an unfailing sense of duty, Golda was not about to allow pain in her leg to stand in the way of political expectations. She left the hospital sooner than the physicians recommended, but not a minute too soon for the Soviets or the Israeli leadership.

Official Relations with Moscow

As early as October, 1943, Golda had received strong indications from the Soviets that they would be willing to establish close relations with the Jews of Palestine. In that year Ivan Maisky, the Soviet minister to Great Britain, had paid a one-day visit to Palestine, where he had met with Golda, who then represented the Histadrut. Golda reported that Maisky "really wanted to find out whether something can be done in this country, so that when the time comes when a stand will have to be taken on the Jewish question and Palestine, he will have firsthand knowledge on the subject. We have the feeling that his visit has been of significant value."

Golda recalled that experience as she and a handful of Israelis set out to establish Israel's first legation in Moscow. Hopes for success were high. Golda and her delegation were euphoric.

However, almost from the very start optimism began to fade. The Israelis arrived in Moscow on September 3, 1948, a day on which the Soviets were burying Andrei Zdanov, a high-ranking associate of Stalin's and a member of the Politburo. The day was dark, gray, rainy, the streets draped with black flags. Zdanov's funeral procession was held up for a few moments to allow the newly arrived

Israeli delegation to pass through with their tiny cavalcade of cars. Without fanfare, the Israelis finally reached their quarters at the Metropole, a five-star establishment that was far from luxurious.

The new minister. In the fall of 1948 Israel's first Minister to Moscow, Golda Meyerson, presented her credentials to Deputy Chairman Valssov of the Supreme Soviet. It was hoped that the Israeli legation's arrrival in the Soviet Union would lead to close Israeli-Soviet relations, but Golda left her assignment feeling disappointed that little movement toward that goal had been made.

Life with the Moscow Delegation

Golda began to organize her troupe of twenty-one Israelis. Simple in her tastes and needs, she vowed that the Israeli legation would live modestly. Her own experience with poverty had trained her to live with few luxuries, and she insisted that the new state's penury meant that there would be little money available for fancy cars, meals, or parties. Golda's modest lifestyle was soon adopted by the entire legation.

The idea was sound but its execution more difficult. The hotel prepared lunch and dinner for the Israeli delegation, but breakfast was ordered through room service on an individual basis. For a week this system continued, until Golda received the hotel's bill. She was astonished. "We can't go on like this," she told the legation staff at a hastily called meeting. "We'll ruin our government if we go on eating twice a day together, and then charge it off to the hotel." As of that day the minister ordered that the staff eat only lunch together. As for the other two meals, they would have to be eaten at a reasonable cost.

Thus, one of the strangest sights in Moscow those days was the shopping tour of the Israeli minister and her assistant, Lou Kaddar. Methodically, during the cold, dark Moscow mornings they would canvas a variety of peasant stalls in search of bread, cheese, butter, and eggs. Golda located a store which sold stolen German war products cheaply, and a hot plate and electric kettle were purchased for each room of the Israeli delegation. On Saturdays, in her room, Golda cooked for the "bachelors," including Lou and herself.

Being unsalaried, the Israelis found it difficult to maintain proper dress and grooming. The men's hair lengthened into curls—quite unfashionable in those days—and their clothing was often soiled and unpressed. Austerity proved tolerable for some, but many could not accept it. Lou Kaddar, for example, discovering that she had too little money for a manicure, led a minor revolt. Soon she won Golda's approval for pocket money to purchase a few specific items.

A Matter of Protocol

Golda's naiveté in matters of protocol helped her score a point with the Soviets at her credentials ceremony. The inexperienced Israeli staff took the ceremony quite seriously, rehearsing like children. It was just as well, for the Russians quickly tried to take advantage of the delegation's inexperience.

Israel's new minister was called upon to deliver a brief speech, and the Russian in charge of protocol suggested to Aryeh Levavi, first secretary of the legation and the man charged with the delicate pre-ceremony negotiations, that Golda speak in English rather than Hebrew. "Mrs. Meyerson speaks English very well," he said.

When Golda was informed of this, she replied caustically, "But I'm not an Englishman or an American. I'm an Israeli."

Levavi passed Golda's view along to the Russians and considered the matter settled. Upon his next visit to the Kremlin, a very apologetic Soviet official took Levavi aside and informed him that the Soviets had been unable to find a translator who could translate Mrs. Meyerson's Hebrew into Russian. "So," he asked meekly, "would the minister mind speaking in English after all?"

Apprised of the latest development, Golda quickly seized upon Levavi as an adequate translator and proposed him to the Soviets. They politely refused and proceeded to hold the ceremony without an official translator—quite a departure from protocol—with Golda's speech delivered in Hebrew but never translated for the benefit of the Soviets present.

Diplomacy, with its emphasis on protocol, its need for the right word—or at least not the wrong word—seemed a sticky thicket of weird ritual and excessive talk. Golda's adjustment had its amusing moments. The first time she paid a courtesy call on another foreign diplomat, she became annoyed both at the time wasted and the triviality of the subject matter discussed. When the diplomat asked

Golda how she arrived in Russia, Lou Kaddar, as French-language interpreter, turned to Golda and repeated the question in Hebrew.

"What?" said Golda testily to Lou. "You don't know? In an airplane."

Dutifully, Lou repeated Golda's answer to the diplomat: *"En aviron."*

A private joke. **Mrs. Meyerson, the New Israeli minister, exchanges a joke with Valssov. To her right is Valerin Zorin, deputy foreign minister. At the extreme left is Gorkin, secretary of the Supreme Soviet.**

The diplomat then asked Golda where she lived, and again Lou put the question to Golda, who snapped even more tartly, "What? You don't know? Tell him in the hotel."

Lou became concerned that Golda might think her translator was an imbecile who deserved to be sent packing. But at the fifth encounter with a diplomat, when Lou turned to Golda and asked, "How did we come?" Golda replied impassively, "We rode white donkeys."

Getting Golda's message, Lou translated: "By plane, Mr. Ambassador." When Lou asked Golda where they lived, Golda's reply, again without batting an eyelash, was "in tents."

Meeting People in Russia

Serving in Moscow was both punishment and opportunity for Golda. Being away from Israel during its first year of existence deprived her of the chance to serve her country at home during a most crucial time. Isolation in Russia put a great strain on her. It was as if she had been exiled to Siberia.

To make matters worse, the Soviets did not allow foreigners to mix freely and to cultivate friends. Golda hoped to bridge this gap by holding open house on Friday evenings. She invited ordinary Russians, including Russian Jews, but none showed up. And so these open-house evenings ended up as a meeting place for the foreign press corps—nothing more.

Friendship with resident diplomats also proved difficult to cultivate. Few nations had recognized the State of Israel. Nonetheless, as per established diplomatic procedure Golda's legation sent out letters to all ambassadors, informing them of the arrival of the Israeli delegation. Anyone who responded was to be invited to meet with Golda.

Almost as if by conspiracy, few responded. Finally, a telephone call came from the representative of Luxembourg, a non-Jew named Bloom. Bloom confessed that he had been uncertain about the proper protocol to be followed in dealing with the Israeli minister, since his country had not recognized the Jewish state. However, he decided, "I'm going to see this woman," no matter what his countrymen might think. Bloom's telephone call had a positive effect on the foreign diplomatic community. The ice had been broken. Other representatives soon called on Golda.

The Moscow Synagogue

If there was an experience that made the entire Moscow exercise worthwhile, it was the response of the Russian Jews to Golda as she met them on several dramatic, memorable occasions in the Moscow synagogue. The new minister visited the synagogue more out of obligation—as the representative of the State of Israel—than personal preference. Delegation members had been instructed before leaving Israel to take with them all religious articles necessary for prayer.

On the first Saturday (the Jewish Sabbath) after presenting her credentials, Golda and her staff appeared at Moscow's Great Synagogue. Informed that some 500,000 Jews lived in Moscow, Golda was disturbed to find barely 300 people in attendance. She was astounded to hear the rabbi invoke a blessing both on her and Stalin, the Soviet leader who was little loved among Russian Jewry. The Soviet leader and the Israeli minister were given full equality at the Jewish prayer service.

A few weeks later, on October 16, Rosh Hashanah (the Jewish New Year) arrived, and Golda again planned to visit the synagogue. This time the crowds were large. At first the assembled Jews were unsure of how to react to this female representative from the Holy Land. But soon the mob outside the synagogue encircled Golda, shouting out her name, giving her a collective embrace. The embassy staff standing nearby worried that their leader might be crushed. But for the most part the crowd treated her gently. Although some pushed and shoved, reached for her clothing, most wanted simply to get near enough to see her, perhaps to touch her.

Golda was overcome by the affection. She felt an electricity in the air, a feeling of Jewishness spilling out all over. She uttered only one thing, and she did so repeatedly, as she turned from side to side to address the mob: *"A dank eich vos ihr seit geblieben Yidden*—Thanks for remaining Jewish."

Only those near Golda could hear the Yiddish words she uttered, but soon her sentiments were passed through the crowd like a precious gift. Some said there were 30,000 present that day, others put the figure at closer to 50,000, but all were aware of Golda's feelings. And those precious moments would be treasured by Golda for the rest of her stay in the Soviet Union, indeed for the rest of her life.

In the short run, the demonstration outside the synagogue had some adverse consequences. Stalin seized upon those few moments of Jewish rejuvenation as a pretext for a new wave of anti-Semitism. An expression was coined to describe those Russian Jews who displayed too much excitement over the presence of the Israeli legation in Moscow or who displayed their Jewishness openly on that Rosh Hashanah day in 1948. They were called "Golda's prisoners."

Golda hoped the Rosh Hashanah awakening would have other, more positive consequences. Perhaps the Israelis could tap that inherently strong Jewish sentiment and lay the foundation for what before had been unthinkable: the immigration of Russian Jews to Israel.

Discreet probes were made, and Golda did what she could to assuage the fear of the Soviets that Israel might drift into the Western orbit. But nothing seemed to help. The gates of Russia were closed to Jews desirous of emigrating to Israel.

Meeting with Mrs. Molotov

There were moments of great elation for Golda during her Russian stay. One occurred on November 7, 1948, the anniversary of the Bolshevik Revolution.

Large numbers of Soviet dignitaries had come to the home of Vyacheslav Molotov, the foreign minister, as part of a holiday reception. Golda arrived with the other foreign diplomats; they were led into a small, private room. To everyone's surprise, in walked Mrs. Molotov. When she approached Golda, the two women began groping for a common language. Though Golda understood Russian, she was unable to speak it. The Soviet woman, through her interpreter, said, "I don't speak Hebrew of course, but I speak Yiddish—do you speak Yiddish?"

Shocked, Golda quickly recovered to ask, "How do you speak Yiddish?"

This time Ivy Molotov answered in Yiddish: "Why, I'm a daughter of Israel."

With Jew talking to Jew, a new ambiance developed. Ivy Molotov introduced her new acquaintance with great pride. "I want you to meet this woman," she said to each dignitary as she introduced Golda, "the minister from the new State of Israel."

Meeting this important member of the Soviet elite, a Jewess proud of her heritage, bolstered Golda' spirits. Reaching out to Russians in general, and Jews in particular, might be easier now, but that was not to be the case. Later, Golda learned that Ivy Molotov had paid a heavy price for her frankness that day. She was arrested soon afterward and exiled to Siberia for two years.

That same week, Golda attended a Russian military parade. She was impressed by the powerful weapons as they were paraded down the avenue. Over a glass of vodka later that day she said to Foreign Minister Molotov, "If we only had a small part of the weapons that I saw at the parade today." Sympathetically, the foreign minister replied, "You will. We also had to start from scratch."

Attempts at Public Relations

Much of Golda's frustration in Moscow came from her inability to perform normal diplomatic functions. While she could make contact with Soviet officialdom at cocktail parties, a meeting with Stalin was ruled out, as it was to virtually all other foreign diplomats. What Golda wanted, what she assumed was her main task, was to explain what her country was all about and to establish firm ties between the Soviet Union and Israel. Opportunities to accomplish this did not exist.

In its naiveté, the Israeli legation to Moscow decided to publish a bulletin describing happenings in the new Jewish state. Of necessity, the Israelis were careful to omit anything that might be construed as anti-Soviet. The bulletin was to be sent to certain Soviet organizations as well as to diplomatic missions.

Almost immediately after publication of the first issue, Golda was called into the office of Valerian Zorin, the deputy foreign minister. Zorin scrutinized her as if she had just assassinated Joseph Stalin. This bulletin, he said, is "a grave offense against Soviet institutions, against Soviet law, and a violation of diplomatic privilege."

Failing to understand his objections, Golda replied calmly, "I was not aware that this would be objectionable." No further explanation was forthcoming, and to avoid additional repercussions issuance of the bulletin was stopped. It seemed that whenever the Israelis wanted to communicate the message of the new state to the Russians, an obstacle arose.

Acting with Golda's permission, one day in the fall of 1948 two embassy staff members, Aryeh Levavi and Aryeh Lapide, translated a telegram from the Israeli foreign ministry, which detailed several victories of the Israeli Army during the War of Independence. Excited over the Israeli triumphs, one of which was the sinking of the Egyptian vessel *King Farouk,* Levavi and Lapide hastily prepared press releases. The two men then drove to the offices of a half dozen Soviet newspapers and submitted a release to each. They then returned home to await arrival of the next morning's papers. Anxiously they flipped through the pages of each paper. Not a word appeared. This time the Soviet foreign ministry was oddly silent. And though Levavi and Lapide were distraught, Golda took the news with equanimity, never having really expected more.

After a few similar incidents, Golda was convinced that the Soviet bureaucracy was not well disposed to foreign diplomats, that her job was in effect meaningless. "One could send a dummy as minister and it would have the same impact," she affirmed.

Nothing corroborated Golda's evaluation more poignantly than the experience she had with a man known simply as Hefetz. Hefetz had left his birthplace, Jerusalem, in 1926 and went off to fight in the Spanish Civil War. Wounded, he escaped to Russia with other injured veterans. One day Hefetz turned up at the Israeli legation in Moscow, asking for help in returning home.

With his thick eyeglasses, Hefetz was a sight to behold: emaciated, dressed in rags, shivering from the cold. He had reached the legation using stolen money.

His story was pitiful enough to warrant a meeting with Golda. As he told her his tale in Hebrew, he struck a responsive chord in the minister. She promised to take up his case with the Soviets without delay.

Soon Golda was on the phone with Molotov, requesting an unprecedented on-the-spot meeting. Warily, the foreign minister agreed. Molotov claimed icily that he knew nothing of the man, and Golda took leave. But keeping her promise to Hefetz, she continued to investigate. Several months passed and nothing happened.

Hefetz came to see Golda for a second time. She learned that after his first visit to the legation, the man had been severely punished by the Russians. Golda was angered. She rushed to see Molotov once more, but her efforts proved fruitless. When he learned that Golda could be of no help, he committed suicide.

The Soviet regime made life for the Israeli delegation difficult in other ways as well. If the legation wanted to open a bank account, it had to receive permission from the foreign ministry. The same held true for sending cables or purchasing theater tickets.

Golda felt trapped. On the issues that really mattered to her—arms deals, cultural and commercial relations—the Russians would not move. Russian Jewish immigration was a dead subject.

The Soviet experience left Golda gravely suspicious about the value of diplomacy. It also left her with a deep sense of mistrust toward the Soviet Union. All the talk of mutual friendship that had been bandied about at the outset of her tour in Moscow had been nothing but sheer rhetoric.

But an excited foreign minister would soon learn that her days of service in Moscow were numbered, that more important and useful work awaited her at home.

6

Back Home After Moscow

The initiative to bring Golda back home from Moscow came from Prime Minister David Ben-Gurion.

On January 24, 1949, Ben-Gurion's Mapai Party captured 35.7 percent of the vote in Israel's first national elections. Of the 120 Knesset (Parliament) seats, 46 went to Mapai, giving it more votes and consequently more power than any other party. Mapai would form the country's first elected government, and Ben-Gurion wanted Golda in the Cabinet.

For some time Ben-Gurion had been of the opinion that Israel could not afford to be without a woman Cabinet minister. On March 14, 1948 he had written to Moshe Sharett, in New York, that "it is unheard of that the first government would be established without a woman because she [Golda] is capable of doing the job as a man."

In February, 1949, Ben-Gurion cabled Moscow, requesting that Golda return home immediately. Golda notified Ben-Gurion that she would require some time to say her farewells. Although she had not mastered all the intricacies of diplomacy, she had learned that foreign diplomats did not leave a country without making a final round of visits.

Golda realized that her response would not be looked upon favorably by the prime minister. Ben-Gurion had little patience with the world of diplomacy; to him forming an effective Cabinet was far more important. A compromise of sorts was reached: Golda would return to Israel, but only for a short while. She would then return to Moscow to say her goodbyes.

Golda Becomes Minister of Labor

Which Cabinet post would be offered her? Ben-Gurion felt she would serve best as deputy prime minister in charge of development. But when Moshe Sharett mentioned the idea to Golda shortly after her arrival at Lod Airport, she balked. "I understand nothing about development matters," she protested. Citing her background in the Histadrut, Golda believed the labor ministry to be the natural place for her. Much to her surprise, Ben-Gurion agreed.

On March 11 Golda was sworn into office along with the other members of Israel's new government. Then, she journeyed back to Moscow. By April 20 the new minister of labor had returned to Israel and was seated at her desk, ready to begin work.

Joining the Cabinet. The minister to Moscow returns to Israel and is greeted by Sheyna and Moshe Sharett, Israel's foreign minister, on February 18, 1949. Soon Golda would assume her new responsibilities as minister of labor. She had wanted to serve as a Cabinet minister from the time the state was established, and now she was about to get her chance.

To Help Build a Nation

The situation Golda found in her homeland would have depressed even the most optimistic soul. The nation had won a great victory against the Arab armies, and there was great joy in, at last, having a state. But the staggering costs of the war were overwhelming. The country had little money. There was inadequate shelter and a scarcity of jobs. Soldiers had been demobilized, only to find that they had to sleep on park benches, for lack of housing.

There was great joy, too, over the fact that immigration into Israel was now unrestrained, but some of this cheer was mitigated by the bitter realities that awaited the new immigrants. The large number of people who poured through the gates was too great for the tiny new state to handle. Between January, 1919 and May, 1948—the period of the British Mandate—only 390,580 Jews had reached Palestine. By the end of 1949, streaming in at a rate of 1,000 per day, the immigrant population totalled one million.

It was a crucial test for the new state. Finances were limited, and competition between Israel's defense and social ministries was fierce. Adding to the burden, the immigrants had come from seventy countries, and many were impoverished

Longtime friends. Golda, minister of labor, with Zalman Shazar, minister of education (and a future president of the State of Israel). The photograph was taken in March, 1949. Shazar was one of Golda's closest acquaintances during their long public careers.

Over a cup of coffee. **Golda, then minister of labor, seated with David Remez, close friend and Cabinet colleague, in September, 1949, exchanges words with Police Chief Sachar. They are seated in the Knesset restaurant.**

Holocaust survivors. To them the new state was a final refuge, and the Israeli government had to provide for them regardless of the difficulties.

Golda Meyerson understood the enormity of the job that faced her as minister of labor, but she was not discouraged. She was familiar with such problems from her Histadrut experience.

No single position in government could have offered Golda a better chance to help build a nation. She now had the opportunity to reach into every area of Israeli life, from housing to employment to social security. Golda had risen steadily to positions of increasing power, but now she was where she wanted to be.

A variety of plans to resolve the financial crisis created by the cost of war and the influx of the destitute immigrants was proposed to the new minister of labor. She listened to the economists but found that they had used reason more than heart to guide them. They tended to oppose programs that would create job opportunities and provide housing as wasteful stop-gap measures. It was the long-

A new political start. **The official opening of the Knesset in Jerusalem on December 28, 1949. Yosef Sprinzak, the first speaker of the Knesset, addresses the deputies. Golda is seated at the Cabinet table.**

term benefits that should be of primary concern, they argued; otherwise the country would bankrupt itself. The economists favored investing in industry, believing that the answer lay in high productivity. Unfortunately for the immigrants, the experts wanted to focus on agriculture, even though few newcomers knew anything about or expressed an interest in farming.

Creating Housing and Jobs

Into this controversy the new minister of labor injected herself. She understood the experts' viewpoint, but she could not agree. To her, the country's immediate needs were of prime importance. Without housing and jobs the new immigrants could not survive.

Her reasoning now clear, Golda issued the first order of her ministry: housing and jobs was to be the top priority. She refused at this crucial moment to concern herself with trade unions, labor-management problems, and the like, matters of concern to labor ministries in the Western world.

At one of the early labor ministry meetings, which included all department

Good Socialist. Golda marches with Histadrut leaders at the 1949 May Day parade in Tel Aviv. At this time the minister of labor firmly believed that the tenets of Socialism could be implemented, and she sought to do that by working toward full employment and the erection of adequate housing.

heads, Golda greeted the director of the ministry's trade union department by inquiring as to his function.

He answered proudly, "My job is to strengthen and foster the growth of trade unions."

"That is one job we certainly do not need to do," Golda sneered.

A country which had the Histadrut, incorporating labor and management into one giant socially-oriented concern, could afford to dispense with such a department. Golda ordered the trade union department abolished.

She insisted, too, that the government find a means of tackling the problems of housing and employment without interrupting the flow of immigration. Some wanted to slow down the rate of immigration, but Golda was adamant about keeping Israel's doors open. Open immigration was what the entire struggle against the British had been about. She still believed what she had always maintained: "A Jewish state that aims at a high standard of living without . . . unrestricted immigration . . . I for one don't see any need for it [a state that would restrict immigration]."

This became Israel's policy. Immigrants came without restriction, but when

Magic Carpet. Yemenite families waiting in November of 1949 at the Aden Airport for their flight to Israel. Israel had fought for the right to gather in hundreds of thousands of Jewish refugees. Now, with the war ended, it had a chance to achieve that goal. In 1949 alone nearly 250,000 Jewish immigrants poured into Israel, and by the end of 1951 Israel's population had increased to 1.5 million, more than double the figure during the War of Independence. These Yemenite families were part of the Magic Carpet program to bring the Jews of Yemen to Israel.

they arrived, more often than not they were housed in tent cities set up in fields that became awash with mud in winter. And there was no hope for immediate relief, and there were few opportunities for employment. Demonstrations with chants of *lechem v'avoda,* "bread and work," were constantly heard.

In an attempt to relieve these pressing problems, Golda traveled to the United States. There, she approached Jewish builders in the hope that they might solve Israel's housing crisis. They could not. Their equipment was not suitable and their prices too high. Golda returned disappointed. She was now convinced that Israelis themselves would have to build the necessary housing; only financial support could be expected from the United States.

The Meyerson Housing Plan

On May 24, 1950, Golda Meyerson appeared before the Knesset with the "Meyerson Plan," a proposal to build 30,000 new housing units. Money was the

The "magic" airlift. Some of the 50,000 Yemenite Jews airlifted to Israel between December, 1948, and September, 1950, in what has come to be called Operation Magic Carpet.

key ingredient. She canvassed American Jewish communities with a confession: "I presented a project for which I don't have the money. In the meantime, we will be happy and they will be happy, even though it means putting a family of two, three, four, or five into one room. But this is better than putting two or three families in a single tent." It took longer than she had hoped, but in time immigrants moved from tents to permanent housing. Golda's imprint on the building of her country (particularly the city of Beersheba) was now visible and enduring.

Golda now turned her attention to the immigrant employment problem. She believed in the dignity of labor. A man had to have a job. No matter how little money he brought home, no matter how little he actually worked each week, he had to be employed. The Socialist within her was expressing itself.

The economists suggested plans that would create employment, but Golda contended that while these plans looked good on paper, they depended on funds

Beginning a new life. Newly-arrived immigrants at the *Sha'ar Ha'aliya* (Gate of Immigration) transit camp near Haifa in 1949.

not yet allocated. The plans would take too long to execute, and the men presently out of work needed an income.

Golda proposed a massive public works program, which she presented to the Knesset in August, 1950. Basic to the plan was a proposal for the building of roads. She met opposition from several quarters, primarily the economists: the country needed productive industry now, they said. A road system was secondary.

But Golda brushed aside their arguments. "If we have to choose between making a road or vegetable-growing," she said, "I'm for vegetables. If we have to choose between a road and clearing land for cultivation—then clearing the land, definitely. If we have to choose between a road and planning new orange groves—I'm for new orange groves. But the upshot is that we haven't one or the other. Not because anyone has ulterior motives, heaven forbid, and not because anyone is trying to hide away from the difficulties."

In the end Golda's roadbuilding program went ahead, and her *goldene wegen,* "golden roads," laced the landscape.

Rough conditions. Here is a view of the tent settlement at Bet Lid in 1949. The new state had little funds and literally no place to house the many immimgrants streaming into the country. Despite this, the country welcomed into its embrace as many immigrants as could reach Israeli shores. These fresh arrivals lived in *ma'abarot* (tents) until more permanent housing could be built.

Golda's Human Touch

In all her efforts Golda was always interested in insuring that the needs of the people were satisfied, especially with regard to housing. She had the uneasy feeling that builders frequently overlooked the human factor. The architects and engineers should have been women instead of men, she often said. A woman understands. A woman is more likely to take into account what is needed in the kitchen: ample work space, a large counter, and not least important, a window above the sink to take in the view while working.

On a visit one day to a housing project under construction in Tiberias, Golda walked into a kitchen and noticed that the window above the sink was above eye level. Suddenly, she began yelling at the contractor. "What? Are you crazy? Are you idiots? A woman stands in the kitchen five hours cooking, and you are forcing her to see the wall and not the Kinneret [Sea of Galilee]?" The contractors lowered the windows.

A conflict also arose over the installation of toilets inside houses. Contractors had told the minister that new immigrants would not know what to do with them; it would be better to leave them outside. That, said Golda angrily, was no excuse. Put them inside, she ordered, and inside they were placed.

She applied the same human touch to other aspects of her work as minister of labor. One day a California businessman visited Israel and announced that the soil was just right for growing melons and cotton. He first approached Levi Eshkol, who was both minister of agriculture and director of the Jewish Agency's settlement department. Believing the man to be slightly out of his mind, Eshkol politely took his leave, and he suggested that the man talk with Golda Meyerson.

Although Golda also thought the man's ideas fantastic, she considered them carefully. People still lived in tents, and there was no work. If the man's ideas were accepted, it would at least put some of the unemployed to work.

As it turned out, the Californian knew of what he spoke, and as a result of his dreams and Golda's imagination, Israel's melon and cotton industries made giant strides.

During the early days of the state, a shortage of funds was perpetually the most pressing problem. One day in 1955 Judy Gottlieb, daughter of Golda's longtime friend Raziel Shapiro, discussed with Golda the problems her daughter Yael was having at a settlement near Beersheba. For her army service, Yael had been sent to teach at the settlement Maslul, inhabited mostly by Iranian immigrants. Yael had appealed unsuccessfully to local authorities for funds to rent a truck so she might take the children to the Ashkelon beach. Golda listened but said nothing. Judy had been careful not to ask the minister to intervene.

The next day, as Golda and Judy were riding to Tel Aviv, Golda handed her a personal check for 50 Israeli pounds. "This will help your daughter get things started," she said quietly. After the local authorities learned of Golda's action, they agreed to finance a recreation program for the settlement's youngsters.

Golda could not use her personal funds to help solve every problem. And she had little leverage with the ministry of finance, which controlled the government's purse strings. To squeeze some funds out of them she often threatened resignation. But how often could she use such tactics successfully?

Once, early in the 1950s, a few days before Passover, Golda was infuriated to find that new immigrants lacked the wherewithal to purchase food for the holiday. She approached Eliezer Kaplan, the finance minister. "I'm not leaving my office until I get the money," she declared bitterly. "I won't prepare for the holiday as long as I know others can't." Kaplan relented and the minister received the funds requested.

New Cabinet. Following the July, 1951 elections for the Second Knesset, the new Cabinet meets for the first time on October 11, 1951. From left, Messrs. Burg, Pinchas, Levine, Shapira, Eshkol, and Sharef; a secretary; Messrs. Ben-Gurion, Naftali, Kaplan, Joseph, and Dinaburg; Mrs. Meyerson, and Mr. Shitreet.

Farewell. Golda at the closing party for visiting students in July, 1953.

Contact with the West. The minister of labor meets students from English-speaking countries in July, 1953. Golda made a point of keeping in touch with American and other English-speaking youth. She shared much in common with them.

Festival of Lights. Prime Minister Ben-Gurion and Minister of Labor Meyerson, along with other ministers, attend a Chanukah lighting ceremony after a Cabinet meeting in December, 1953.

A moment of relaxation. The minister of labor in her Jerusalem apartment in the mid 1950s.

The minister of labor. The time is July, 1950. In her new Cabinet role, Golda Meyerson would be responsible for some of the most far-reaching social legislation in the nation's history. Through her efforts, housing and employment became priority issues of the government despite the scarcity of public funds.

Golda was under constant attack for bringing the nation to the brink of bankruptcy. One such instance occurred in January 1952 when she proposed the country's first national insurance legislation. When the treasury department informed her that the legislation would result in economic disaster, she replied, "but it will be a social disaster if we don't do it."

Among those same treasury officials she engendered a certain fear because of her obduracy. One day a finance ministry official was advising a colleague in his ministry about the best way to approach the labor ministry to insist that it pare the costs of a proposal. "You better settle things with Zvi Bar-Niv [Bar-Niv was legal advisor in Golda's ministry]," he advised. "If you don't, he'll go to the *balabusta* [boss] and she'll go to Ben-Gurion. Then it will cost more money."

During Golda's term as labor minister she lived with a personal tragedy that she kept buried inside herself. Although she never allowed her private anguish to detract from the joy and satisfaction of her work, it weighed on her like the albatross of the Ancient Mariner.

7

Golda's Albatross

During her long and varied career, Golda Meir was able to deal courageously and most often effectively with every problem she encountered. In her private life, however, there was one problem she was never willing to face. The problem, which remained a closely guarded secret for years, concerned her son, Menachem, and his wife, Channa.

In 1949, Menachem, a music student in New York, met Channa Lutsky, the 18-year-old daughter of Golda's longtime friend, Sara Kessler Lutsky. They fell in love and after a whirlwind courtship were married on June 3, 1950.

The marriage was ill-fated. Crisis followed crisis, and by 1955 Menachem and Channa decided to divorce. Before proceeding with the divorce, however, the couple thought that perhaps, if they had a child, the marriage could be saved.

In the spring of 1955 Channa became pregnant, and shortly thereafter Menachem made arrangements to travel to Yugoslavia for a few months of study with the famous cellist Antonio Janigro, an Italian living in Zagreb. He wanted Channa to accompany him, but her doctor advised against it: the travel might be too taxing. Golda intervened, urging her daughter-in-law to go with Menachem for moral support. Channa considered her mother-in-law's request selfish; nevertheless she made the trip.

The Birth of Meira

In Zagreb, several months later, the pregnant Channa began to hemorrhage. After a brief hospitalization, she and Menachem returned to Tel Aviv. By then Channa was convinced that the marriage was doomed.

On January 3, 1956, in Belinson Hospital, Channa gave birth to a girl after only eight months of pregnancy. The baby was named Meira, after her paternal grandfather, Morris.

Golda Meir now had three grandchildren, two having been born earlier to her daughter, Sarah, and Sarah's husband, Zechariah.

Channa was alarmed when baby Meira was not brought to her soon after the delivery. Thoughts about the misfortune suffered by her sister-in-law, Sarah, ran through her mind. Sarah had lost an infant baby only recently. When the baby was finally carried in by the nurses, Channa's fears were allayed. The child seemed perfectly normal.

Menachem's first wedding. Just before Golda's son, Menachem, married Channa on June 3, 1950, they posed for this photograph in Channa's home in Passaic, New Jersey. From there, the couple went to Temple Emanuel, also in Passaic, for the ceremony. From left to right: Golda, Menachem, Channa, and Channa's mother, Sara Lutsky. Sara was a girlhood friend of Golda's from Milwaukee.

Several days later, Golda visited Channa in the hospital. This was a rare get-together. When the two had last met—a few weeks earlier—a stormy session ensued. Golda felt the marriage was deteriorating, and she tried to convince her daughter-in-law to make every effort to effect a reconciliation. The Golda-Channa meeting had not been a friendly one, and after that conversation Channa set up house on her own.

Golda's Distress

When Golda had visited the hospital on that cold January morning, Channa was sedated, but she later recalled her mother-in-law's words: "I hope now you're satisfied."

At the time those words meant little to Channa. That was the way Golda talked. But Channa later came to believe that Golda already knew that something was wrong with the child—a fact of which Channa was still ignorant. Was Golda trying to say that Channa was responsible for the misfortune? Did Golda mean that Channa was being punished for leaving her son, Menachem, for breaking up the marriage?

Meira was born a mongoloid. The doctor knew the condition of the child from the outset, and although Menachem had been told, that information was kept from Channa for several months. Everyone concerned—mother, father, and Golda—were devastated when the condition of the infant was no longer in doubt.

Soon thereafter a dispute arose: should the child be institutionalized? Menachem and Golda felt strongly that this was the proper course to follow. Channa disagreed. Menachem argued that there was no reason for Channa to sacrifice herself by keeping the child at home. She was only twenty-four years old; her life was still ahead of her; she needed the freedom to build a life for herself. But Channa wanted to give Meira a home and the love and attention she would require to develop to her maximum potential.

Channa prevailed. Meira was kept at home. And six months after Meira's birth, her mother and father were divorced.

From the very beginning Golda refused to have contact with her new grandchild. Whether she saw Meira on her visit to the hospital a few days after the child's birth is not known, but from the day of that visit until Golda's death in December, 1978—when Meira was twenty-two years old—the two never came face to face. Nor did Golda ever mention her publicly.

Through the years Meira's condition and whereabouts were a closely guarded family secret. Some members of the press knew of it, but they chose to respect Golda's privacy. Only after Golda's death did Menachem finally reveal what had been bottled up inside him for many years.

Obviously siding with his mother, Menachem said, "Mother didn't consider the child as her obligation in any way—especially since Channa wouldn't have anything to do with my mother . . . She [Meira] had very little bearing on my mother's life. The other grandchildren were part and parcel of her life. And when the gap [between Menachem and Channa] widened, my mother didn't give Meira much thought at all. Her other grandchildren were part of her everyday life."

Channa's view of the situation was in sharp counterpoint. Golda, she believed, had disowned Meira not because of the divorce, as Menachem had suggested, but rather because of the child's affliction.

Meira as a baby. Two-and-a-half-year-old Meira, in June, 1958, on the back porch of Channa's home in Jerusalem. There was disagreement between Channa and Menachem (with Golda taking Menachem's side) over whether to institutionalize Meira. Channa prevailed: the child remained in Channa's home.

As Meira grew up, Menachem contributed to the child's support, paying half the cost of her maintenance. In the early years he visited her occasionally, but after Channa remarried, it was uncomfortable for him to visit the child in his former wife's household. Gradually, Menachem's visits became less frequent, and finally they stopped.

When Menachem remarried, he claims, he and his wife, Aya, offered to take Meira into their home temporarily, or even permanently, should Channa find it too burdensome to care for the child. Channa disputes that such an offer was ever made.

As a young child. Ten-year-old Meira in Channa's home in Tel Aviv.

With three grandsons. Golda with Menachem's sons at a Haifa flower show in 1966. Left to right: Danny, Amnon, Gidi.

While the existence of Meira was for the most part kept secret, Golda's friends of longstanding—Ze'ev Sharef and his wife, Henya—knew of the situation. When Henya asked Channa why Golda had no contact with her grandchild, Channa suggested that she ask Golda herself, and then added bitterly, "Tell her, if she wants to see Meira, it doesn't have to be a package deal; it doesn't have to include me. I can bring the child to some neutral place."

Henya approached Golda with Channa's suggestions. She received Golda's answer, which she found distressing to divulge to the young mother. After much beseeching on Channa's part, Henya revealed what Golda had told her. "Golda," declared Henya hesitantly, "said that the decision to have no contact other than a financial one with Meira is Menachem's, and she must respect his decision and act accordingly." But Channa was convinced that it was Golda, not Menachem, who had vetoed a relationship with Meira.

Golda never budged from this position. When Meira turned eighteen, Channa pressed Menachem to establish a joint trust fund for their daughter so that the handicapped child would not prove financially burdensome to the offspring of either of them in the future. Channa suggested that she and Menachem contribute equally to the trust fund. Menachem pleaded inability to pay, and the matter was not pursued further.

Making the Truth Known

In 1975 the newspapers reported that Golda Meir's memoirs were soon to be published and that Golda was to receive a substantial amount of money as an advance against royalties. Channa now wondered whether this change in Golda's financial status might make Menachem agree to establish the trust fund for Meira.

Channa knew that royalties could conceivably continue to be paid for many years into the future. This triggered many thoughts in Channa's mind, especially one: Would Meira be a beneficiary along with the other grandchildren? Equally important: If she (Meira) were not named a beneficiary, would Menachem's

Golda's family. **Golda and Sheyna with their children and grandchildren. Back row, left to right: Sheyna's son, Chaim, and his son, Yitzhak; Menachem Meir and his wife, Aya; Sheyna's daughter-in-law, Sara, and Sara's husband, Yona; Sheyna's granddaughter, Ruth. Front: Sarah Meir Rehabi, Golda's daughter; Yona's son, Allon; Golda; Yona's daughter, Nira (standing at Golda's right); Naomi Rehabi, Sarah Rehabi's daughter; Sheyna; Roni (eyes closed), Chaim's daughter; Bella, Chaim's wife.**

At Kfar Tikva. **Twenty-year-old Meira does some exercises in a gym class at Kfar Tikva in 1976. She moved to Kfar Tikva in June, 1974, to join other young handicapped adults in this community near Haifa.**

children eventually assume some kind of financial responsibility for Meira, as Israeli law obligated?

Channa, calling on Menachem and Aya, raised these questions.

"But our children don't know of Meira's existence," said Aya. She was apparently trying to beg off.

"Coming from you," said Channa, looking directly at Aya, "that rather surprises me." Aya then acknowledged that fundamentally Channa was correct. "We need to find a suitable opportunity to tell them about Meira," she conceded.

Much later Menachem revealed that his children had been told of Meira but "not all the details." They were probably informed only after this conversation between Channá, Menachem, and Aya.

For years, Channa had hoped that one day Golda would establish a relationship with her granddaughter in order to make up for the pain Meira had suffered for having been rejected by her grandmother. Channa cherished that hope until the very end, but when Golda died in 1978, Channa knew the time for hoping was over. Now she would have to *act.* "I have to put Meira on the map," she told her closest friends.

One old friend, Nomi Zuckerman, who knew every detail of the situation, had advised Channa to take action three years earlier—in 1975—when Golda's memoirs appeared. The fact that in her memoirs Golda had totally ignored Meira, that she had spoken only of five grandchildren (two from her daughter, Sarah, and three from Menachem's second marriage) was a clear signal that the public had to be informed of the truth.

But Channa had ignored Nomi's advice, still hoping that one day Golda could be brought around to accepting Meira into her life.

When Golda died on December 8, 1978, Channa felt the time had come to tell the world about Meira, granddaughter of Golda, equal in every way to the other five.

On December 10, she placed a mourning notice in the newspaper *Ha'aretz*. She signed it simply: GRANDDAUGHTER MEIRA, KFAR TIKVAH. (Kfar Tikvah, located near Haifa, is the community of young handicapped adults where Meira has been living since June 17, 1974.)

That same day, Channa discussed the idea with Paula Moses, wife of the publisher of *Yediot Aharonot*. As a result, a mourning notice was also placed in this newspaper. It appeared on December 12, the day of Golda's funeral:

ON THE DEATH OF MY DEAR GRANDMOTHER, GOLDA MEIR. HER BEREAVED GRANDDAUGHTER, MEIRA MEYERSON WEINBERG. [Weinberg was Channa's surname after her remarriage.]

Thus the secret was out, and news of the hitherto unpublicized granddaughter of Golda Meir reached the public. It was startling news. Very few people had actually been aware that Golda had a sixth grandchild, let alone that the child was a mongoloid.

At one point, some years earlier, Channa had granted an interview to an Israeli magazine, in which she told of her retarded daughter, noting that the child's grandparent was a "known personality," but nobody connected this with Golda Meir.

Details of this unhappy aspect of Golda's life were not disclosed immediately after the appearance of the mourning notices. None of the participants in the drama chose to talk about Meira, nor were the newspapers overly anxious to play it up.

Shalom Rosenfeld, editor of Israel's popular newspaper *Maariv*, had known Channa and Meira for years, but he had chosen never to write about Meira's relationship to Golda. One of his reporters, who had also known the truth for some time, asked Rosenfeld shortly after Golda's funeral if it would be appropriate now to write a story about Meira. "Don't touch it," he ordered—out of respect for Golda.

Meira was aware of what had transpired in her life. She was retarded but not severely—and she was sensitive.

About one month before her grandmother's death, the Kfar Tikvah social worker had tried to coax Meira into expressing her feelings about Golda, but she

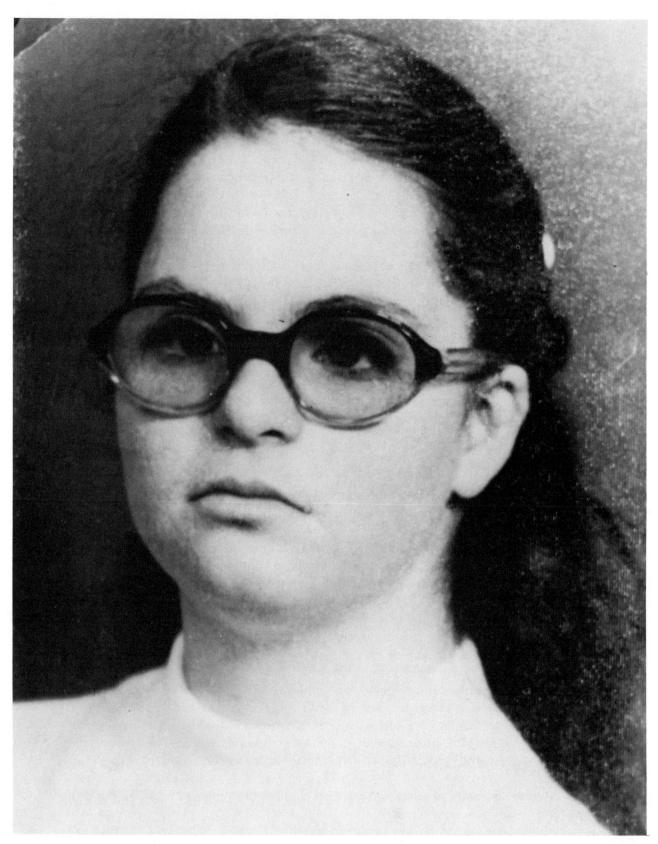

The Forgotten One. Meira Meyerson Weinberg, Golda's "other" granddaughter.

A discreet editor. **Shalom Rosenfeld, editor of *Maariv*, was aware of the hostility between Golda and Meira, but he preferred not to publicize it.**

refused. She would talk openly about her stepfather's mother, with whom she had direct contact, but not about her father's mother.

A short article in *Yediot Aharonot*—on December 13, 1978, the day after Golda's funeral—referred to the relationship between Golda and Meira. The same social worker again visited Meira, asking if she had seen the article. Meira acknowledged that she had.

"Why then won't you talk to me about this part of your life?"

"Look," said Meira, "whenever I told anyone Golda Meir was my grandmother, they laughed at me. They said it wasn't true. They said I was making it up. They said, if it was true, why didn't she visit me and send me presents. Now they ask me why I wasn't invited to the funeral. I don't want to talk about it, because I don't want people to go on laughing at me."

Meira, who had lived with Channa and Channa's second husband, Jesaja (Isaiah), until she was 18, continues to reside at Kfar Tikvah to this day. She has a boyfriend, also a resident of the community, and she takes special pride in the ceramic pottery she makes.

8

Early Years as Foreign Minister

When, in 1956, Golda learned that Ben-Gurion wanted her to leave the labor ministry and become foreign minister, she looked upon the change more as punishment than promotion. She had come to think of the labor ministry as her home; it was inconceivable that she would find greater satisfaction in another Cabinet post.

Much of Golda's bias toward the labor ministry rested on the spurious notion that a foreign minister can contribute little to the national effort. "What does Ben-Gurion want with me?" she asked a member of her staff one day in manifest frustration. "All a foreign minister does is talk and talk more. One day this way, another day that way. . . . Here at the labor ministry, at least I can make a house, I can build a road, or get a law passed. I do something and I can see it with my own eyes. Over here in the foreign ministry all they do is talk."

Her disaffection with Ben-Gurion was understandable. She had built up an enviable record in the labor ministry. The programs she had initiated would serve as blueprints for the future.

When Golda was ready to move her belongings to the foreign minister's official residence, Zalman Chen, a member of her ministry, came to her home on Marcus Street to help. As he and Golda exited the house, and he was about to close the door after her, Golda glanced back for a moment. Gloomily she pronounced, "I don't want to go."

Ben-Gurion vs. Sharett

Golda's appointment as foreign minister in June, 1956 had less to do with ability than with events and personalities. The selection of Golda was actually secondary.

Ben-Gurion had decided that the moderate Sharett was an impediment to his policies toward the Arabs; he *had* to be replaced. Sharett had mustered respectable majorities in the Cabinet to oppose a few of Ben-Gurion's planned retaliatory strikes against Arab Fedayeen infiltrators. If Israel had to go to war to silence the Fedayeen, would the foreign minister stand in the way? questioned Ben-Gurion.

Ben-Gurion was not inclined to gamble on being able to control Sharett, and when the opportunity to oust him arose—as it did, quite unexpectedly—Ben-Gurion seized it. The initiative, paradoxically, came from the foreign minister himself.

"Goldene Wegen." Golda appears at the opening of the Beersheba-Dimona road in December, 1955. Projects such as this one helped the burgeoning nation overcome a vast unemployment problem. They also generated economic activity by linking the nation's distant parts.

Building the nation. The minister of labor appears at the founding of a Youth Aliyah institution at Kfar Vitkin in 1954. Foremost among Golda Meyerson's interests was the transport of Jewish refugees to Israel. Upon the refugees' arrival, she took an equally strong interest in their successful integration into the new country.

Ben-Gurion's Mapai Party had fared poorly in the Knesset elections of July 26, 1955, losing five of the forty-five seats it had won in the 1951 elections. A new secretary-general of the party was needed. Ben-Gurion had approached Golda about the job. Reluctant to leave the labor ministry, she begged off. A meeting had been arranged in the prime minister's home in Jerusalem. Ben-Gurion raised the question of who ought to be the next secretary-general. Half joking, Sharett proposed himself. Ben-Gurion cheerfully agreed and the matter was settled, never giving Sharett a chance to protest. A few days later the prime minister spoke with Golda, mentioning how fortunate it was that Sharett had taken the party job.

"But," said the minister of labor inquisitively, "who will be foreign minister?"

Without the slightest hesitation Ben-Gurion said, "You."

Golda protested, but she knew her objections would count for little. "That's that," Ben-Gurion insisted, dismissing her protestations with a wave of the hand.

Meyerson Becomes Meir

Golda's acceptance of the new job meant that she would have to change her name at last. Ever since 1948 she had kept the name Meyerson despite Sharett's orders that all foreign service personnel Hebraicize their names. In 1956 Ben-Gurion insisted that the orders be followed, and Golda chose the surname "Meir," meaning "illuminate."

Sharett's Fury

Sharett was bitter over his ouster. Although he reserved most of his wrath for Ben-Gurion, Golda felt some of the sting as well. Sharett earnestly believed that he was on the verge of establishing rapport with Gamal Abdul Nasser, the Egyptian leader, and his unexpected dismissal by Ben-Gurion put an end to the opportunity.

Golda could say nothing that would appease Sharett. The two were neighbors, and she was constantly afraid that she would meet him in the street. A chance meeting would be highly uncomfortable.

Sharett expressed his venom in his diary. "All those days," he recorded, "Ziama [Aranne, the minister of education], Ze'ev Sharef, and others are telling me how very miserable Golda is, that she had no alternative other than to give up her wish in favor of B-G's [Ben-Gurion's]. I remained unimpressed by all the deliberations and soul-searchings. Perhaps Golda feels deep in her heart that she deserves the post. Or she's convinced in her heart of hearts that B-G was justified in throwing me out and that it's really best for the country that I cease serving as foreign minister. In any event, another friendship was burned by the avalanche of the crisis B-G created."

Sharett's fury reached its peak just before he was supposed to hand over the foreign ministry to Golda. Ze'ev Sharef, a Mapai Party colleague who served as minister of finance and minister of housing, had visited Sharett one evening to ask if he would formally turn the office over to Golda the next morning. Sharett said no, explaining that he was in the midst of three days of private briefings with her.

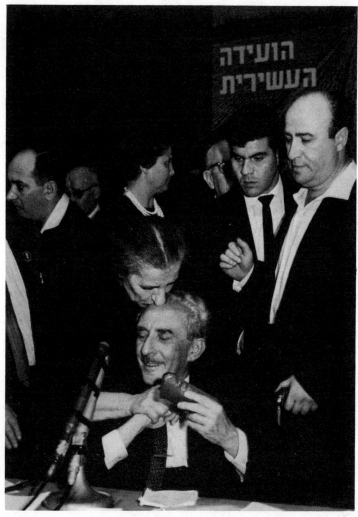

הועידה
העשירית

A bittersweet moment.
**Golda kisses an aging Moshe
Sharett. Once Golda be-
came foreign minister in
June, 1956, replacing Sharett, relations with him
steadily worsened. Sharett
always thought Golda was
at least partly responsible
for his dismissal by Ben-
Gurion.**

To his diary Sharett complained, "To appear with her in the office in front of all
the workers will be leaving a false impression of forgiving her, and of a friendship
that doesn't exist."

First Days in the Foreign Ministry

As Golda settled into the foreign ministry, the times were growing increasingly perilous. With the last British soldiers leaving Egypt, the final restraint
on Nasser in his campaign against Israel was removed. In addition, the Soviet
foreign minister was being feted in Cairo, a brutal reminder that Israel's enemies
were being supported by a mighty war-making machine. And no less of a worry
were the Fedayeen attacks, which had reached significant proportions.

In those first few days on the job, Golda pondered just how she could make an
impact on such events. The daily routine of a foreign minister seemed so
ephemeral: much conversation but no way of knowing if progress was being

Sisters. Golda and Sheyna in Sheyna's backyard in Holon, Israel.

made. Golda also gave thought to her relationship with the prime minister. She was fearful that Ben-Gurion might try to keep her from taking full charge. She knew that as long as she followed his activist policy toward the Arabs in general, and the Fedayeen in particular, she had little cause for concern. Still, she was apprehensive that Ben-Gurion would insist upon deciding all policy.

Oddly, the earliest problems arose from a different quarter. From the outset, Golda's personal relations with the foreign ministry staff were poor. Some staff members felt strongly that Golda was not qualified for the job, that she had no business accepting it, that she lacked the skill of a polished diplomat like Sharett.

Sharett had surrounded himself with men of intellectual sophistication and cosmopolitan outlook who understood the art of diplomacy. Because of Golda's simple manner of speaking, her tendency to inject emotion into arguments, and because of her generally hardline approach to foreign affairs, Sharett's appointees had little in common with Golda. And Golda's early battles in the foreign ministry were often devoted to attacking the soft attitude toward foreign policy that Sharett's holdovers tried to impose on the ministry.

Trouble brewing. Ambassadors to the four major powers meet with Foreign Minister Golda Meir in September, 1956, a month before the Suez Campaign. Golda was one of the few high Israeli officials who participated in the prewar planning. Left to right: Yosef Avidor, ambassador the the Soviet Union; Ya'acov Tzur (France); Abba Eban (United States); and Eliahu Elath (Great Britain).

The Suez Crisis

Golda Meir's first political crisis as foreign minister was Suez—a brief but complicated military campaign in which the armies of Israel, Great Britain, France, and Egypt were involved. It proved to be the great watershed in Golda's thinking about the Israeli-Arab conflict. Its lessons were painful, but she was determined that they would be learned well.

The crisis actually was brewing before Golda was appointed to the foreign ministry. Egypt had already started to entertain serious thoughts of a second round of war with Israel. Fedayeen attacks launched from Egypt increased steadily. In 1955 Nasser signed an arms deal with the Czechs, and in that same year he blocked non-Israeli vessels from reaching the Israeli port of Eilat. Since 1953 Israeli shipping had been prevented from passing through the Straits of Tiran to Eilat.

The final straw came in July of 1956 when Nasser nationalized the Suez Canal, a serious blow to the British since nearly one-quarter of its imports passed through this waterway. There was little doubt that war was imminent. Nasser had been provocative enough. The only uncertainty was who would strike the first blow.

Israel decided to strike first. Coordinating its war strategy with Britain and France, the planned attack was a closely-guarded secret. Only ten people in Israel knew of the planned attack; Golda was one of them. On September 29, she went to Paris with Moshe Dayan, then chief of staff, to finalize war plans with the French.

At first Golda was not concerned that she had no time between meetings to take in some of the city's famous sites, but when she discovered that Dayan had endangered the secrecy of their journey by strolling around Paris, she became annoyed.

The Israelis planned to surprise the Egyptians. Otherwise, they felt, they might be the victims of a preemptive strike. So, on October 24 the Israelis clandestinely began to mobilize reserve troops for an assault five days later. That same day Egypt, Syria, and Jordan unified their military commands and set as their goal Israel's destruction. Time seemed to be running out.

On a visit to her daughter, Sarah, at Kibbutz Revivim, Golda had to exercise great restraint to contain the secret. Even so, when asked by the kibbutz security man if it would be wise to begin digging ditches, the foreign minister responded solemnly, "If I were you, I would."

The Suez War

The war began on October 29. It proceeded like clockwork. In less than 100 hours the Israelis had seized the entire Sinai Peninsula and all of the Gaza Strip, an area three and a half times the size of Israel. Casualties were at a minimum (172 killed, 800 wounded), and only one Israeli had been taken prisoner.

As the enormity of the Israeli victory became clear, pressures began to mount that the Middle East return to its prewar status quo.

Painful withdrawal. Israeli soldiers take a last look at Sharm el-Sheikh as they prepare to withdraw after the 1956 Sinai campaign. Smoke still rises from blown-up military installations. American pressure forced the Israelis to withdraw from the Sinai.

"A comfortable division has been made," Golda told the United Nations General Assembly angrily. "The Arab states unilaterally enjoy the rights of war; Israel has the unilateral responsibility of keeping the peace. But belligerency is not a one-way street. Is it surprising if a people laboring under this monstrous distinction should finally become restive and at least seek a week of rescuing its life from the perils of a regulated war conducted against it from all sides?"

But pressure continued to mount, particularly from the United States under President Dwight D. Eisenhower. U.S. Undersecretary of State Edward Hoover, in a November 8 letter to Golda, threatened to impose economic sanctions and to initiate proceedings for Israel's ouster from the U.N. if it did not withdraw its troops from the Sinai. And so, on that very day Israel announced that it would withdraw its forces on condition that its security would be assured and acts of belligerency by land and sea terminated.

During the ensuing days Golda was in a state of inner turmoil. The Israelis had come under intense international pressure, and they lacked the inner strength to stand up to the great world powers. The demands for withdrawal and compromise were overwhelming. Though there were countless talks with the American secretary of state, John Foster Dulles, during that frustrating winter, ultimately Israel had little choice but to announce a full military withdrawal.

On March 1, 1957, a day Golda called "not one of the finest moments in my life," she planned to announce from the United Nations rostrum that Israel would complete its pullout of forces. Upon learning this, Israeli diplomat Emile Najar was enraged. "If you give that statement," he told her bitterly, "you will be a traitor."

By telephone, Golda again begged Ben-Gurion to allow her to delay the announcement. Ben-Gurion refused and the announcement was made.

Disappointment at the U.N.

Much of Golda's anguish was over the vague language the United States had employed to propitiate Israel. Rather than offering guarantees or commitments, the United States offered "expectations and assumptions," a phrase that obligated the United States to take no action. The United States "expected" that the U.N. would protect Israel's right of free and innocent passage through the Gulf of Aqaba, and it "assumed" that Egyptian Army units would not be permitted to return to the Gaza Strip.

Just how much value could be attached to such language became manifestly clear when the American delegate to the U.N., Henry Cabot Lodge, rose to speak after Golda. Lodge agreed to Israel's demands with respect to the Gulf of Aqaba, but on the crucial issue of Gaza he dropped a bombshell. Its future, he asserted, should be worked out in the framework of future armistice agreements. In effect, he was guaranteeing that the Egyptians would return to Gaza.

Stunned, enraged, Golda sat in her U.N. seat. Her emotions told her to march to the rostrum immediately to retract Israel's promise of withdrawal. Her mind reasoned that a public retraction would only humiliate Israel. So she sat and did nothing. Again she was reminded why diplomacy bothered her so much: the emphasis on words, the insincerity of the diplomats using them, the utter futility of all those negotiating exercises.

With the former First Lady. Golda and Eleanor Roosevelt at the U.N. in 1956.

The nation's number one diplomat. **Foreign Minister Meir with Regina Medzini at the United Nations in 1957. Golda spent much time at the U.N. representing Israel in the Middle East dispute.**

The drama at the U.N. in New York on that March day in 1957 was Golda Meir's baptism under fire. And she would never forget it, never forget the behavior of the United States, never forget how irrelevant and fraught with peril that piece of theater played out before the U.N. had been, never forget its true significance for Israel.

That evening after her U.N. speech, Golda Meir spent a long time washing her clothes. A member of the Israeli delegation to the U.N. asked her the next morning why she had spent so much time doing her clothes. "At least," she replied, "something should be clean around me."

U.N. Reception. Foreign Minister Meir and her sister Sheyna at a reception for the Israeli mission to the U.N.

Golda Contacts the Arabs

For years it had been difficult for Israel to make even the most casual contact with the Arabs. Even those Arabs who desired to do so refrained, fearing retribution from their Arab brethren.

As foreign minister in the late 1950s, Golda Meir put out a number of feelers to the Arab states through third parties at the United Nations, hoping that somehow the ice might be broken. Golda was pleased when one day the deputy head of the Pakistani delegation, a woman, approached her, saying, "Look, if we women are involved in politics, we ought to do something for peace." Golda smiled back: "Wonderful, let's do something about it. You're Pakistani, you have no diplomatic relations with Israel. Certainly, you cannot be accused of being anti-Arab. You call to your apartment anyone you want from the Arab delegation. Invite me. This will not be peace negotiations. I'm not fooling myself. But let's get into one room and talk."

The woman reacted with excitement, calling it a brilliant idea. She asked Golda to wait until she had something to report. Weeks passed and nothing happened. One morning the Pakistani woman and Golda sat down for tea in the U.N. dining room. Golda waited for an explanation. At that moment the Iraqi foreign minister passed their table, frightening the Pakistani. "Oh, he sees I'm sitting with you," she said weakly.

Although Golda sensed it was bad timing, she asked the Pakistani about the proposed meeting. "I'm sorry," said the woman, "I can't do it." And that was that.

The Arabs were determined not to be seen in the company of an Israeli. In September, 1958, CBS-TV had invited Golda, then foreign minister, and Mohammed Ahmed Mahgoub, the foreign minister of Sudan, to appear on its program "U.N. in Action." The Sudanese minister had not been told that Golda would appear on the same show.

When the time came to air the show, the two ministers were escorted to separate rooms. The commentator planned to race back and forth between the two to maintain a discussion on tensions in the Middle East. Prior to show time Golda was ushered into Mahgoub's studio to say hello. When the Sudanese realized who she was, he bolted for the door. The producer was able to salvage his program only by deleting that part of the show which showed Golda greeting Mahgoub. The Sudanese agreed to be interviewed in a separate room from the Israeli foreign minister.

All of Golda's efforts to establish a meaningful relationship with the Arabs proved futile.

9

A Seasoned Foreign Minister

The years 1956 and 1957 marked a low point in relations between Israel and the United States. Not until the 1960s did a thaw set in.

America Warms Up to Golda

As Golda's contacts with the United States grew, Americans began to find a warm place for her in their hearts. Her early years in the Midwest and her midwestern American accent combined to give her special appeal. They liked the way she spoke.

"She speaks my language," the American labor leader George Meany once said. "For Abba Eban I have to take a dictionary."

Golda had her own gallery of American favorites. Understandably, Dwight D. Eisenhower and John Foster Dulles were not among them, nor was Henry Cabot Lodge. Lyndon Johnson was, for he was one of the few who opposed threatened American sanctions against Israel after Suez.

A Meeting with JFK

Golda had an amiable relationship with John F. Kennedy. Her one meeting with the President, during a Kennedy vacation in Palm Beach, Florida, in December, 1962, came at a time of growing American interest in Israel. In keeping with diplomatic practice, Golda's aide, Mordechai Gazit, proposed a sentence or two for Kennedy to speak in Golda's presence. She could not know, of course, if the President would accept Gazit's language, which sought to put into Kennedy's mouth a strong American commitment to the preservation of Israeli security.

To Golda's astonishment, the President agreed. "Madame Foreign Minister," he said, addressing her publicly, "I wish to tell you, I'm aware of your problems, and the United States has the willingness and capability to assist you if attacked."

As they left the meeting, Golda and Gazit smiled at one another. It marked the first time an American president had spoken such words, a far cry from the wishy-washy "assumptions" voiced by Henry Cabot Lodge in 1957. "I felt that we were talking to a friend," Golda remarked upon her return to Israel.

Kennedy failed to follow through on his strong language by delivering sophisticated weapons to Israel, although an apocryphal story, widely and often repeated, would have it otherwise. According to this story Golda Meir called on John F. Kennedy sometime in 1961.

"Mr. President," she said, "I want to talk to you about weapons. Israel needs weapons for its security."

"Why talk about weapons?" said Kennedy. "Let's talk about something else."

"No," said Mrs. Meir, "I want to talk about weapons."

"You come from the land of the Bible," said Kennedy. "Let's talk about the Bible."

"No," said Golda Meir. "We can talk about the Bible some other time. Today we must talk about weapons."

"I'll give you money," said Kennedy.

"Money you can give to the UJA," said Mrs. Meir. "We must have weapons. We need protection."

"I'll protect you with the Sixth Fleet," said Kennedy.

"No," persisted Golda. "We must have weapons!"

Finally, Kennedy became angry: "Why are you so obsessed with weapons? Whenever I meet you, you talk about weapons! Whenever I talk to other Jewish leaders, they talk about weapons! What's *wrong* with you people?!"

Memorial to a slain leader. Admirers of President John F. Kennedy contributed to the erection of this magnificent memorial located on a high spot in the outskirts of Jerusalem. It consists of fifty-one spokes, representing the fifty states of the United States and the District of Columbia. An eternal light is the centerpiece of its interior.

"I'll tell you what's wrong," said Golda Meir after a long silence.

"You see, Mr. President, I belong to an ancient people. Twice in our history our country has been destroyed, our Temple reduced to ashes, our people dispersed to the four corners of the earth—yet, somehow, we have managed to remain alive.

"Do you know how? I will tell you.

"We stayed alive because of the shopkeeper in Bialystock and the tailor in Kiev, the industrialist in New York and the diamond merchant in Amsterdam, the student in Paris and the visionary in Safed. Though they came from different backgrounds—from different lands, speaking different tongues—they had one thing in common: a dream that one day the world would be at peace and our sovereignty would be restored, our children would be gathered in, and our Temple would be rebuilt . . .

"Mr. President, our Temple has not yet been rebuilt. We have just *begun* to see the light . . . And should this beginning be erased, then the shopkeeper in Bialystock and the watchmaker in Paris, the tailor in Kiev, and the rebel in Leningrad, the talmudist in Brooklyn and the visionary in Safed—all these Jews who have a dream in common—will no longer even be capable of dreaming."

President Kennedy didn't say a word for a long moment. Then he pushed a button on his desk and gave an order which resulted in Israel's receiving its first Hawk missiles.

When Golda was told about this rumored conversation between herself and Kennedy, she remarked: "If I had spoken to Kennedy so beautifully, I would have gotten more arms."

Difficulties with Ben-Gurion

Serving as David Ben-Gurion's foreign minister was not easy. As Israel's international stature began to grow after Suez, so did Ben-Gurion's interest in foreign affairs. He traveled abroad more often too. Rather than ask Golda, Ben-Gurion had his personal secretary, Yitzhak Navon, draft cables touching on foreign affairs. Major foreign policy statements often came directly from Ben-Gurion's office without Golda's advance knowledge. Incredibly, Golda was only told about the plan to have Israeli agents capture Adolf Eichmann *after* the prime minister had granted his approval.

Incompatibility with Shimon Peres

The prime minister's activism in foreign affairs had a chilling effect on Golda's independence. She was determined, however, to play a major role in cultivating Israel's relations with France, its most important ally. But even here she was stymied, indirectly by Ben-Gurion and directly by his agent, a young man named Shimon Peres.

Golda Meir and Shimon Peres belonged to two different worlds. Both came to Palestine as immigrants (Peres from Poland in 1934), and both had their roots in the labor movement. But there the similarities ended.

Golda was 60 years old in 1958; Peres was 34. Golda was extroverted,

The people have their turn. Adolf Eichmann sits in the dock as Gideon Hausner, the Israeli prosecutor, enumerates the Nazi leader's crimes against the Jewish people in April, 1961. Eichmann was eventually found guilty and was executed, the first time the State of Israel had imposed the death penalty on anyone.

sentimental, intuitive. Peres was secretive, rational, intellectual. Golda was of the old world, Peres of the new. She clung to the ideals of the pioneer; Peres was more interested in the new world of technology. Peres believed that the time had come for the older generation to step aside; Golda disagreed.

Golda Clashes with Peres

The first unfriendly encounter between Golda and Peres occurred in 1946, at the Zionist Congress in Basel, Switzerland, where Golda was a delegate and Peres an observer. Peres had been writing articles for publication in a party daily newspaper back home. In one article he attacked Haganah leader Dr. Moshe Sneh, accusing him of Communist inclinations.

Thinking the idea preposterous, Golda was furious. "How dare you do it," she fumed bitterly. Although the allegations created a mild stir at the Congress, it was the first round in a feud which assumed serious proportions a decade later.

When Golda Meir was foreign minister, Peres was director-general of the ministry of defense, a ministry headed by Ben-Gurion. Golda had the reputation of being a tried-and-true Ben-Gurionite. Peres, the whiz kid, was the new kid on the block. The fine line between the authority belonging to the ministry for foreign affairs and the ministry of defense was often blurred. What was not in doubt at that time, however, was the critical importance of France to Israel's national security.

France had warmed up to Israel in the 1950s largely as a result of the fight for independence by Algerian nationalists. Algeria had been a part of France since 1848. By late 1955 Egypt had begun allocating funds and transshipping Soviet weapons to the FLN nationalists in Algeria. With Nasser engaged in a struggle against Israel, it was natural for France to closely ally itself with Israel. Israel, for its part, was delighted to do business with the French. If the French were willing to sell arms, Israel would buy.

When African leaders chided Golda for dealing with "imperialist" France, she said candidly, "If DeGaulle were the devil himself, I would regard it as the duty of my government to buy arms from the only source available to us."

Before Golda became foreign minister in 1956, Israeli-French relations had already begun to blossom. In 1954 Peres, as director-general, had signed Israel's first military agreement with the French, involving the sale of tanks to Israel. And during Golda's term as foreign minister, Peres strengthened his hold over the French connection.

The first real clash between Peres and Golda came over Peres' meeting with Jean Monnet, architect of the European Common Market. Peres held Monnet in great esteem and regarded his meeting with him as something of a personal coup. "Monnet told me I was the first Israeli to meet with him since Chaim Weizmann," Peres said later.

Golda was distressed over Peres' achievement, convinced that Israel's foreign minister should have been the one to meet with Monnet. But this was only one of a number of other equally distressing incidents.

Perhaps the most embarrassing incident occurred when Golda showed up one day for an appointment at the French ministry of defense. Ben-Gurion and Peres were in Paris at the same time. Upon entering her host's office, Golda learned to her great embarrassment that her two fellow countrymen had been to see the official the day before—and she had never been informed.

Peres used his close rapport with Ben-Gurion and his own not inconsiderable charms to enhance his favor with the French. Golda spoke no French and had a thinly disguised contempt for the people of France and their manners. Peres felt comfortable in their company. It was understandable that the French would pay closer attention to Peres, the man close to the prime minister who had the power to sign contracts on the spot, contracts valued in the millions of dollars.

To the French, Golda was the Israeli with whom you chatted; Peres was the official with whom you did business. Golda could, and she did, complain to the prime minister, but Ben-Gurion took no real interest in the jurisdictional dispute. Golda was bewildered. She could not take Peres' toe-stepping to the public. The Israeli defense ministry operated in secret: the arms contracts required neither Knesset scrutiny nor public approval. To whom could she turn?

Ben-Gurion, Peres, and Golda

The man responsible for Golda's clashes with Peres was Ben-Gurion. It was he who launched Peres on independent, secret missions to France and Germany. In 1958 Peres' defense ministry again made arrangements behind Golda's back, this time selling Uzi machine guns to the Germans. The foreign minister was hesitant about complaining too strongly.

To protect himself from personal tiffs like this one, Ben-Gurion shrewdly feigned ignorance and innocence. Whenever Golda raised the issue of Peres' behavior to the prime minister, Ben-Gurion would dispatch his secretary, Yitzhak Navon, to placate her.

Once, Ya'acov Tzur, the Israeli ambassador to France, phoned Golda from Paris with a complaint about Peres. Navon happened to be meeting with Golda. "Here," she said, turning the receiver over to Navon, "listen to what Tzur has to say. I can't go on like that. Let Ben-Gurion make Peres foreign minister and be done with it."

Allies of Golda tried to effect a reconciliation between her and Peres. Isser Harel, then director of the Mossad, Israel's intelligence agency, approached Peres in an attempt to make peace. Peres was intractable. Why didn't he report to Golda about his activities? Harel had asked Peres. "I've got approval from Ben-Gurion," he replied, "and that's that."

Golda's only remaining weapon, one she could use sparingly, was the threat of resignation. She didn't truly desire to resign, and this was evident to those around her. Emile Najar, a close friend of Golda and Israel's ambassador to Japan in 1949, took a ride with the foreign minister in a small boat down the Seine in Paris. He was on leave, visiting family.

"I want to quit," Golda said dejectedly. She spoke of the running feud with Peres, of his meetings behind her back, and of her inability to put a halt to them. "I'm fed up!"

Najar smiled knowingly: "You will never quit."

"Why do you say that?" she asked.

"Because," he replied with supreme confidence, "you adore what you are doing. So everything you say I don't take seriously."

One of Golda Meir's major weaknesses was her unwillingness to forgive or forget. It was of little importance how old the offense or how minor the transgression or snub. She simply could not forget it. She carried grudges, as if they were badges of honor—particularly those against Shimon Peres. Those she carried to the end of her days.

Before making decisions, Peres normally calculated the risks carefully. But with Golda he did not calculate well. And he paid for his miscalculation when years later, determined to become prime minister, Peres was denied the prize largely because of one immovable obstacle—Golda Meir—a person who did not forget and could not forgive.

10

Golda's African Adventure

Golda had a romance with the people of Africa. Before 1956 this continent was a place of mystery to her, but it was in Africa that she scored her greatest personal triumphs as foreign minister.

Golda Pursues Africa

The African adventure got its start under prime minister Moshe Sharett. Both Ben-Gurion and Sharett had sensed the kinship between Israel and the under-developed African countries, yet neither knew how to translate those feelings into action.

As Golda searched for areas where Israel's foreign policy could have an immediate and noticeable impact, her thoughts turned to Africa. Ben-Gurion himself dealt with the Arabs. As for the U.N. and Washington, the prime minister simply bypassed Golda, dealing directly with Abba Eban. Relations with France and West Germany were handled by the defense ministry. The continent of Asia was largely unfathomable; neither China nor India had established diplomatic relations with Israel. Africa was pure, virgin territory.

In the winter of 1957 Golda was in the doldrums over the burdens of office: the Sinai negotiations, conflict with Shimon Peres, confrontation with Ben-Gurion over the manner in which he decided policy. Each in its own way drained her energies and enthusiasm. After a seminar for Afro-Asian peoples in Tel Aviv, where she first encountered Africans and their problems, Golda knew where she must place her energies.

Early in 1958 the foreign minister paid her first visit to Africa; it was a great success. This was followed by more visits. Wherever she went, she enchanted the natives.

Golda entered the African arena unhampered by any of Israel's other agencies, and she managed to establish good, wholesome relations with the natives. Had she tried to relate to them only as a diplomat, trying to win their votes on important U.N. issues for instance, she might have failed. But her approach was unique.

Although there was no doubt in anyone's mind that Golda was anxious to win over the African nations to Israel's side, she avoided the formal, diplomatic approach. She spoke to them in simple terms about how Israel was willing to help the natives improve their skills in the areas of farming, education, land settlement, and community development.

Great friend of Africa. The foreign minister welcomes Mr. Batsio, minister of trade and industry from Ghana, to her Jerusalem home in August, 1957. Golda developed a strong personal interest in the African nations, traveled throughout the continent frequently, and had a lasting effect on the peoples there. Israel's flourishing relationship with these nations was perhaps Golda's most significant accomplishment as foreign minister.

Incident at Victoria Falls

A white woman in her early 60s, fresh from the land of the Bible, Golda described to the Africans the fascinating way of life in Israel, where many people lived on kibbutzim and moshavim. She showed both her toughness and her compassion, and whether she praised the Africans or criticized them, they adored her. And they called her Golda.

One event in 1963 brought Golda much respect. She had been invited to Zambia's independence celebrations, and while there neighboring Rhodesia extended an invitation to all visiting dignitaries to cross over the border for a visit to the magnificent Victoria Falls, the highest in the world. The border police asked whites and blacks to form separate lines to show their passports. "No, thank you," steamed Golda defiantly. "I can do without the falls." Her angry departure proved so moving to the other visitors that they quickly followed suit. On the way back to the Zambian capital, deeply affected by what had just transpired, Golda grew weak and fainted.

The closeness Golda Meir felt for the Africans led her to dress in their tribal robes during native ceremonies. She felt enough kinship to lecture them on their meandering from Socialist principles. In fact, when she learned that a certain group of African students was enjoying the benefits of fully paid government tuition and that the students had servants to clean their dormitories, she berated them for their laziness. They accepted the criticism.

Adoration for Golda

The Africans loved her. Many letters of testimony poured into her office in Israel. One man from the Congo asked her to send him pictures of girls aged 25 to 26, women he might consider as candidates for marriage. She politely turned him down. A worker in the Monrovia Bureau of Internal Revenue asked Golda to become his godmother. Sorrowfully, she answered that Jewish religion forbade such relationships.

The Africans always gave Golda the benefit of the doubt. Normally they had little patience for long-winded speeches, but when Golda held forth about Israel or any other subject, they listened attentively. Once, in New York's Waldorf-Astoria Hotel in the early 1970s, Haile Selassie, king of Ethiopia, cornered an Israeli foreign ministry specialist on Africa, Hanan Aynor. "Now," said Selassie, gesturing to a chair, "you sit down and I'll give you an answer to Mrs. Meir."

Aynor was baffled. "Why your Imperial Majesty?" he asked.

"Because," said the emperor, "when I last saw her I couldn't get a word in."

The Africans recognized Golda's weaknesses, but they forgave her. They forgave her because her motherly, protective attitude toward Africans shone through. Her genuine interest and compassion had earned her many friends and admirers, perhaps more than any European or American before her.

Back in Israel, African leaders paraded through Jerusalem with increasing frequency. This led Ben-Gurion to raise his bushy white eyebrows in perplexity.

A true love affair. S.E. Jean-Marie Jone, vice-president of the Mali Republic, receives Israeli transistors from the foreign minister after signing technical, economic, and cultural agreements. November, 1960.

Ministers meet. Tanganyika's minister of agriculture meets the foreign minister in June, 1961.

More than politics. Members of Liberian President Tubman's entourage join Foreign Minister Meir in Israeli folkdancing at her home in June, 1962.

Special friend. President Felix Houphouet-Boigny of the Ivory Coast was a close friend of Mrs. Meir. Here, in July, 1962, he bestows the order of "Grand Officer" of his country upon the foreign minister.

Why was it necessary for Israel to plunge into Africa with such zeal, to host the African leaders with such abandon.

The prime minister informed the foreign minister of his growing weariness with the goings-on in Jerusalem. Golda was prepared; she had a response ready: "Imagine," she said to him, "that instead of coming to see us, all these presidents went to Nasser. That would worry you, wouldn't it?"

Statistics reveal Golda's success in Africa. In 1956 Israel had a single representative in all of black Africa, in Ghana. A decade later, after Golda had made her personal impact felt, the number of missions had grown to thirty.

In the first five years of her personal diplomacy in Africa, the foreign minister had logged 100,000 miles, and an almost legendary aura grew up around her. She became the best-known white woman in Africa; African mothers named their children after her; Africans from all walks of life wrote her letters; she became a kind of honorary queen or godmother for the African villager.

Although Golda became a legend and remained a legend in Africa, Arab oil and

A warm welcome. The foreign minister welcomes Mrs. Smart, wife of the foreign
minister of Sierre Leone, in May, 1963.

Israeli foothold in Africa. The foreign minister and Jomo Kenyata, prime minister of Kenya, are shown at the ceremony for laying the cornerstone of the Israeli embassy in Nairobi in December, 1963. Israel established thirty embassies in Africa during Golda's term as foreign minister, symbolizing the development of close relations between the Jewish state and the African continent.

An old acquaintance. The prime minister greets an old acquaintance, Angie Brooks of Liberia, at the United Nations in April, 1970.

Friends are not forever. **Prime Minister Meir and Foreign Minister Abba Eban with Idi Amin, the president of Uganda, at a time (July, 1971) when relations between Israel and Uganda were warm. Those relations would eventually deteriorate, and Amin would become vehemently hostile towards Israel.**

the need for Arab money eventually lured African politicans away from Israel. One by one, the African states that Golda had so assiduously cultivated began to inch toward the Arab embrace. They were embarrassed as they did it, but they could not alter their course, and the final curtain began to fall with the onset of the Yom Kippur War, in 1973. By the time the full aftereffects were felt, nearly all of the thirty African states won over during Golda's term as foreign minister had severed ties with the Jewish state. The African adventure was over—at least temporarily.

Idi Amin and Golda

The most exasperating instance of the African turn-around was Uganda. Its oversized, explosive leader, Idi Amin, had once acquired his paratroop wings in the Jewish state, and he had been a welcome visitor in Jerusalem. But his behavior during his final visit to Israel in the spring of 1972 greatly annoyed Golda (then prime minister). Amin's domineering personality and the sheer audacity of his

Meir and Yancy. **Prime Minister Meir greets Ambassador Ernest J. Yancy of Liberia in January, 1970.**

demands confounded her. Standing next to her, the towering black mountain of a man made Golda a bit fearful, especially when he insisted on speaking to her alone.

Lou Kaddar, Golda's personal secretary, ever protective of her boss, waited outside the prime minister's office, ready to come to Golda's aid if necessary. If Golda should scream, Lou and the security men would charge into the office.

The conversation with the African president went as follows:

Amin: "I have come to see you because I want a few Phantoms from you."

Golda: "We don't manufacture Phantoms. We buy them from the United States, when we can—which is not always, or often enough. They aren't things that you buy and sell. Anyway, why do you need Phantoms?"

Amin: "Oh, to use against Tanzania."

Later, during Amin's same visit, he sent Golda a message requesting ten million pounds sterling. When Golda refused, the Ugandan turned to the Libyans and received financial help from them.

11

Ben-Gurion and Golda

Golda's influence and popularity in Africa were unrivalled, but her political strength at home was not firm. Ben-Gurion was the fulcrum of Israeli politics for nearly two decades, and Golda's strength was dependent upon him. He was the father of the country, a man with many faces. He could be domineering, stubborn, impulsive, insensitive, but more often than not, when it came to the major issues of the day, he was far wiser than any of his peers. Although Ben-Gurion was in his early sixties when Israel was founded, no one considered his age a liability.

As the State of Israel grew, Ben-Gurion became untouchable. He moved in and out of office as if power was his to use as he pleased. But Ben-Gurion was too sagacious, too charismatic, too much the father of his people to be challenged.

The Battle for Succession

So powerful was the "Old Man" in those early days of the republic that it was almost taken for granted that he would *anoint* his own successor. The landscape of Israeli politics was strewn with a whole array of hopefuls eager for Ben-Gurion's blessing, and Golda was aware that his attention was riveted on the younger members of his party, including Moshe Dayan and Shimon Peres. Men in their thirties and forties, they had vision and daring, qualities valued by Ben-Gurion.

But Ben-Gurion did not overlook the older politicians, the ideologues and pioneers who had ploughed their visions into the building of the state. Now in their fifties and sixties, they included such individuals as Pinchas Sapir, Levi Eshkol and Zalman Aranne—and Golda Meir. Ben-Gurion had a soft spot in his heart for these veterans, particularly Golda, and he was aware that they considered themselves his rightful heirs. And so, in effect, the battle for the mantle of political leadership in the 1950s became a battle between two generations—and a battle to win over the heart of the Father of the Nation.

Although she would never say it publicly, Golda believed that she was best suited to assume the prime ministership upon Ben-Gurion's retirement. She resented the brashness and independence of the Young Guard. "Why are you pushing so far?" she asked Moshe Dayan, their unofficial leader. "By simple biology, you will prevail over us."

Dayan answered bluntly, "We can't rely on you."

Mutual Admiration

To win the battle for succession, Golda knew that she would have to capture the mind and heart of Ben-Gurion, whom she considered strange, complicated yet appealing. She understood his politics far better than his personality. Activism against the Arabs, disdain for the United Nations, a healthy respect for the United States—these were attitudes that she could endorse, making her seem more of a

In the Parliament building. **The prime minister and the foreign minister in the Knesset in 1962.**

Ben-Gurionite than Ben-Gurion himself. Yet she could not understand his antisocial nature. At a gathering he would keep to himself, leaving the rambling conversations to others. He would much rather spend his leisure time perusing the Bible or studying Greek, which he started at a ripe old age.

Golda admired the Old Man for his wisdom, for his uncanny ability to sense what had to be done for the Jewish people. He had so effectively cast a spell over her that she remained loyal to him despite their differences. Even when she felt he was wrecking her beloved Mapai Pary, she bore him no malice and extolled him as "the greatest Jewish figure in modern history." She freely admitted to friends in the 1950s that she would accept Ben-Gurion's verdict on most political issues "even if it went against my instincts." To Yitzhak Ben-Aharon, a labor leader as well as a one-time Cabinet minister, she once said that if Ben-Gurion requested it, she would gladly leap out of the eighteenth floor of New York's Essex House.

Ben-Gurion had deep respect for Golda's talents. He especially admired her political toughness and her ability to move an audience. In March of 1948 he wrote to Sharett that she is "capable of doing the job as a man." And again, years later, he is reported to have remarked that Golda Meir "is the only man in my Cabinet." Golda doubted that Ben-Gurion ever made such a statement. Nevertheless, the public related to the comment, and it has become part of Israeli folklore.

In public, Ben-Gurion never praised Golda in flowery terms. And when he did assess her activity, it was always a bit begrudgingly. "Not bad at all" was the way he praised her as acting director of the Jewish Agency's political department.

But deep inside, the prime minister did have genuine feelings of affection for her. Concerned that Golda's health might not be up to the fundraising burden placed on her while in America, early in 1948 he wrote a letter to Abba Eban in the United States that "everything must be done that she won't work more than her measure. After all," the letter continued, "Golda is more important to Israel than several million dollars."

Despite Ben-Gurion's deep affection for the woman, he was not averse to deflating her ego when necessary. One of Ben-Gurion's more bizarre attempts at doing so came during the early days of her foreign ministership. Prime Minister Ben-Gurion offered Abba Eban the position of chief adviser on foreign affairs. Eban and Golda both thought the idea unwise, sensing that almost every day they would clash over who had ultimate responsibility for foreign affairs. Rather than taking the job, Eban agreed to remain in Washington as head of the Israeli Embassy. At a luncheon in Jerusalem, he and Golda agreed that "they could best cooperate across the ocean," as Eban put it in his memoirs.

Again, in November 1959, Ben-Gurion tried to assign to Eban foreign affairs responsibilities as part of his job as minister without portfolio; he was to become a kind of deputy to Golda. Understandably angered, Golda informed Eban tactfully that he was capable one day of being a foreign minister, but he should wait his turn. But it was clear that there was more than a simple jurisdictional problem here: with her low regard for all intellectuals, Golda had never particularly cared for the professorial Eban.

The German Debate

But no matter how tight the reins held by Ben-Gurion over Golda, he could not silence her over the controversial issue of Germany. Heated debate had swept the nation in the early 1950s over whether to accept German reparations.

Ironically, West Germany, in the 1950s, was one of the few nations prepared to sell arms to Israel. Because of this, Ben-Gurion was ready to sweep all bitter

The good old days. Mrs. Meir and the Russian ambassador M. Bodrov at an Independence Day reception (May, 1959) for the diplomatic corps. The U.S.S.R. broke off diplomatic relations with Israel during the Six Day War of June, 1967, and since then the two countries have had no formal relations.

memories under the rug. Golda could not adjust to the idea. She had opposed reparations when the issue came to a head in 1952. In the end she bowed to Ben-Gurion's judgment, but insisted that reparations be regarded as Israel's by right. Their acceptance should in no way be construed as forgiveness of Germans for their past barbarity.

Golda's bitterness toward Germany was deep-rooted. In 1948, she urged that the new government refuse to designate the Tel Aviv quarter of Sarona (since renamed Hakirya) as the new capital because it would be located in German housing. She proposed instead Mount Carmel in Haifa, recalling that Herzl had mentioned this as the site he preferred. Sarona was eventually chosen, but only temporarily, until Jerusalem could be made the permanent site.

Golda made sure always to express her disdain for German-made products. She refused to ride in a Volkswagen, nor would she board a West German airplane. Golda knew German from her Milwaukee days, but she refused to utter a word of it.

Shortly after Golda became foreign minister, Ya'acov Tzur came to visit her in Jerusalem. He raised the painful subject of diplomatic relations with West Germany.

"Golda," he began delicately, "now I know what it means to you, but I have to tell you that we must find a way to renew relations with West Germany."

"Not me," she snapped disdainfully.

Although as foreign minister she was compelled to modify her position, Golda never failed to express regret that Middle East diplomacy made her land on German soil on two occasions.

Golda opposed the establishment of diplomatic relations with West Germany, but there was little she could do to prevent it. Her attempts to undercut Ben-Gurion's wishes met with little success. Aryeh Levavi, her director-general at the foreign ministry, found himself having to choose between two conflicting sets of orders, those of the prime minister and those of the foreign minister. "What should I do?" he finally asked the foreign minister.

"Do what you like," said Golda.

In that case, said Levavi, he would comply with Ben-Gurion's wishes, not only because he was prime minister, but also because he was in agreement that it was in Israel's interest that relations with the Germans be established.

As Levavi began to leave the room, Golda called to him, "Why don't you all understand that apart from the moral aspect of coming to terms with Germany so early, even from a tactical aspect, it's a mistake to bargain too easily."

Over her objections, relations with West Germany were established in 1965.

Deteriorating Relations with Ben-Gurion

Golda's relations with Ben-Gurion began to deteriorate in 1958 when the Old Man finally appeared ready to anoint the younger generation of Mapai leaders as his successors. This deeply anguished Golda, for she and the prime minister had been so close in political thinking. They had shared so many important moments.

The first indication that Ben-Gurion considered Golda expendable came at a crucial party conference at the Kfar Hayarok Agricultural School in December, 1958. Embittered by rumors that Ben-Gurion planned to abandon her, Golda confronted him with an ultimatum: if he elevated the Young Guard to positions of leadership, she would resign her post.

Her timing was perfect; the threat worked. The prime minister knew that losing Golda was bad politics. A number of his coalition partners would simply not accept a Mapai-run government with so much "young blood." In no mood to turn his back on Golda or the other party veterans, Ben-Gurion capitulated.

One real clash between Ben-Gurion and Golda came in the Knesset elections of November, 1959. Reaping the political fruits of the Sinai victory, Ben-Gurion's popularity swept the Mapai to its greatest triumph, increasing the number of

Mapai seats in the parliament to forty-seven. Having pledged to introduce new faces into his government to offset criticism that he and his colleagues had held power for too long, the prime minister planned to appoint Moshe Dayan, Abba Eban, and Shimon Peres to senior positions. But Ben-Gurion also wanted Golda to remain a part of the government.

Golda was apprehensive. If so many of the Young Guard were added to the new government, in time she and her veteran colleagues would surely be put out to pasture. So, she decided to take a stand. If Ben-Gurion truly wanted her in his Cabinet, he would have to pay a price. Long negotiations were conducted in November and December, with the result that Golda remained as foreign minister; Peres was dropped from consideration as deputy minister of defense; and Dayan was given the politically unimportant post of minister of agriculture. Golda's political astuteness had kept the neophytes at bay.

The Lavon Affair

Ben-Gurion's desire to place members of the Young Guard in leadership positions was greatly hampered by the Lavon Affair. One of the most divisive aspects of domestic Israeli politics, the affair lasted for eleven long, painful years. Most of the facts have since come to light, but not all.

As far as is known, the affair began in 1954, the year Britain announced its intention to evacuate Suez as soon as it signed a treaty with Egypt. Until that time the Israelis had felt secure in the knowledge that the British were exerting a restraining influence on the Egyptians. Now they were anxiety-ridden. What would prevent Egypt from engaging in provocative acts against Israel now? In answer, a plan to forestall an early British evacuation was devised.

The plan, designed to discredit Egypt, called for the dynamiting of a number of American and British buildings in Egypt. The Israelis hoped this would prove Nasser's "irresponsibility" and thus, it was hoped, the British would be convinced to remain.

There seemed to be no question that Colonel Benjamin Gibli, chief of army intelligence, had issued the order. What was unclear was whether Pinchas Lavon, the minister of defense, had given his approval. Lavon maintained that he had no knowledge of the operation.

Lavon was forced to resign, although he managed to win what he considered an official apology for what he insisted were false accusations. Had Ben-Gurion not considered the apology an affront to the army, of which the prime minister was commander-in-chief, the matter might have been laid to rest. But Ben-Gurion considered this an attempt by Lavon to strike out against the prime minister's protégés, particularly Moshe Dayan.

Over the next decade, until 1965, Ben-Gurion was obsessed with the affair. He wanted to see "justice" done. He therefore activated the legal machinery that he hoped would confirm the guilt of Lavon. In the process, he dissipated much of the good will that he had managed to create over the years, and in his last years in politics the affair led him to attack some of the men and women with whom he had worked for decades—including Golda Meir.

Protagonists in the Lavon Affair. **Golda meets with Pinchas Lavon in the Knesset restaurant on November 30, 1959. (161)**

The Lavon Affair had no real bearing on Golda Meir, except that it served her politically in a most propitious way. It had been suggested that neither Lavon nor Gibli had been responsible for issuing orders to the Israeli spies in Egypt. Golda joined others in expressing the suspicion that Moshe Dayan or Shimon Peres—either individually or jointly—had issued those orders. Eager to destroy the political futures of both these men, Golda now had an issue that could be used to discredit them.

But to succeed, she needed time. A speedy resolution of the affair would almost certainly mean that Gibli would have been found solely responsible for having issued the order. From Golda's viewpoint this would have been disastrous. She needed time to accumulate evidence—against Dayan or Peres—and possibly against Ben-Gurion himself.

Golda was careful to work behind the scenes so that her role in the affair could never be properly established. Golda knew that, if she could discredit Dayan and Peres, she would also, indirectly, discredit Ben-Gurion. The Lavon Affair was the last straw in her deteriorating relationship with Ben-Gurion. It became clear to her that she must do everything possible to deny him political leadership and the power to handpick his successors.

Another Cabinet. Golda, now foreign minister, sits in on the portrait of the new Cabinet of June 26, 1963. With his back to the camera is Levi Eshkol, the prime minister. The photograph was taken at the president's residence in Jerusalem.

Afraid that Ben-Gurion would ignore her and choose Dayan as his successor, Golda stepped up her attacks. She continued to criticize the Old Man on the Lavon matter.

Ben-Gurion's attempts to conciliate his Mapai colleagues were unsuccessful. At a meeting designed to effect a reconciliation, he lost his temper at Golda and shouted, "You're destroying Mapai!" She left the room in tears.

Ben-Gurion retained a certain blindness toward Golda. "I can't understand why she is against me?" he asked his aides in all innocence. He scoffed at their suggestion that she wanted to unseat him. He could blame her for her unseemly fits of temper, but never for political ambition at his expense. "She had a poor childhood," he would say in explaining her rebelliousness. Or, he would say, "She suffers in the leg," referring to her injuries from the 1948 taxi accident.

Matters came to a head in early 1965. At the annual Mapai conference in Tel Aviv, Golda and some of her associates lashed out at Ben-Gurion for insisting on keeping the Lavon Affair alive. Soon thereafter, Ben-Gurion bolted Mapai to set up his own Rafi Party, Rafi being an acronym for the Hebrew of "Israel Labor List." With him he took many of the bright young men whom he had been grooming for leadership.

In the June, 1965 elections, Ben-Gurion's Rafi Party ran as a separate list. Garnering only 10 Knesset seats, Rafi had little clout in the new Knesset. Ben-Gurion's colleagues, Dayan and Peres, eventually realized their political futures would be handicapped unless they returned to the Mapai fold—which in time they did. Ben-Gurion never rejoined Mapai.

Off to Washington. Prime Minister Levi Eshkol (far right) receives a warm send-off from Foreign Minister Meir at Lod International Airport on May 31, 1964. Eshkol was about to leave for the United States, where he would meet with President Lyndon B. Johnson. At the meeting with Johnson, Eshkol would speak these memorable words: "My people are the last station in history. If the nation of Israel does not survive, the Jewish people will not survive." Others in the photograph (left to right): Minister of Communications Bar-Yehuda; Minister of Justice Joseph; and Deputy Prime Minister Eban.

Golda's New, Unexpected Enemy

By the spring of 1965 Golda was ready to retire, both for political and personal reasons. She had been debating retirement for several years, but now she was determined to leave the foreign ministry.

The political reason had to do with Levi Eshkol, who had succeeded Ben-Gurion as prime minister in 1963. Though Ben-Gurion had handpicked Eshkol as his successor, the two men soon drifted apart largely over the Lavon Affair. Eshkol, therefore, became a sort of political bedfellow of Golda's.

In truth, Golda had little desire to serve as foreign minister under Prime Minister Eshkol. She resented the fact that the Old Man had passed over her to give Eshkol the premiership. Nevertheless, she decided to continue to serve as foreign minister despite her bitter feelings toward Eshkol and Ben-Gurion.

Now that Eshkol was on her side in the Lavon Affair, she wanted to do nothing that would weaken his political position. She feared that if she left the foreign ministry right after Eshkol took power, it would be interpreted as a sign of Eshkol's weakness. Such an interpretation might hurt Golda's and Eshkol's struggle against Ben-Gurion in the Lavon Affair.

Eventually, she changed her mind about leaving office, for personal reasons. In 1963, Golda's doctors had discovered that she had been stricken with cancer. The prognosis was not good. But, because she was not prepared to step down, she was careful to keep her illness a carefully-guarded secret, even though she was continually visiting hospitals for treatment.

With all the party bickering over Ben-Gurion and the Lavon Affair, and with a question mark hanging over her health, Golda eventually decided to end the hectic lifestyle she had been leading. In the autumn of 1965, at age sixty-seven, she resigned from the foreign ministry. "Why do I need it all?" she asked her friends.

12

Recall to Party Leadership

Despite retirement, Golda Meir enjoyed more prestige than any Mapai Party member. Although she often felt and behaved like a sickly, old woman in need of a long if not permanent rest from public life, she remained an active member of the Mapai executive and retained her Knesset seat. Therefore, when friends of longstanding, such as Pinchas Sapir and Zalman Aranne, approached her in the winter of 1966, requesting that she assume the party leadership, she was prepared. Weakened by the Rafi walkout, having lost some of its most active, energetic members, Mapai was no longer the mighty force it had been.

The task of rebuilding Mapai was a most difficult one. When Golda became its secretary-general in February, 1966, she feared that both holding a seat in the Knesset and running a political party might be too great a burden. Her associates convinced her otherwise.

The party was like family to her, and as with families differences were to be settled internally. When party gadfly Shulamit Aloni used her own radio program to air her grievances about Mapai, Golda treated her like an errant daughter who had complained to the neighbors about mother's ill treatment. "If you're not happy with what's going on in the party or the country," she scolded Aloni brusquely, "bring it to the party. Don't let the public know about it before we settle it in the party."

Repeatedly Golda demonstrated her belief that the party was sacrosanct, that only its members deserved to occupy government posts, for only they were capable of leading the nation. The strength of this belief became even more obvious when some time later, during Golda's term as prime minister, Shmuel Toledano, the prime minister's assistant for Arab affairs, asked that a Druze be appointed consul to a mission abroad. The prime minister rebuked him for selecting a member of the Herut opposition: "Why didn't you take a Mapai man?" she inquired with annoyance.

Eshkol and Golda

As party secretary-general, Golda was not really entitled to as much power as she wielded. After all, Levi Eshkol, also a Mapai leader, was *the* prime minister. By virtue of that position alone he should have been the most powerful figure in Israeli politics. But he was not. Golda was.

One of the reasons for Eshkol's failure to become the dominant political figure of his time is to be found in Golda's attitude toward the man that Ben-Gurion had selected as his successor. To Golda, Eshkol could never replace her mentor, Ben-Gurion. She regarded Eshkol as an upstart. Although Ben-Gurion had caused her great anguish, she never ceased to admire the Old Man for his great wisdom and foresight. Ben-Gurion had founded a state; Eshkol was a simple bureaucrat. Ben-Gurion welcomed decision-making; Eshkol was not always able to reach conclusions expeditiously. Eshkol, schooled only in agriculture and economics, was a Johnny-come-lately to foreign affairs.

When Ben-Gurion chose Eshkol as his successor in 1963, a choice the Old Man soon came to regret, Golda Meir wept privately. The early 1960s had witnessed no real improvement in Israel's situation vis-à-vis the Arabs; indeed there were signs that relations would worsen. The nation needed a foreign affairs specialist at the helm, not a man versed only in farming and finance. Golda was convinced that she was the person who should be in charge, not Eshkol, the unsophisticated kibbutznik.

Embittered over having been bypassed for the prime ministership, uneasy over her subordination to Eshkol, Golda nevertheless felt buoyed by the esteem in which she continued to be held. As party secretary-general she was determined to be a more effective force in government than the prime minister himself.

When Ben-Gurion headed the government, no Mapai leader would have dared challenge his authority. But those now attending party meetings devoted to foreign affairs would find Golda lecturing Eshkol. When Eshkol wanted to see Golda, it was he who called on her. Senior government officials frequently came to her office to explain why certain programs were lagging.

Anti-Ben-Gurion Forces Coalesce

In her struggle to prevent Ben-Gurion from transferring power to the younger members of Mapai, Golda needed Eshkol's support, and she was able to enlist it. Eshkol soon became the spearhead of the anti-Ben-Gurion forces, largely because of the Old Man's stand on the Lavon Affair.

Golda became fanatical in defending Eshkol against Ben-Gurion. When serious charges were leveled at the prime minister in 1966, charges that might have led to his political downfall, she was prepared to defend him whether or not the charges were grounded in truth.

Throughout her life Golda would insist that she had no political ambitions, but the facts belied the claim. Her instincts for survival in politics were keen, and she emerged as one of the nation's most adept political practitioners. Although the public was not privy to all her performances, insiders often noted how she fought like a lioness at the slightest prospect of losing power.

No better display of Golda Meir's innate political instincts is to be found than in her defense of Prime Minister Levi Eshkol at this time. Some have suggested that the charges leveled against Eshkol revolved around the disappearance of Mehdi Ben Barka. Ben Barka was an exiled Moroccan nationalist with wide connections in Arab diplomatic and intelligence circles. On October 29, 1965, he was kidnapped outside a café on the Boulevard Saint Germain in Paris and was never again seen. It was presumed that he was murdered.

In early 1966, Isser Harel, then the prime minister's advisor on security affairs, learned that several months earlier a serious breach in Israel's security had taken place and that Eshkol had not informed him of it. When interviewed for this book, Harel would say nothing to confirm that the security mishap was connected with the Ben Barka affair. Harel believed that Eshkol should resign, as should Meir Amit (Harel's successor as head of the Mossad—the Israeli intelligence agency). If the prime minister did not resign, Harel vowed that he would resign as Eshkol's adviser.

Harel than approached Golda Meir for support. Fearing that the political position of her "ally," Eshkol, might be endangered if Harel resigned, she urged him to stay. Golda understood that the only one to gain from Eshkol's downfall would be Ben-Gurion. The Old Man would have the moral victory over Eshkol that he had been seeking.

"Let's assume that you are correct," she said to Harel, play-acting more than making political calculations. "What do you suggest? Who will be prime minister?"

With hesitation Harel declared, "You!"

Golda stared at him and then laughed nervously. "Me become prime minister? An old lady who visits the hospital so much?"

Harel was in a quandary. Were he not to raise his voice against Eshkol, and were he not to quit, he might be opening himself to later charges that he was an accomplice to the security breach of which the prime minister had never advised him.

Golda was not impressed with such logic. She appealed to his sense of loyalty. His resignation, she argued, would be desertion; this would be tantamount to accusing those of his colleagues who remained loyal to the prime minister of being dishonest.

Eshkol did not clear himself, and eventually, on June 29, 1966, Harel tendered his resignation. Contrary to Golda's fears, his departure did not spark a political crisis.

Under ordinary circumstances the episode might have been forgotten, especially since Golda was unwilling to oppose the prime minister. Without her support no move against Eshkol could have succeeded. But now that Golda had protected Levi Eshkol from his accusers, she would always worry that others might one day accuse her of being a party to the security mishap. Its details were kept from the public not only for the sake of national security, but to protect Golda Meir as well.

However, in the autumn of 1966 a news organization outside Israel learned the details of the incident and planned to publish them. Advised of this unfortunate turn of events, Golda sensed danger to her reputation. She turned to Isser Harel. Golda wanted him to issue a public statement in which he would assert that his resignation had been due to some event other than the episode involving the Eshkol charges. For some unfathomable reason she was certain that this would induce the news organization to drop the story.

Harel was astonished at her. "How can I do something I've never done before?"

he asked her. "Lie about this? That's what my fight was all about in the first place. And apart from that no one would believe this denial."

Golda was indignant. She glared at him coldly and pronounced decisively, "Our friendship is at an end."

Golda vs. Dayan

The feeling throughout the country was that Eshkol was weak and indecisive. In his dual role as prime minister and defense minister he came under the most intense criticism in May, 1967 for failing to act when an Arab attack seemed imminent. During this famous "waiting period" in Israeli history, the public began a search for heroes, and Moshe Dayan was propelled into the limelight.

Golda was anxious to quench the fires of enthusiasm for Dayan, her goal being to deny Ben-Gurion and the Young Guard a political victory over the Arabs, although she felt certain that if war came, Israel would win, with or without Moshe Dayan as defense minister.

By the end of May, 1967, the Straits of Tiran were closed by Nasser, making war inevitable. The nation was not at ease knowing that the defense ministry was in the hands of Eshkol. Pressure for a change began to mount. Not only were strong voices heard within the government, but a vocal crescendo of "We want Dayan. We want Dayan!" was heard on the streets. On June 1 a group of Tel Aviv housewives demonstrated outside the Mapai Party headquarters on Tel Aviv's Hayarkon Street. The target of the protest was Golda Meir.

Of all Mapai leaders Golda had been most vocal in opposing Dayan, whose appointment as minister of defense was being demanded. Privately she labeled Dayan and his followers "neo-fascists." But although she made every effort to steer the party away from his election, Golda's friends within the Old Guard favored him. Golda was virtually alone in her opposition to Dayan. Yet, despite her isolation, she worried the Dayan camp. "As long as the Old Lady is there," Dayan said to friends, "she controls the party, and she won't let me in the Cabinet."

But Dayan was wrong in his estimation of Golda's strength. He had the support of the entire nation, and Golda lacked the political influence necessary to maneuver his defeat.

Resigned to the fact that Dayan would soon become defense minister, Golda was determined to lessen some of the credit that would accrue to him if the war that lay ahead were successfully executed. She appealed to the nation's leaders to start the war on June 1—before Dayan would assume full charge of the defense establishment. She was overruled.

The Six Day War

The war exploded with lightning speed. On Monday morning, June 5, wave after wave of Israeli bombers swept over nine Egyptian airfields. Within three

Almost over before it began. Egyptian planes were destroyed on the ground by devastating Israeli raids in the opening hours of the Six Day War of June, 1967. Few believed it possible, but the Israeli Air Force had effectively brought the war to an end with these lightning raids on the first day of the war, June 5, 1967.

Push toward the Canal. Israeli military units advance along the southern sector on June 7, 1967, the third day of the Six Day War. Here, they are shown deep in Sinai on their way to the Suez Canal.

Triumphal entry. The date: June 7, 1967. The event: the Israeli conquest of the Old City of Jerusalem. Here, Israel's military leaders—Defense Minister Moshe Dayan (center); Uzi Narkiss, Central Front Commander (left); and Yitzhak Rabin, Chief of Staff (right)—enter the Lion's Gate of the Old City shortly after Israeli troops took control of the Old City.

Historic moment. Israeli parachutists reach the Western Wall in the Old City of Jerusalem on June 7, 1967. The Wall, actually part of the outer courtyard wall of the Second Temple, is the holiest site in Judaism.

We've returned. The Israeli flag flies above a military outpost at Sharm el-Sheikh on June 8, 1967. This time the Israelis did not intend to withdraw from the conquered land. Only with the signing of the Israel-Egypt Peace Treaty of March 26, 1979 did Israel agree to relinquish the Sinai, which it had captured in the Six Day War. As for Sharm el-Sheikh, Israel would only give that up in April, 1982, at the very end of the three-year implementation process of the treaty.

At the Suez. Israeli soldiers on the east bank of the Suez Canal on June 9, 1967.

hours word reached Israeli headquarters that the raids had been a huge success. In the afternoon of that same day, with equal success, Israeli planes attacked two Jordanian and five Syrian air bases. By nightfall on that first day of the war, Israel was assured of victory.

On June 10, after six days of battle, the war was over. Israel had won a remarkable victory. The conquered Arab territory was three and a half times the size of Israel. One million Arabs were now under Israeli occupation. Israeli troops now controlled the western bank of the Suez Canal and the western bank of the Jordan River. But the price for Israel was high: 803 dead; 3,006 wounded. Egypt reportedly lost 10,000 to 12,000 men, with 20,000 wounded. Jordan suffered 1,000 dead and 2,000 wounded.

Rejoicing in Victory

Golda shared in the euphoria that swept the country. Prayerful that the magnitude of the Israeli victory would certainly bring the Arabs to the peace table, she rushed to the Western Wall in Jerusalem to express thankfulness and joy. She had a warm embrace and kiss for her escort, Chaim Herzog, the newly appointed military governor of the West Bank. Emotions ran high at the Wall, which was open to visitation from Jews for the first time since 1948.

Post-war Labor Alignment

Victory in war made Moshe Dayan the most popular man in Israel. As one of the leading figures of Ben-Gurion's Rafi group (which had split off from Mapai in 1965), his popularity, and hence the importance of Rafi, could no longer be ignored. For Golda and her fellow Mapai Party leaders, the task ahead centered upon reuniting the party. For the maverick Rafi members the central question was whether or not to return to the mainstream of the Party.

The Six Day War removed all Rafi doubts. In January, 1968, after much negotiating, a new political party came into being, an amalgam of three very different political groups; Mapai, with its Old Guard veterans, not quite centrist in its political makeup but neither excessively hawkish nor dovish; Ahdut Avoda, normally considered the repository of left-wing sentiment, although the rather hawkish views of some of its leaders, such as Israel Galili, ran counter to such labeling; and Rafi, with its collection of unrepentant Ben-Gurionites who were activist and right-wing.

Bringing these factions together was not easy; and standing at the very top of this political crazy-quilt was Golda Meir. She was the miracle worker, creating unity out of chaos, and when the new coalition turned to her to assume leadership of this new Labor Party, she agreed.

Having Rafi on the inside proved as troublesome as Golda had feared. Shortly after the merger, Rafi chieftains organized a frontal attack against the party, urging it to be more democratic. Direct elections for mayors were proposed, as was secret balloting for party delegates. These two resolutions were drafted, and despite Golda's opposition they were adopted.

Golda and Eban. After the 1967 Six Day War, Golda joins Abba Eban, head of the Israel delegation, at a United Nations session. Seated next to Eban is Gideon Rafael.

Golda never recovered from these setbacks. In July, 1968, 70 years old, she resigned as secretary-general of the Labor Party. Worn out by the infighting, she resolved to devote her new-found leisure to family and friends. "I want to be able to read a book without feeling guilty or go to a concert when I like," she said.

Still, tired as she was, she had to let the Rafi people know she was still alive. "I do not intend to retire to a political nunnery" was her final statement before settling down to a brief hiatus.

13

Ascent to Power

Had Golda Meir been a younger woman, in better health, virtually nothing could have kept the Labor Party from regarding her as the natural successor to Levi Eshkol. But her frequent visits to the hospital had continued while she was secretary-general, giving her a public image of a sickly, old woman, one who could not hold high office again.

The two other likely candidates for Eshkol's job were Moshe Dayan, riding a great wave of popularity as the hero of the Six Day War, and Yigal Allon, hero of the 1948 War of Independence, a highly respected leader of the former Ahdut Avoda wing. Because Mapai—now Labor—had won every national election since the state was established, whoever became the party's candidate for prime minister was almost certain to be elected.

Pinchas Sapir: Kingmaker

At this juncture, the power within Labor rested almost exclusively in one man's hands: Pinchas Sapir, a bookkeeper by trade and by mentality. Heavyset, bald, with a strong, husky voice and an autocratic sneer for underlings, he was the closest thing Israel had to a party boss. Because of his position in the party, which gave him the authority to dispense large sums of money, people frequently but mistakenly assumed that he relished power, that his objective was to become prime minister. On the contrary, he preferred to be a kingmaker.

In his search for a successor to Eshkol—whose health was failing faster than was generally known—Sapir, a dove, could be forgiven if he were to confess that virtually no one met his standard. The field was crowded with hawks. Golda Meir, Moshe Dayan, even the leaders of Ahdut Avoda—Yigal Allon and Israel Galili— were too rightist. Dayan was particularly anathema to Sapir, for Dayan's policies toward the occupied territories, he believed, would keep Israel inextricably involved in the region.

Golda had cast a spell over Sapir for much of his public life. To him her appeal was not rooted in her politics or her shrewdness, but in the way she managed to win the favor of Jews around the world. Though only ten years apart in age, theirs was a mother-son relationship, and in matter of policy Sapir would often bow to Golda's judgment. At this juncture, with no other choice available, Sapir regarded Golda as the one Labor politician capable of denying Dayan the prime ministership.

Party boss. When this photograph was taken in February, 1968, Golda had just been elected secretary-general of the newly-united labor Party. Though she had desperately wanted to retire in the fall of 1965, the Labor Party's veterans insisted that she assume the running of the party. Golda remained in that post until the summer of 1968.

A State of Crisis

In December, 1968, while visiting New York, Sapir stayed at the Essex House. Yossi Sarid, one of his young Israeli protégés, was studying for a Masters degree in New York at the time, and Sapir phoned him one night and arranged for them to meet at the hotel's barber shop at seven the next morning. Before expressing what was on his mind, Sapir and Sarid made light conversation—in Hebrew. Confident that the barber did not understand them, Sapir confided to his protégé that Israeli politics was in a state of extreme crisis.

"Eshkol is very sick," he announced somberly. "He's dying. He has no chance of surviving. It's only a matter of weeks."

At the time few people knew the truth about Levi Eshkol. Although the public had been told that he was suffering from a serious heart condition, he was, in fact, dying of cancer. Sarid was shocked. He asked Sapir if it had been decided who would replace the prime minister.

Sapir answered promptly: "Golda is going to be the next prime minister." Then, moving closer to Sarid, Sapir whispered: "Yossi, this is between us. It's final and decided."

Over the next two months Sapir told others in the party: "Only she can hold the party together. There is no other possibility."

And, indeed, as long as Sapir felt that way, it appeared all but decided. As Sapir canvassed members of Eshkol's Cabinet during the months before the prime minister's death, he encountered little opposition to Golda's candidacy.

As long as Eshkol was alive, Golda did not want to make a decision about her own political future. To her, death would be the only valid reason for Eshkol's departure from politics. In no way did she want to appear opportunistic.

Four days before suffering a third heart attack, on February 7, 1969, Eshkol informed Golda of his desire to step down. She would not permit it. The prime minister did not make known his choice as a successor, but it seemed that he considered Sapir his likely heir. The prime minister was aware that Golda Meir was also a likely candidate; his feelings about that were not clear. What was clear, however, was that Eshkol favored neither Moshe Dayan nor Yigal Allon.

Eshkol Succumbs

Prime Minister Levi Eshkol died at 8:15 A.M. on February 26, 1969. His death came as a shock to the nation, which had been generally unaware of the critical nature of his illness. Golda herself was taken by surprise; she had an appointment to meet with him the next day.

Yigal Allon learned of Eshkol's death as he was driving through the outskirts of Jerusalem. Two secretaries flagged him down to convey the news. "Now it will be Golda" was his immediate reaction.

Pinchas Sapir was en route to Haifa when a policeman caught up with him and relayed the news. Sapir quickly phoned Abba Khoushy, the mayor of Haifa, with whom he was scheduled to meet. He cancelled the meeting and informed the mayor that Golda was his choice to replace Eshkol. Khoushy quickly offered his support.

In the Knesset dining room, just one hour after Eshkol's passing, a number of Mapai veterans, after brief consultations, were in nearly total agreement that Golda should be the next prime minister. Golda would not discuss the subject. She insisted that politics and mourning should not be mixed.

A public opinion poll published after Eshkol's death showed that the public favored Dayan (45 percent) over Allon (32 percent) for prime minister. The poll also showed that the public expected Dayan to be selected. Golda had very little support. But what mattered was what a handful of Labor Party leaders would decide; the public at large had no voice in selecting Eshkol's successor.

(In Israeli politics, upon the death of a prime minister the Cabinet must resign automatically. The president of the state has thirty-five days within which to confer with the various political parties and to then select one party to form a new government. The largest party is always assigned this role.)

The acknowledged kingmaker, Pinchas Sapir, was busy trying to rally support behind a single candidate. Israel Galili, the Ahdut Avoda leader, favored Allon. He asked Sapir to discuss his choice with Golda. Sapir agreed, but he warned Galili that the Dayan forces would oppose Allon's candidacy to the end, resulting in a party split, which would have dire consequences on the elections scheduled for the following fall. To give the prize to Allon, Sapir reasoned, was political suicide.

Sapir discussed a possible Allon candidacy with Golda, and she granted a fairly warm endorsement. She was distressed, however, when Sapir reminded her that Allon had been selected by the Cabinet to serve as acting prime minister on the day Eshkol died, and that when he had appealed to party leaders to make the appointment permanent, they refused. As an act of remorse for his transparent grab for power, Allon retreated somewhat by promising to support Golda should his own bid fail.

Employing more cunning than grace, Sapir held Allon to his pledge. He spread the word that both Galili and Allon had stated a preference for her candidacy. In fact both had only grudgingly conceded that she was at best an acceptable second choice. After Sapir's legerdemain the ploy worked, and Allon's chances quickly evaporated.

The door was opening wider for Golda. Despite her attempts to downplay the possibility that she might become prime minister, Golda enjoyed the political game too much to let such an opportunity pass her by. She protested lightly at times, but always lightly. In Belinson Hospital one day she listened quietly as a doctor proposed her as a future prime minister. "How can I become prime minister?" she teased. "I don't know enough Bible or Hebrew."

With Eshkol's passing there was almost automatic deference to Golda as the leader of the Labor Party. She was deluged by party delegations urging her to take on the job.

Golda's Primacy

One event in those solemn hours in February of 1969 symbolized Golda's primacy. It was one of those subtle moments when actions spoke louder than words. The date was February 26, 10:30 A.M. The prime minister was dead but two

What does the future hold? Golda at the gravesite of the late Prime Minister Levi Eshkol on March 6, 1969. Both Moshe Dayan and Yigal Allon seemed to be frontrunners for Eshkol's post. However, to avoid splitting the party, Labor Party leaders turned to Golda.

Final home. The father of modern Zionism, Theodor Herzl, comes to his final resting place in the land of Israel. Herzl died at the age of forty-four after a lengthy struggle to establish a Jewish state in Palestine. "The Jewish state is a world necessity," he once wrote. Herzl's remains arrived at Lod Airport near Tel Aviv on August 16, 1949. They were later buried on a ridge overlooking Jerusalem, which is called Mt. Herzl.

hours and the important figures of the government and Labor Party had begun to gather at Eshkol's Jerusalem home. Sapir, Allon, and Dayan were there. They discussed Eshkol's burial place. He had been a founding member of Kibbutz Degania Bet near Lake Kinneret (the Sea of Galilee).

Eshkol's wish had been to be buried at the kibbutz, next to his first wife. However, Jordan had been shelling the region repeatedly, and fears were voiced that a funeral at Degania, with the attendant television cameras and newsmen, might become the kind of media event that could invite a Jordanian attack.

Dayan thought that Mount Herzl, in Jerusalem, would be the logical burial site. After all, Theodor Herzl and other dignitaries of the Jewish state were buried there. But no one was prepared to make the final decision.

At 11 A.M., Golda Meir, looking sad but with a regal air, entered the Eshkol home. She took what seemed to be her natural place: in the center of a large sofa. Half of those gathered in the room were now seated to her right, the other half to her left.

"Is there a problem?" she asked quietly, with slightly belligerent overtones.

The matter under discussion was reviewed for Golda's benefit, and she immediately proceeded to take charge. No one challenged her. No one thought the "meeting"—for that's what it had become—should be chaired by anyone else.

"What does Dayan say?" she asked pensively.

An answer was given.

"And Allon?"

Again she was informed.

"And Sapir?"

Another opinion.

Then, acting as judge and final arbiter, she made the ruling: "He will be buried in Jerusalem."

No one questioned her judgment or her authority. From the moment Golda Meir had entered the room, she had assumed full charge. At that very moment she had also been "elected" prime minister.

Golda continued to have personal reservations about accepting the prime ministership, even after the office was hers for the asking. At Eshkol's funeral tears streamed down her cheeks: "I didn't know whether I was crying for Eshkol or for me," she said later. As she watched Eshkol being lowered into the ground, she wondered about him and about herself. His problems were ending. Were hers beginning?

Even as she feebly tried to avoid it, the mantle of responsibility was being thrust upon Golda. It was becoming increasingly difficult to escape what seemed the inevitable. At a reception for foreign delegations after the funeral, she met Walworth Barbour, the American ambassador to Israel. "Sapir and I said you're the only one to do it," he declared with a twinkle in his eye.

Golda smiled back and said quietly, "You flatter me."

The pressure was growing for Golda to announce her willingness to accept the prime ministership. All signs seemed to point to Golda. Allon may have wished for power, but he lacked the clout. Even Dayan sounded convincing when he said that he didn't want to contest her appointment to the prime ministership.

"These two generals," wrote Sylvie Keshet, a columnist for *Ha'aretz*, "are only good to fight and frighten Arabs. But they're afraid to say 'boo' to one old Jewish lady." The "old Jewish lady" had in effect sewed up the nomination before the generals, Dayan and Allon, could even leap into battle.

Golda's ill will toward Dayan played no small part in her arriving at a final decision. Indeed, she would take the job largely to stop him from getting it. She had fought Dayan once before—in May, 1967—and had, in effect, been overruled by the will of the nation. But this time, she asserted, "The decision on who will be the next prime minister will not be made in the street."

Could she withstand the rigors of the job? The question haunted her. Few people knew specifically of her bout with cancer, although the general state of her health was no secret. It bothered Golda to hear of the doubts raised in some influential quarters. "The people of Israel," wrote *Ha'aretz* in an editorial, "have the right to expect that the helm will be given to a younger person, whose power of action will not be restricted by age or health."

Golda sought the advice of her family. The day after Eshkol's death she said to her nephew Yonah (Sheyna's son), "If my mother and father were alive, I would have consulted with them, but since they are not, I want your thoughts." Yonah advised her to accept the job, as did her children, Menachem and Sarah. Both children knew about the cancer, yet neither thought it was serious enough to disqualify her. Sapir and Galili (who now supported Golda) cagily put pressure on the children to give their mother the encouragement she needed.

The family made the final decision. Had Menachem and Sarah been opposed, she would have declined the prime ministership. When they said yes, she felt reassured.

Although she regarded the post as temporary, Golda was nevertheless annoyed when she heard people complain that she was too old for the job: "I know 70-years-olds who are full of energy and I know 40-year-olds who are worth nothing." But her age did worry her, and so she pleaded with Lou Kaddar, her longtime secretary and confidant, to continue to work with her so as to lighten the burden.

Lou and Golda

The relationship between these two women was quite special. No one was closer to Golda than Lou Kaddar. She looked after Golda's personal needs and much, much more. Lou listened to Golda tirelessly and often times offered her opinions on matters of importance. The two women trusted each other and shared many secrets—political and personal. Someone once asked Lou if she thought that Golda loved her. She replied, "I don't know."

One of Lou's most important tasks was to shield Golda from some of the pressures as well as annoyances of public life. One such occasion arose in 1963, when Golda was foreign minister. She and Golda were in New York's Essex House when the telephone rang and the switchboard asked for the foreign minister. To spare Golda, Lou, who had taken the call, announced that it was Golda Meir who was speaking.

The party at the other end of the line hung up, refusing to give a name. This happened a second time, and again Lou pretended to be Golda. The party hung up once more.

The telephone rang a third time, and this time Golda agreed to speak. The hysterical voice she heard was that of Clara, her sister, calling from Bridgeport, Connecticut.

"Zipke!" shouted Golda, using the name by which her family called Clara. "Calm down. That's my secretary. I'm not being kidnapped by the Egyptians. She's not an Egyptian. She's an Israeli."

When, on a spring day in 1969, Golda informed Lou that she had been asked to become prime minister and that she doubted whether she could refuse the opportunity, Lou made her feelings clear: to refuse the offer would be foolish.

"I'll take it," said Golda, "if you'll come with me."

Lou declined, arguing that at this point in her life she didn't want to work such long hours. Golda coaxed her, promising that the job would last only for a little while. Lou, reluctantly, finally consented. She would be Golda's aide.

At that first press conference. To Golda's left is Lou Kaddar, her confidante and personal secretary.

The Elections

The party's machinery began cranking up for the elections. Golda first won the backing of the Labor Party Cabinet ministers—despite the abstention of Moshe Dayan. Next she received the support of the party's leadership bureau, 40-7. The dissenters came from the Dayan camp. Only the party's Central Committee had yet to give its stamp of approval, but since Sapir held the committee in his iron grip, Golda's nomination was assured.

The committee met on March 7 at 9:30 A.M. in Tel Aviv's Ohel Theatre. The vote went according to plan. Golda Meir received 287 votes, none against, with 45 Dayan supporters abstaining. Dayan later explained that he had abstained because he did not consider Golda "the kind of personality who would open new vistas in the leadership of the state and the party."

Wearing a simple dark blue suit, Golda cried when the vote was announced. Her acceptance speech was modest: "I never dreamt that I would be a prime minister. I never thought the day would come when I would be obliged to accept a judgment of this kind from the movement. I am not sure I will succeed."

The new government. President Zalman Shazar and Prime Minister Golda Meir drink a toast to the Cabinet which Golda had just formed. The date is March 11, 1969. Golda took over the country as a war of attrition between Israel and Egypt continued. Nearly two years after the Six Day War peace with the Arab world seemed as distant as ever. Still Golda vowed to do all in her power to achieve peace.

Conferring with defense chiefs. Golda deliberates on April 23, 1969 with Chief of Staff Haim Bar-Lev and Defense Minister Moshe Dayan about the latest events in the war of attrition between Israel and Egypt. Golda was a novice in military affairs when she assumed office, but she learned quickly. Dayan privately doubted her abilities as a military strategist, but others, like Bar-Lev, gave her high marks.

The nation's premier spokesman. On March 18, 1969, at her first press conference as prime minster, Golda addresses members of the press.

First woman prime minister. President Zalman Shazar asked Golda Meir to
form a Labor Government following Labor's election victory in October, 1969.

Jerusalem Book Fair. Accompanied by Teddy Kollek (left), mayor of Jerusalem, Golda visits the 1969 International Jerusalem Book Fair. Here she examines *Bible Gems,* a publication of Pitman Publishing Corporation. Moshe Dayan once kidded Golda that she did not know a great deal about the Bible.

She was greeted with an expansive ovation, embraces and kisses, and as she walked down the aisle and out of the hall, the crowd shouted after her, "Golda, Golda!" The police cleared a path so the prime minister-designate could enter Pinchas Sapir's waiting car.

Among the many letters of congratulations received by Golda was a touching note from her sister Clara, admonishing the prime minister-to-be to remember her humble beginnings: "Whatever you do, never forget that you are the daughter of a carpenter."

Golda reiterated to one and all that she would serve as prime minister only until the October elections. Sapir had his mind made up otherwise: he was determined to keep Dayan from becoming prime minister. Golda understood this and accepted it, and soon she ceased making statements about her intended length of service.

Transient or not, Golda was intent upon savoring those first few moments as prime minister-designate—and she did.

14

The Peak of a Career

In March of 1969, the month Golda assumed office, a war of attrition, initiated by the Eygptians the year before, was raging at the Suez Canal. Egyptian troops had moved up to the western bank of the canal to begin artillery duels with Israeli troops on the other side. In response, the Israelis had constructed a series of fortifications along the canal's eastern bank. This became known as the Bar-Lev Line, after Haim Bar-Lev, Israeli chief of staff between 1968 and 1971.

While the conflict with Egypt persisted, Golda also faced the problem of contending with the Palestinian Arabs, who were intensifying their terrorist activities. The week Golda took office two pounds of plastic TNT were exploded in a crowded cafeteria at Jerusalem's Hebrew University, leaving twenty-nine people wounded.

A New Relationship

Prime Minister Meir had decided to make no changes in the Cabinet she had inherited from Eshkol. Moshe Dayan continued to serve as minister of defense. Although she had agreed to assume the prime ministership primarily to prevent Dayan from occupying that office, Golda now was forced into a new relationship with him. A novice in military affairs, she was more in need of the expertise of Dayan, a former chief of staff and a war hero, than that of any other member of her staff. She became increasingly dependent on him in defense matters, an ironic turnabout considering her evaluation of his importance during the Six Day War.

Golda had once despised Dayan, but she now began to view him in a different light. His charisma, which had always attracted others, now began to attract her as well. She now shared with the entire nation a view of Dayan as the authentic Jewish soldier, the Sabra warrior.

In the prime minister's eyes, Dayan's unique qualities endowed him with special virtue. His judgment could be trusted completely; his mastery of military subjects was unquestionable. She loved him, and she needed him. Dayan, however, reciprocated by dismissing her lightly, often cynically.

The New Lands

The Arab lands conquered by Israel during the Six Day War were providing a demographic and economic liability for the young nation. One million Arabs on the West Bank and the Gaza Strip diluted the Jewishness of the Jewish state and

The agony of office. **The prime minister at the May 10, 1970 funeral of an eighteen-year-old Israeli killed in a terrorist attack at Kiryat Shemona, a border town in the northern part of the country.**

became a burden on the national treasury. How could a Jewish state afford to support so large an Arab minority?

The Arab world was unrelenting in its anger and bitterness toward Israel. Egypt was intent upon reestablishing the pride it had lost in the Six Day War. Palestinian Arabs wanted a state of their own—on the Occupied West Bank and Gaza Strip.

The occupied Arab lands won during the 1967 war were regarded by most Israelis as bargaining chips for peace, but after the Arab summit at Khartoum in August, 1967, it became clear that the Arabs had no interest whatsoever in negotiating a peace settlement. Golda's reaction to the Arab attitude was clear: "As long as there is no peace agreement between us and our Arab neighbors," she stated at a press conference, "we stand where we are." She was referring not only to the West Bank but the rest of the conquered lands as well.

The Demands of Office

For Prime Minister Golda Meir the day was never long enough. The appointments, the commotion, the constant interruptions were incessant. The burdens of office were great, and there was little time to think.

Golda grew to cherish the evening and night hours. It was then that the important meetings were held. It was then, when the pressures of office lessened, that Simcha Dinitz, Golda's aide, would read her the most recent cables.

These demands placed by the prime minister on her aides caused them much consternation. Dinitz, a family man, had been led to believe that he could simply leave the evening cables with Golda at 5:00 P.M. and pick them up at the office the next morning, by which time they would have been read. But Golda's eyes were the eyes of an old woman, and she made it clear to Dinitz that his presence was required every evening.

The prime minister wanted more from Dinitz than cable-reading. His wit, his relaxed manner, his keen intelligence, made him good company, and she appreciated the amusement he could supply. Dinitz was a great mimic, and when in a light mood Golda delighted in his imitations. His Abba Eban, already a classic, was a particular favorite of Golda's.

Golda's sleeping habits were erratic. One night she would find herself having conversations into the early hours of the morning; the following day she might sleep through the daylight hours. On one occasion, while in New York visiting her close friend Rebecca Shulman, a former president of Hadassah, she slept so soundly that Rebecca became frightened: "I was scared to death. I'd go to see if she was still breathing."

Breakfast was nearly always spent in the company of Lou Kaddar, but conversation was minimal. While eating a hard-boiled egg, toast, and coffee or tea, Golda would scan the morning press, beginning always with the Labor Party daily *Davar*. She had an uncanny ability to discover almost immediately some article that proved irritating.

Golda's world was simple. There were the heroes and the villains. The Jews, if not always heroic, were her people; they were a force for good. Those who wanted to harm the Jews, either overtly or by indifference, were a negative force. The world—Golda Meir's world—was black and white; there were no gray shadings. The skeptic, the cynic, the intellectual were nonexistent in that world.

Golda's wisdom was homespun, practical. There were few absolutes. Often she would tell friends that morality and beauty are in the eye of the beholder. Love, she said, is always beautiful, but making love to a prostitute ugly. The highest form of morality for Jews, she believed, is the preservation of the people. Only slightly less in importance is one's fidelity to the institutions and people who work on behalf of Jews. If one wants to be moral, said Golda, one has to become a teacher, a philosopher—someone who can explain the Jewish cause. The main task of concerned Jews is to preach, to inform both the converted and the unconverted. According to these principles, Golda conducted her life. Whether dealing with Richard Nixon or Henry Kissinger or the American ambassador to Israel (the most accessible of the three) she put her personal code into practice.

Every time the prime minister summoned Walworth Barbour, the American envoy, for a chat, she would begin by expounding on Jewish history. After the tenth meeting, Barbour exclaimed, "Listen, I know all that. You've been through it many times before . . . I don't mind the first few times, but every time I want to find where Israeli troops were in a raid, we have to start in Russia."

Jewish Loyalty

Golda believed that just as her fellow Jews owed unwavering loyalty to the cause of the Jewish people and to Israel, they also owed loyalty to her as she pursued their cause. When someone was disloyal to the Jewish cause, she felt pity. When they were disloyal or offended her, she felt anger.

One such case involved an Israeli consul-general stationed in Turkey who had become the victim of an unfortunate set of circumstances. Crossing the Bosporus in a ferry, he met the wife of a Jewish community leader. When the boat docked at Istanbul, the two were seen debarking together. This was duly reported to Golda, and she accepted the gossip as sufficient evidence of indiscretion, to warrant the recall of the Israeli official. Those who investigated the matter soon learned that the official was no stranger to Golda. In the 1930s, as a minor Histadrut official, he had once offended a Histadrut executive named Golda Meyerson—and from that point on the reason for Golda's overreaction was obvious to those who knew her.

Similar incidents were known to the inner circle. In Zurich, in the early 1950s, the consul-general had been alerted that Menachem, Golda's son, would be passing through. He was advised that Menachem's mother expected the Israeli mission to entertain him while in town. The independent-minded counsul-general treated Menachem as he would any Israeli, rather than like the son of the minister of labor. To Golda this was a serious snub, one that she would never forget. During her entire term as foreign minister that diplomat was never promoted. Only after she left the foreign ministry did he achieve an advancement in rank.

Getting around the country. As prime minister, Golda made a point of visiting various parts of the country. Here, on January 20, 1971, she and a young mother admire a newborn baby at Kibbutz Ein Gedi, near the Dead Sea.

Despite Golda's tendency to speak her mind freely, she often suffered silently, inwardly. Her steel-gray eyes staring straight ahead, the creases on her wrinkled face, the slight curve of her lips often spoke volumes.

Although it was rare, when Golda did lose control of her temper the fury was spent on those closest to her. One day when a hectic schedule threatened to keep her from accompanying Sheyna to the airport to welcome Clara, due in from the United States, she screamed at her two aides, Lou Kaddar and Simcha Dinitz, "What are you doing to me? I've never seen a more stupid schedule than the one you've organized for me!" In her pique, Golda picked up an ashtray and hurled it onto the floor.

Dinitz, convinced that he would be fired, appealed to Lou, whom he thought had some influence with Golda. "We're both in the garbage can," responded Lou.

Later, Golda summoned both her assistants for what Dinitz feared might be the fatal announcement. Her eyes fixed on the floor, Golda begged their forgiveness: "I don't know what happened. I don't know how to explain it."

Golda's Kitchen Cabinet

Golda Meir the decision-maker was anxious to hear the opinions of others. As she listened, she gulped down many cups of coffee and smoked cigarette after cigarette. She soaked in the collective judgment of her colleagues, which sometimes led her to challenge her own instincts. She probed her advisers for weaknesses in argument and, at times, guided them to conclusions that would support her own.

The unlikely place where this deliberative process took place was Golda's kitchen. There her permanent entourage of Labor Party advisers gathered, usually on Saturday evenings, to prepare for the regular Sunday Cabinet meeting.

The kitchen meetings led cynics to remark that decisions which rightly belonged to the whole Cabinet had been "baked" in advance. It was a case of too few cooks, not too many. But the number of participants in the Kitchen Cabinet was intentionally small. Non-Labor persons were automatically excluded. Each permanent member was there either for his expertise—as with Dayan, the minister of defense, or Sapir, the minister of finance—or because Golda trusted his judgment—as with Galili, the minister without portfolio, or Ya'acov Shimshon Shapira, the minister of justice. Galili could draft official communiqués skillfully. Shapira had considerable legal talents.

The Kitchen Cabinet meetings were far more frank than those of the full Cabinet. There were no stenographers, formal votes, or leaks to the press. The charge that the Kitchen Cabinet was fundamentally undemocratic mattered little to Golda. She ruled her government with an iron hand, and it phased her not at all that major decisions were made around her green formica kitchen table the night before the issues at hand would be brought up for consideration by the formal Cabinet. At home or in her office Golda was the boss.

Leisure Activities

The prime minister had little time for relaxation. She often yearned for the

A good crop. On January 20, 1971, Golda visited Kibbutz Ein Yahav in the Aravah region. She is shown here examining one of the fresh tomatoes grown on the kibbutz.

privacy she was denied: "I like going to the movies without a bodyguard trailing behind. It sounds impossible, but if I want to see a film, they send the Israeli Army Reserves to escort me."

She had little time for reading but took great pleasure in listening to classical music, which Morris had taught her to appreciate. For Golda, television was often a means of relaxation. She enjoyed the American detective series, particularly *Ironside*, and American commercials were particularly amusing to her. In the intimate company of someone like Rebecca Shulman of New York, Golda sometimes would recite the Maxwell House "coffier coffee" commercial, after which they would both laugh uncontrollably.

Golda's Chicken Soup

Golda found herself most relaxed when at work in her kitchen. Her chicken soup became famous and Golda herself came to be known as the world's most famous Jewish grandmother. More than one visitor had the experience of being invited to stay for a meal at Golda's house, only to find the prime minister herself taking charge of the cooking. Chicken soup was invariably served.

Golda also enjoyed preparing and serving other Jewish dishes, such as heavily-peppered *gefilte* (stuffed) fish and luscious cheese blintzes. And she never would fail to serve tea (in a cup)—tea so hot that it would burn one's tongue. Following the old Russian style, Golda herself put cubes of sugar in her cheek and then drank the tea through them. But she did that only when alone, never in company.

Golda and the Role of Women

Golda came to power just as the feminist movement was gaining momentum. Many feminists regarded her as a prime example of feminist success, but she was uncomfortable with the designation. In the Palestine of the 1920s, long before the feminist movement in the United States or elsewhere had established itself, Jewish women had begun taking on new roles, moving out of their households and into the fields. They were searching for a new lifestyle, not because they were women but because they believed that the old ways of European Jewish women no longer applied. These women appealed to Golda. She saw them not as pioneers of feminism but as pathfinders in the Jewish cause.

Promoting women's causes per se made no real sense to Golda. When she arrived in Palestine, a "man's world" awaited her, and she was determined to penetrate it because it was there, in that world of men, where the crucial business of Zionism and nation-building was being transacted.

Golda did not identify with the tiny women's liberation movement of the 1920s, for she found its ideas and positions constricting. Later, when addressing American Jewish women in the United States, she did not mention the role of women in the Yishuv. Of greater import to her were the problems of the Yishuv at large.

As the years passed, Golda seemed less and less interested in her own femininity. The deep, gravelly voice, the prominent nose, the unstylish dress

Woman to women. Israel's female prime minister, Golda Meir, reviews the honor guard of female soldiers before departing for the United States in October, 1970. Golda became a symbol of feminist success, but ironically she had little admiration for the women's liberation movement. She considered its ideas extreme and unrealistic.

suggested masculinity to many who saw her in person. Someone remarked that she had the face of what the French called a *bellelaide,* a beautiful ugly one.

Golda realized that she was not beautiful, and in her later years she spoke about it: "I'm a realist. And I suppose if I believed that if I could go to a beauty parlor, and I would really become beautiful, I suppose I would have done it. But I knew that wouldn't help. This is it. I have to live with it."

Golda paid especial attention to certain aspects of grooming: she gave particular care to her hair. She kept it long all her life. When asked why, she simply said, "because Morris and Menachem liked it that way." And she put on a pomade to make it shine. Once another woman asked Golda who her hairdresser was (by way of complimenting her on the dye she used), and Golda only laughed. Her hair had never been dyed.

Golda seemed determined to avoid calling attention to her femininity. Her dresses were simple—usually black or gray—and even on television she rarely wore jewelry or lipstick. She carried only a plain handbag.

Golda wanted to be thought of as more than a woman. As she climbed the

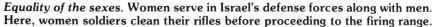

Equality of the sexes. Women serve in Israel's defense forces along with men. Here, women soldiers clean their rifles before proceeding to the firing range.

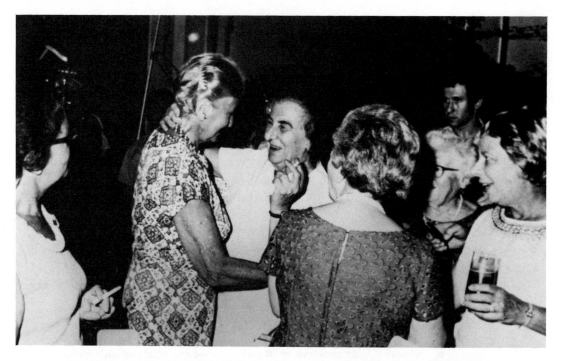

Another reunion. The prime minister relaxes with an old friend, Regina Medzini, at the fiftieth anniversary celebration (1971) of the arrival of the *Pocahontas* in Palestine. Of those who came on the ship as part of Golda's group of immigrant friends, fully half soon returned to the United States, unable to endure the hardships of pioneer life in Palestine. Regina and Golda stayed on.

political ladder, she was invariably incensed when her success was attributed to her gender. When it was reported to her that Ben-Gurion had described her as "the only man in my Cabinet," she was enraged. And in 1969, when called upon to form a new government, she felt obligated to defend herself: "The president didn't send for me because I was a woman. He sent for me because he thought I had the support of the majority of the Parliament."

Golda was an emotional woman who displayed her feelings openly and freely. Although labeled "hard" by her detractors, she was in fact very sensitive. It was not unusual to hear her charged with conducting affairs of state with her heart rather than her head, to which Golda would reply, "So what harm was there in that?" To Golda, people who hid their emotions were to be pitied. After the Yom Kippur War in 1973, Golda said with a full heart: "When peace comes, we will perhaps in time be able to forgive the Arabs for killing our sons. But it will be harder for us to forgive them for having forced us to kill their sons." The public appreciated her emotion-packed words.

That Golda could weep with her whole heart was politically beneficial. Audiences responded to her ability to express herself honestly. At that dramatic moment when the Labor Party Central Committee chose her as its candidate for prime minister in March, 1969, she wept openly. The tears were genuine, and the effect on those present was powerful. To Golda's colleagues her ability to show tears was an indication of humility and sensitivity.

Golda expressed her womanhood in yet another way: she disdained coarse humor. She was straight-laced, almost puritanical in her conception of how Israeli foreign service personnel should conduct themselves abroad. As foreign minister she insisted that male foreign service officers have no girlfriends or mistresses. What they did on home soil, however, Golda considered their own business. She let Walter Eytan, her director-general at the foreign ministry, know that she herself had participated now and then in such distractions when she said to him with a wink, "You know, I was never a nun."

Golda's attitude toward other women was not always kindly. Although conscious of the difficulty faced by women in building a career, she rarely offered a helping hand. One was not likely to hear Golda praise women in public service. She knew that she was unique in Israeli politics, and she intended to keep it that way. In her nearly ten years as foreign minister, never once did she recommend a single woman as ambassador.

Grudgingly, Golda Meir was known to admit that women did have some enviable qualities. They got to the point more quickly; they did not beat around the bush. They were more practical, more realistic.

The women Golda admired most were those who succeeded by virtue of their skill rather than their womanhood. Ironically, this woman who detested the style and ideology of the feminist movement became a worldwide feminist symbol. She had, after all, achieved great political success. To Golda, the women's liberation movement was comprised of nuts, bra-burners, and other undesirable man-haters. They were not for her.

Golda was astonished that she had become a positive symbol of the feminist movement. What appealed to the feminists about Golda was clearly not her views on men, whom she liked, or child-bearing, which she considered a privilege. It was that she had sacrificed husband and children for her career. In 1976, while visiting a college bookstore in the United States, she was startled to find a photograph of her younger self on a wall poster sponsored by a woman's liberation group. The poster showed her taking the Israeli oath of office. The legend read: "But can she type?"

Golda approached the poster for a closer look. Then, to a group of students milling around her, she commented: "You know, I never did learn to type."

Golda and the Orthodox Establishment

As Golda became an active member of the labor movement, she managed to escape the notice of observant Jews. None of her early positions were considered terribly important. But when she was appointed acting director of the Jewish Agency's political department in 1946, the Orthodox establishment began to protest. An August 28, 1946 editorial in the National Religious Party's newspaper, *Hatsofeh*, described Golda Meyerson as "intelligent, energetic, dedicated, a torchbearer," but despite all these estimable qualities, "a woman." It was difficult to believe that the same Jewish nation that had "fixed a woman's honored place inside the tent" could elevate Golda Meyerson to this post in the Jewish Agency, the editorial maintained.

In 1949, when Golda became Israel's first woman Cabinet minister, the opposition of the Orthodox Jewish Community meant little. But in 1955, when Golda, then minister of labor, had been proposed by Ben-Gurion to become the party's candidate for mayor of Tel Aviv, two religious members of the Tel Aviv City Council withheld their support (one because she was a woman). Golda did not receive the party's nomination.

In 1969 there were again rumblings of discontent within the Orthodox bloc. Eager to join Golda's government but reluctant to take Jewish law less than literally, the Orthodox politicians of the National Religious Party were in a quandary. They appealed to rabbinic authorities with a question: in the State of Israel, who was head of state, the president or the prime minister? The sages made it easy for the religious politicians to join Golda Meir's government. They ruled that the president, not the prime minister, was head of state.

Golda and the Military

Never in modern times had so elderly a woman been called upon to head a nation. This sickly 71-year-old grandmother was most decidedly without the background or the temperament to make military decisions. As a young mother she had even objected to her son, Menachem, playing with tanks and guns.

What Golda knew of military affairs she had learned from generals as they deliberated a variety of military operations in the 1950s and early 1960s. She had listened and absorbed and learned from what she heard.

Golda enjoyed conveying the impression that the complexity of military affairs was beyond her understanding. By so doing, she was free to transfer to her generals some of the heavy responsibility for carrying out a war. Once, just before assuming the prime ministership, after attending a military exercise on the West Bank, she was asked by a reporter to comment on what she had just witnessed. "Do you think that an old lady like myself would have anything to say about things like this?" she answered.

In truth, Golda was enamored of the military. The sight of a young Jewish boy in a military uniform moved her deeply. In the uniform she saw a dramatic reversal of the Jewish past; she was reminded of the time when Jews were not in a position to defend themselves.

Despite her lack of a military background, Golda did not hesitate to make tough decisions during the War of Attrition with Egypt. Egypt kept chipping away at Israel, and delicate political decisions, more difficult than the strictly operational ones, had to be arrived at. Did Israel have the courage to see this confrontation through to its bitter conclusion? Would seeking an early ceasefire be a wiser course? Would the price that would have to be paid in casualties be justified? Could arms be found in sufficient quantity?

Golda's mind was clear on all these points. The war would be prosecuted; the arms would be found; the prospect of numerous casualties would not keep the nation from defending itself. No one—not the Egyptians, not the Russians—

would prevent the Israelis from taking the war home to the enemy. "The War of Attrition," she said in September of 1969, "can be a two-way street. It isn't something we wish for. But if it has to go on, if that's the position of the Arabs and they won't stop, it has to go on. We can take more than they believe we can take. And we can fight back."

Golda did not take lightly the responsibility of war. She recalled that Prime Minister Eshkol had instructed his military attaché, Israel Lior, to awaken him the first thing in the morning to inform him of military engagements that had taken place the night before. Golda, however, insisted that Lior keep her abreast of battle results and the number of Israeli casualties incurred as he learned of them. She ordered that she be awakened at any time of the night, as often as necessary.

Indeed, Golda's sleep was often interrupted. One morning she complained to Lou Kaddar about the night she had just endured: "He called me eight times. I've been sleeping only minutes from one call to the other." Sympathetic, Lou suggested that Golda let Lior use his judgment on whether to awaken her during the night. Golda dismissed the idea. Absurd, she thought.

On occasion those middle-of-the-night telephone calls were comic. Golda once picked up the phone at 3 A.M. only to hear the message from an operator (Lior was apparently off duty): "26 sheep were killed." Golda had wanted to know about all casualties, but this seemed a bit excessive. Trying to return to sleep, the prime minister was awakened by the ring of the phone some time later. The same operator reported a slight change: "Sorry, Mrs. Meir. It was only 25."

For Golda, war brought with it few light moments. Its implications obsessed her. "You cannot liberate yourself from it," she said. "It does not leave you. You cannot get rid of it for a single second. There is always this consciousness that there is a war, that we are still not out of it, that it may begin anew."

15

Golda's Secret Cancer

Golda Meir's fifteen-year struggle with cancer is little known, and until the day of her death she was determined that it stay that way. She had been unable to conceal the fact that she was ailing, for she frequented hospitals on a regular basis. Yet, for her own private reasons Golda insisted that her affliction with cancer remain a secret which she shared only with her children and a few close associates. Although some government officials had guessed correctly about her illness, only on the day of her death, December 8, 1978, did doctors admit for the first time that she had been suffering from malignant lymphoma, cancer of the lymphatic system.

To Golda, illness was a private matter. One did not discuss such things with others; she wanted no pity. And, furthermore, she feared that if the state of her health were made public, she would be judged unfit for office.

As long as she felt she could perform, Golda had no intention of retiring from public service. In the mid-1960s a Labor Party member raised the subject of her cancer at a private meeting in Israel with American Jews. "Look," he asked rather brazenly, "why are you running after this lady? She's very sick with cancer. Her future is in the past. You should contact the younger generation." The American Jews who heard this remark were astonished. They recounted it to her shortly thereafter. She was enraged.

Incredibly, Golda's secret was kept from most members of her family and from almost all of her friends and associates. Explaining her frequent hospital visits, Golda told her good friend Regina Medzini that she had long suffered recurrent dehydration. Myrie Syrkin, another close friend, only learned the truth in the final months of Golda's life.

Beginning as far back as 1947 Golda suffered from illnesses sufficiently serious for physicians to advise her to leave public life. At one time or another, she suffered from pneumonia, kidney stones, phlebitis, an injured foot, cardiovascular complications. Frequently, she collapsed from exhaustion.

When the cancer struck, Golda's doctors saw no reason to advise that she abandon public office, so long as the cancer remained in remission. They did, however, advise that she rest whenever possible, advice which largely went unheeded. The doctors asked the family to urge Golda to take it easy. "After all," one physician explained to Clara, "this is a very serious illness. Her chances for living long are very small." All to no avail. Golda was not about to give up.

Rejuvenation

When Golda assumed the prime ministership, the highest office in Israel, she seemed to be imbued with a new vitality. Danny Bloch, the *Davar* political correspondent, on the day of Levi Eshkol's death, spotted Golda in a Jerusalem restaurant talking with Zalman Aranne. She looked gaunt, run-down, sickly. Ten days later, when it was clear that Golda would be the next prime minister, she looked as robust as a woman twenty years younger. "The matter is very simple," she said when questioned about her amazing rejuvenation, "my illness was that I wanted to be prime minister. The moment I was made prime minister all my health problems were solved."

As prime minister, Golda bore up well to the office, although she continued to receive hospital treatment on a regular basis. Those in the hospital who knew of her condition—a few doctors and nurses—were sworn to secrecy. The public was told only that she had a cold, or that she was suffering from fatigue, anything but the truth.

The duties of the prime ministership demanded of Golda great mental strength, and she was more than equipped for the job. She led a nation in wartime with all its manifold problems, without uttering a complaint. She refused to let her ailments interfere with her work.

One Independence Day Golda was suffering from one of her recurring unbearable migraine headaches. Her schedule called for her to speak that evening before a group of paratroopers in Ramat Gan, outside Tel Aviv. At Golda's Tel Aviv home, Lou Kaddar and Yonah, Sheyna's son, discussed whether or not Golda should make the scheduled appearance. Both agreed that the plans should be canceled. Yonah suggested that he inform the organizers, but Lou, knowing Golda, said that it would be best that she speak to Golda first. Told of their plans, Golda exploded: "What are you talking about?" Not only did she address the paratroopers, migraine and all, she sat through an entire musical program.

New Elections

The politicans worried about the prime minister's health, often for the most practical of reasons. Were she to leave the political scene, their own power would be in jeopardy. As the October, 1969 elections approached, Golda was prevailed upon to run once again and thereby prevent a party split, for only she could keep Moshe Dayan from becoming prime minister.

Golda was now the party's top vote-getter. Thousands of posters with a large color portrait of a well-groomed matriarchal Golda Meir appeared on walls. The legend it bore consisted of a single word: "Golda!" That said it all. And the voters related to it.

Labor suffered a minor setback in the 1969 elections: the Labor-Mapam alignment lost its majority; the number of Knesset seats it held fell from 63 to 56. Actually, the alignment commanded 60 votes, for it could count on the support of the Druze Arab Knesset members.

Golda was now prime minister in her own right. For the first time she had been elected to the post by the entire nation. All talk of retirement ceased.

Getting around the country. **Golda at a Druze ceremony in the Galilee in 1970. The Druze, part of the Arab community, live mostly in northern Israel.**

Although Golda had delighted in her victory, in time she grew increasingly weary of the job. All during 1972 and into 1973 she sounded like a leader about to step down. Privately, she told Aharon Yariv, the director of military intelligence, "I'm like a prisoner who knows his date of release." A doubting Yariv cast a cynical look at her: "The party won't let you quit." It would have no effect, she insisted. "Let the party stand on its head, individually and collectively. It won't help."

Rumors began to circulate as to who would be Golda's successor in 1973. The most widely reported of the rumors focused on Pinchas Sapir, but he had other ideas. Another, less likely prospect was Moshe Dayan.

Early in 1973 Golda came under pressure from Sapir to remain in office. Sapir attempted to extinguish small brush fires of dissent within her family as well. When Sheyna's son, Yonah, appealed to Golda not to be a candidate for re-election in October, 1973, he felt the full force of Sapir's pressure.

The Cancer Spreads

While all these maneuverings were taking place, Golda was quietly enduring one of the worst ordeals of her life. She was contemplating resignation.

Nonstop smoker. Informal photographs taken in 1973 during an interview with the Israel Defense Forces' journal *Bemachaneh.*

In April, 1973 Golda's doctors suspected that her cancer had spread again, and though Golda was in no pain, they felt a thorough examination necessary. After a day or two in the hospital the prime minister was advised that the situation was serious, that cobalt radiation treatments would be necessary. She would require massive doses, at least five, and up to ten sessions, possibly more. There would be almost certain, unpleasant side effects. The doctors wanted to begin immediately with a large dose of cobalt three times a week.

The news jolted Golda. Could she receive the treatments and continue to execute her duties as prime minister? She decided to try. The treatments were to be given in complete secrecy. If the treatments proved too debilitating, she would announce her intention to retire from public office immediately. The only people to be told of the situation, aside from her children, were Lou Kaddar and Israel Galili. Golda wanted at least one party member, Galili, to know the truth.

Lou made the complicated arrangements for treatment. Golda's appointments secretary was told by Lou that the prime minister would be visiting Hadassah Hospital in Jerusalem a few evenings a week, and under no circumstances were any meetings to be scheduled for her during those hours. The secretary was not told the purpose of the hospital visits.

Golda sometimes underwent treatment in the mornings and reported for work in the afternoon, as if nothing had taken place. Finding excuses for the prime minister to visit the hospital so frequently became less of a problem when Lou collapsed and had to be hospitalized for emergency surgery. Now Golda could pass off her hospital visits as trips to see her personal assistant.

Cooperating in the ruse, the doctors kept Lou in the hospital longer than necessary, so that Golda would be able to receive treatment without having to be so secretive.

Golda's pain was not negligible, but she managed to continue with her official duties. Unlike many patients who undergo cobalt treatment, Golda refused to be confined to bed for several days after each hospital visit. She insisted on maintaining her regular work schedule.

In early June Willy Brandt, chancellor of West Germany, paid an official visit to Israel. Golda continued the treatments during the visit and, remarkably, she made an appearance at the state dinner in Brandt's honor immediately following a cobalt session. No one in the room suspected what Golda was going through and how often she had considered resigning.

In June Golda began to feel that the treatments were having a positive effect. This buoyed her spirits and led her to conclude that she would not, after all, have to step down from office. In fact, if her condition remained unchanged, she would seek re-election in October!

The reaction of the party's rank-and-file was one of relief. Golda's decision to seek re-election was conveyed to the party's secretary-general, Aharon Yadlin, in a letter written in mid-June. To an overjoyed central committee meeting in Tel Aviv, he read aloud: "I have decided not to end my public life against the will and the consent of my colleagues who carry with me the burden of responsibility." Upon hearing the news, the audience broke into applause.

16

Golda Faces the Issues

The fear of war and its terrifying prospects for Israel led Golda Meir into the embrace of a man who was to become the first American president to resign from office. Richard M. Nixon had encountered a barrage of criticism both for his policies in Vietnam and for the mushrooming scandal called Watergate. Golda did not care; to her these were issues that had little impact on her. She chose to judge the president strictly in terms of how he performed for the Jewish state.

The First Meeting

The first meeting between Golda Meir as prime minister and Richard Nixon as president took place in the White House in September, 1969. Golda was unduly nervous. Golda's shopping list of needed arms was long; she was concerned that Nixon might think the requests excessive. She felt that the relationship that would be established between Israel and the United States would depend on her personal relationship with the president.

Golda began the conversation by reminding Nixon of a statement made by him when visiting Israel in 1966. If he were an Israeli, Nixon had said, he would not want to give up the Golan Heights. The president did not deny the statement. "I repeat, Madame Prime Minister," he said, choosing his words carefully, "if I were an Israeli, I would find it truly difficult to give up the Golan Heights." In the conversation that followed Nixon made it clear that the United States planned to insure Israel's capacity to fight its present battles, and that the prime minister need not worry about the length of her shopping list. Israel would also receive low-interest loans of $200 million for up to five years.

The American president was captivated by Golda Meir. In his memoirs, Nixon wrote that she conveyed "simultaneously the qualities of extreme toughness and warmth." To his daughter Julie the president noted that Golda "used her emotions. They didn't use her."

Nixon revealed that the ice was broken at the state dinner held in Golda's honor. The president tried to set her mind at ease about American-Soviet détente: the United States, he assured her, had no illusions about Soviet motives. "Our Golden Rule as far as international diplomacy is concerned is, 'Do unto others as they do unto you.'" Listening in, Henry Kissinger interjected diabolically, "Plus ten per cent." Smiling, Golda remarked: "As long as you approach things that way, we have no fears."

Crucial meeting. Golda leaves for her first meeting as prime minister with President Richard Nixon of the United States. She carried a "shopping bag" full of arms requests, but just as important, she wanted to make sure that the United States commitment to Israel's security was intact. Here, Golda bids farewell to three Cabinet colleagues before leaving for the United States on September 24, 1969. Left to right: Menachem Begin, Pinchas Sapir, and Israel Galili.

Farewell. The prime minister, her military attaché, Israel Lior, at her left, and Deputy Prime Minister Yigal Allon stand for the national anthem at airport farewell ceremonies on September 24, 1969.

At the White House. President Nixon greets Golda on the White House lawn on September 25, 1969. Secretary of State William Rogers, whose name would become synonymous with the Rogers Plan, stands beside Mrs. Nixon. Israelis winced at the Rogers Plan when it was announced in December 1969, for it declared that Israel should give up most of the territories it had occupied during the 1967 Six Day War.

But not long after this meeting Golda discovered that she did have cause to worry. In early 1970 the Soviets began sending military advisers to Egypt. Still, the United States hesitated to provide Israel with sophisticated weaponry, reasoning that withholding aid might induce the Israelis to become more flexible on the question of peace with the Arabs. Nixon wanted to be the peacemaker.

Golda knew that such logic was spurious. All that it would accomplish, she argued, would be to weaken Israel. When advised that the Americans planned to delay the latest Israeli request for sophisticated arms, she turned to Nixon in a letter dated March 12, 1970: "It is true that our pilots are very good, but they can be good only when they have planes. Lately some rumors have reached me that your decision may be negative or at best postponed. I absolutely refused to believe it. If, God forbid, this were true, then we would feel really forsaken."

The rumors were true. On March 23 Secretary of State William Rogers announced that the United States had decided to deny Israel's request for twenty-five more Phantoms and 100 Skyhawks. To soften the blow, he added that the

The president and the prime minister. Nixon meets with Golda on September 25, 1969. Golda made a favorable impression on the American president, and he responded by informing her early on that Israel would receive all it had asked of the United States.

United States would provide Israel with $100 million in economic credit. It took Golda Meir's personal intervention during a number of visits to the United States to convince the president to alter U.S. policy, to help Israel close the arms gap that was now favoring the Arabs.

Nothing was more important to Golda than preserving the continued flow of American arms to Israel—not even Watergate. When the scandal first came to light, she pretended to be unaware of it. Actually, however, the prime minister found it difficult to fault the president personally. Political dirty tricks had never distressed her; she had been in politics too long for that. Where she considered Nixon's behavior indefensible was in his lying to the American people.

As Watergate was unraveling, the drama of the Yom Kippur War took place, and from that point on Golda judged Richard Nixon only on his attitude toward

State dinner. President and Mrs. Nixon and Prime Minister Meir on the way to the state dinner given in Mrs. Meir's honor on September 25, 1969.

Meeting journalists. Golda Meir and President Nixon at their White House press conference on September 26, 1969.

With the ambassador. Sabbath dinner at Ambassador Yitzhak Rabin's Washington residence, on September 26, 1969. United States Senator Edward Kennedy is seated to Golda's left. Rabin is to her right. United States Senator Abraham Ribicoff is second from the right.

Honoring Golda. Ronald Reagan, then governor of California, speaks at a dinner in the prime minister's honor in Los Angeles on October 1, 1969.

Greeting at JFK. New York City Mayor John V. Lindsay (left) and New York City Commissioner of Cultural Affairs Dore Schary (lower right) greet Golda upon her arrival at John F. Kennedy International Airport on September 29, 1969. Standing directly behind Mayor Lindsay is his wife, Mary.

Israel. To Golda, Nixon was a savior on a white horse. She found tiresome the debate over whether the president deserved her high praise in view of the Watergate scandal. To Clara she said flatly: "Look, Clara, you're an American. You don't like Nixon. I'm an Israeli. I'll never forget that if it hadn't been for Nixon, we would have been destroyed."

A nostalgic step backward. Prime Minister Meir meets pupils at her alma mater, the Fourth Street Elementary School, in Milwaukee, on October 3, 1969. The school was renamed the Golda Meir School for Gifted and Talented Children.

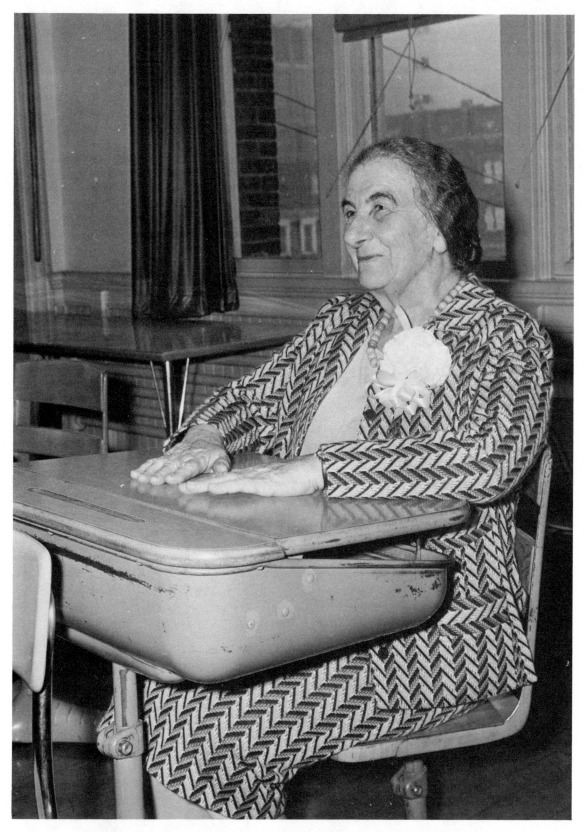

Reading writing, and 'rithmetic. Golda at her old school desk in Milwaukee on October 3, 1969. (80)

Recalling the past. Seated aboard a special El Al jet on a flight from Milwaukee to New York, Golda recounts to Yitzhak Rabin some of her experiences as a young girl growing up in Milwaukee. Rabin at the time of this flight, October 3, 1969, was Israel's ambassador to Washington. Golda was prime minister.

Old friends. The prime minister appears with Zalman Aranne in November, 1969. Aranne was one of Golda's closest political allies during her rise to power in the 1960s.

Golda and the Palestinian Issue

In 1969 the Palestinians were becoming a political force. The Arabs made their plight the central issue in the Arab-Israeli dispute. The Israelis countered that the issue was secondary. Golda Meir tried to wish them out of existence.

Nonetheless Palestinian Arab nationalism had taken root. Its chief spokesman was Yasser Arafat. Through his Palestine Liberation Organization he hoped to create an Arab state on the West Bank and the Gaza Strip.

When Golda assumed power in 1969, it still seemed to make sense to attempt to curb the growing nationalist feeling of Palestinian Arabs. She feared that the establishment of a PLO-dominated Palestinian state would become dependent on outside intruders and most probably would fall prey to Soviet designs.

After much thought, Golda settled on a very simple tactic: she would declare that there was no such thing as a Palestinian Arab. The dragon would be slain by

Golda at the U.N. Secretary-General U Thant of the United Nations meets Prime Minister Golda Meir at the United Nations on September 29, 1969. This was Golda's first visit to the United States as prime minister. She came for crucial talks with U.S. President Richard Nixon.

Sheyna's memoirs. Golda reads from Sheyna's memoirs at the celebration of Sheyna's eightieth birthday. Golda had encouraged her sister to write her memoirs not only for posterity but in order to use her later years productively.

Happy reunion. Sheyna's eightieth birthday (1969) is celebrated at the prime minister's home. Left to right: Bella, Sheyna's daughter-in-law; Sarah, Sheyna's daughter-in-law; Sarah Rehabi; Sheyna's son Chaim; Sheyna; Sheyna's other son, Yona; Golda; Menachem Meir; Aya Meir; Zechariah Rehabi.

the power of her words. In time, she hoped, the view that Palestinians did not exist would be accepted by the world; the Palestinian "issue" would eventually die a natural death.

On June 15, 1969, in an interview with the *Sunday Times* of London, the prime minister expressed her attitude publicly: "There was no such thing as Palestinians. When was there an independent Palestinian people with a Palestinian state? It was either southern Syria before the first World War, and then it was a Palestine including Jordan. It was not as though there was a Palestinian people and we came and threw them out and took their country away from them. They did not exist."

Some argued that Golda's tactic of denying a Palestinian existence helped her to resolve a personal dilemma. If they existed, any good liberal Socialist, Golda included, would have difficulty justifying those Israeli actions that kept Palestinians from attaining their "rights." By arguing that there were no Palestinians, there was no need to feel guilty about Israeli policy because no "Palestinian" was being deprived of his "rights."

Golda's policy backfired. Rather than crush the movement, it stirred in them a new Palestinian pride. By attempting to ignore their existence, she had inadvertently challenged them into accepting themselves as Palestinians.

As the Palestinian national movement gathered momentum, Golda tried to retract some of her earlier public pronouncements. Although the record belied the words, she tried to deny that she really meant that there was no Palestinian nation. She declared: "I am a Palestinian. From 1921 to 1948 I held a Palestinian passport. And I was aware that there were Arabs and Jews in Palestine and that all were Palestinians."

She accused the Palestinians of sleeping through the period between 1948 and 1967, when Jordan ruled the West Bank: "Why did the West Bank Palestinians accept this annexation [by Jordan]—willingly or unwillingly, but in any event without an uprising of explosives and mines? Why did they awaken as a Palestinian entity only after the Six Day War?" Her personal solution was for the Palestinians to band together with their brethren in Jordan in some amalgam under Jordanian sovereignty, and Jordan's King Hussein could, if he wished, change the name of his state to Palestine.

Despite her strong stand on the Palestinian issue, some moderate Palestinian Arabs wanted to talk to Golda Meir. Aziz Shehadeh, a prominent attorney from Ramallah, a West Bank town, was one such individual. Shmuel Toledano, Golda's adviser on Arab affairs, sought to coax the prime minister into meeting with Shehadeh and other Palestinians. He appealed to her on humanitarian grounds. The Palestinian refugee problem could not be overlooked by Israel, he insisted. Golda turned on him angrily: "Look, the way I feel, if I'm walking on the roadside and see someone hurt in a car accident, I'm sorry, but I don't feel guilty. So I don't feel responsible for solving the refugee problem."

The Palestinians understood Golda's message. They became more committed to the struggle. Even moderate Palestinians found her dismissal of them distasteful. Elias Freij, the mayor of Bethlehem, another West Bank town, maintained that "her denial of our national status had in fact given us the incentive to fight for our rights." Mahmud Abu-Zuluf, editor of *El Kuds,* the most important newspaper on the West Bank and in Gaza, published an editorial soon after Golda Meir's comments to the *Sunday Times,* in which he charged: "This woman from Russia and America had a Palestinian passport, but she cannot change history. Statements like hers do not bring peace or understanding between Arabs and Israelis."

If Golda's language was bellicose, it was also clear. Palestinians begrudgingly respected Golda for her outspokenness. She was open, frank. They knew where they stood with her.

So did the prime minister's own Labor Party colleagues. Golda demanded that her doctrine on the Palestinians become party and national dogma. Reading *Time* magazine on January 26, 1970, she came across an article about the new secretary-general of the Labor Party, Aryeh Eliav. It discussed at length his well-known pro-Palestinian views. Israel and the Palestinians, he maintained, like Holland and Belgium, could exist side by side. "The first thing we have to do," Eliav told *Time,* "is to recognize that the Palestinian Arabs exist as an infant nation."

Golda was not amused. Shortly after the article appeared, Eliav was called into her kitchen, *Time* magazine in front of her, the article filled with the customary red pencil marks. "Did they quote you right?" she asked belligerently. "Yes," Eliav replied, but he insisted there was nothing new in his remarks; in fact, they had been drawn from an old pamphlet of his, a copy of which had been sent to Golda.

She was not assuaged. "There's no Palestinian issue," she asserted. "Why are you putting it as the focus of everything?" Eliav answered: "Because it is. We have to tackle it."

Not Golda. Contending that the views of the new secretary-general clashed with those of the party, she vowed to take the matter to the party's central committee. "I will say to them," she told Eliav, "you have an old and foolish woman as prime minister, and you have just elected a young and wise secretary-general who happens to disagree with me on a central issue. You will have to choose between us."

Seeking peace. **Prime Minister Meir with Special Mediator Gunnar Jarring to her left and Foreign Minister Abba Eban. They appear in the garden of Golda's Jerusalem residence on January 8, 1971. Jarring had come to the Middle East to try to bring the parties to the Arab-Israeli dispute to a peace agreement, but he ultimately failed. His failure left the region in a diplomatic deadlock, a situation that led to the Yom Kippur War of 1973.**

Eliav explained to Golda that it was not his intention to make political hay out of his position as secretary-general. Rather than take the matter to the central committee, he proposed that they agree to disagree. Golda accepted the suggestion.

In time the prime minister softened her views on the Palestinians, but only ever so slightly. The first inkling of such a shift came in October 1973. Israel Galili, the master wordsmith of the Labor Party, drafted a new resolution for the party platform, and Golda reluctantly approved it. The party was now on record as recognizing "the independent identity of the Palestinian Arabs." But although Golda felt compelled to accept the resolution, no one believed that she had really had a change of heart. For her, the Palestinians still did not exist.

Golda Meets the Pope

Golda had always believed that a meeting with the Pope might bring about improved relations between Israel and the Vatican. Instead, the meeting resulted in a crisis.

Scheduling a meeting between Golda and Pope Paul VI was first discussed in 1969, after Foreign Minister Abba Eban had met with him. But not until January 15, 1973 did that meeting take place. Truly a historic occasion, it would mark the seventh time in the twentieth century that the Pontiff would meet with a member of the Zionist movement. It would be the first time, however, that an audience would be given to an Israeli prime minister.

Relations between the Vatican and Israel had never been warm. Traditionally, the Catholic Church did not look favorably upon Israel's hold over Jerusalem, with its many Catholic holy sites. Partly for this reason the Vatican had persistently refused to recognize the Jewish state. It believed that the holy places in Jerusalem ought to be internationalized.

Immediately before the historic encounter there was considerable tension among those in Golda's party. When it was discovered that the prime minister would need a hat, a frantic last-minute effort was made to rush her one suitable black hat by plane from Israel. As Golda was about to enter the quarters where she would face the Pope, she turned to Lou Kaddar and Simcha Dinitz. "What's going on here?" she asked. "Me, the daughter of Moshe Mabovitch the carpenter, going to meet the Pope of the Catholics?" To which one of her aides quickly replied, "Just a minute, Golda, carpentry is a very respected profession around here."

The conversation between Golda and the Pope opened on a decidedly unfortunate note. The Pope, speaking in Italian, with the aid of an interpreter, made it clear to the prime minister that he found it hard to fathom how the Jewish people, "which should be so merciful," behaves so harshly in its own country.

Golda, speaking in English, had a quick rejoinder: "Your Holiness, do you know what my own very earliest memory is? It is waiting for a pogrom in Kiev. Let me assure you that my people know all about real harshness, and also that we learned all about real mercy when we were being led to the gas chambers of the Nazis."

The bluntness of the Pope's opening comments took the prime minister by surprise, but she would not be cowed. "His eyes bored deep into me," she later told the newspaper Ma'ariv, "and I looked back with an open, straight, strong gaze."

The conversation progressed to other subjects. The Pope praised Israel for its care of the holy places in Jerusalem. He requested permission to open a new college in the Holy City, and then deferentially he noted that unlike his predecessors he had not issued an encyclical proclaiming the need to internationalize Jerusalem's holy places.

After sixty-five minutes, Golda exited from the meeting. She shrugged off the Pope's opening remarks as mere lip service to the Arabs. Later, she told Emile Najar, Israel's ambassador to Italy, who had arranged the audience, that she had found the Pope to be "a political man, very sensitive, very intelligent."

All seemed to have gone remarkably well. The Vatican had released an official communiqué drawn up in advance by Najar and Vatican officials. According to the rather bland, innocuous document, Golda and the Pope recalled "the history and sufferings of the Jewish people." The communiqué went on to explain the Vatican position on Jerusalem's holy places, the question of Palestinian refugees, and Middle East peace efforts. To the press, Golda described her audience as "an historic event of great value." She added optimistically: "In the quest for peace and good will all over the world, there is an identity of views between the Pope and the Jews."

Najar and the Pope. Emile Najar, Israel's ambassador to Italy, shakes hands with the Pope.

Momentous audience. Golda meets Pope Paul VI at the Vatican on January 15, 1973. At first she had been elated at the audience, but following the release of a dismaying Vatican communiqué which had a pro-Arab tone, the prime minister grew disheartened with the Pope.

Then the bombshell struck. Vatican spokesman Professor Federico Alessandrini, gave the press a "verbal note," the tone of which was markedly different from the official Vatican communiqué. The statement observed that the Pope's meeting with Golda was "not a gesture of preference or exclusive treatment. The Pope accepted the request of Mrs. Meir because he considers it his duty not to let slip any opportunity to act in favor of peace, in defense of all religious interest, particularly the weakest and most defenseless, and most of all the Palestinian refugees."

Which was the real Vatican view? The official communiqué or Alessandrini's "verbal note"?

When Najar learned of Alessandrini's statement, he was distraught. It was a stab in the back. An official protest, he felt, would be necessary.

Golda cautioned Najar against this. "Don't exaggerate it," she instructed him with a wave of the hand. "Don't give too much importance to the whole thing."

Meeting some newsmen a while later, the prime minister refused to display disappointment. "Was it a slap in the face?" she was asked. "I am not sensitive enough," she replied aggressively. "I did not break into the Vatican. I came because the meeting was arranged. If someone feels they have to explain something to someone, it's their affair. I have no reason to like it or dislike it."

After Golda left Italy, by the time she reached her next stop, Geneva, she knew it would be necessary to react more definitively to the second statement that emerged from the Vatican. By this time, cables from Israel had arrived. Orthodox circles were outraged over the Alessandrini statement.

Thinking in political terms, as always, Golda sensed that the fury of the Orthodox Jews could have grave implications that she would have to consider carefully. She could not afford to incur the wrath of the National Religious Party, an important element in her government coalition. If piqued enough, the NRP could stage a walkout, resulting in the collapse of her government.

What the Orthodox resented was that the Pope had slighted their leader. Although Golda was not terribly offended, she understood why oversensitive Orthodox Jews might be. Therefore, in her public report on the audience with the Pope, she decided to downplay the elation she truly felt. Instead she would present what she felt needed to be said. She chose the Israeli press as her vehicle.

In an interview with *Ma'ariv*'s Dov Goldstein she said: "I didn't like the opening of the conversation at all. I can't stand it when we are talked to like that. I've had previous experiences of this sort, and when someone opens a conversation in that way, I won't give in. Oh no." The meaning of Golda's words was clear: the audience had not gone well but the prime minister had at least done her duty by standing up to the insulting Pope. The religious community in Israel was satisfied. The fury subsided.

Next came some behind-the-scenes maneuvering designed to repair the damage done to Vatican-Israeli relations by the second communiqué. To a Vatican official with whom he had labored over the first communiqué, Najar now lamented, "Much china has been broken. You and I must try to repair it. We must find an opportunity."

Najar suggested that the forthcoming visit to Israel by the Italian foreign minister might be used to mend some fences. Najar, scheduled to return home for the occasion, said, "I must have something in hand for Mrs. Meir. I must have some gesture from the Pope to show that no lasting harm had been done."

"Maybe," said the Vatican official, "we could bring pictures of the meeting, signed by the Pope." "Yes," responded the Israeli ambassador, adding quickly, "and a letter from him as well. That would do it."

The two officials pledged themselves to secrecy. They had no desire to expose the rift between the Vatican and Jerusalem. In March, the photographs and the Pope's letter—brief, no more than ten lines—were hand-delivered to Golda by Najar. The letter was cordial. It spoke warmly of their meeting in January. It did not refer to the unfortunate events that had transpired in its aftermath.

Golda smiled at Najar, acknowledging with her glance that the affair now seemed to have closed on a happy note.

Najar drafted a note to the Pope in Golda's name. He would deliver it to the Pontiff upon his return to Italy. Golda's reply was warm. The nasty exchanges had come to an end.

Neither of the letters was ever made public. Their existence has remained a secret until now.

Golda and Peace

Despite their defeats in the Six Day War of 1967, the Arabs showed no desire for peace with the Israelis. This became clear at the Arab summit conference held in August, 1967, in Khartoum, where it was agreed not to recognize Israel, not to negotiate with Israel, not to make peace with Israel.

Golda was disheartened. "Our Arab neighbors speak about a hundred years' war," she observed. "It won't be a hundred years, but how long it will be I honestly don't know."

Golda did know that she was doing all she could to bring about peace. And of all the assaults on Golda, the one that wounded her most was the charge that as prime minister she had not done enough for the cause of peace. She blamed the Arabs entirely. She said it a thousand times in many different ways: the moment the Arabs express a readiness to talk peace, Israel will be there, pen in hand.

In public, Golda often took an intractable line toward the Arabs, but she never ceased believing that the Arab *public* position might not be the *real* one, that a more moderate attitude existed. And she traveled thousands of miles to try to meet such Arabs, to find the answer.

All these efforts were carried out secretly, and such secrecy often had its lighter moments. One incident occurred in 1965 while Golda, then foreign minister, and Lou Kaddar were airborne [destination classified as of this writing]. Golda and Lou were seated behind the cockpit. A curtain separated them from the other passengers. Two hours into the flight Golda signaled Lou that she wanted to use the bathroom. Lou in turn called the stewardess. A few moments later the captain's voice came over the intercom, asking everyone to take their seats due to turbulent weather. Lou then notified Golda that she could go to the bathroom. Three times this sequence of events was repeated.

Golda and Lou arrived and remained at their destination undiscovered for a few days. As they were about to board their return flight to Israel, Lou suggested that they use the ladies' room now so that the other passengers would not be disturbed. "What do you mean?" Golda asked in all innocence. Only then did Lou realize that Golda had never connected the captain's fictitious announcements with her personal needs!

Another Washington visit. Simcha Dinitz, Golda's aide (between Golda and President Richard Nixon), and Ambassador Rabin follow the prime minister and the president after a White House meeting on March 1, 1973. Golda's meeting with Nixon was stormier than usual, coming as it did in the wake of the Libyan plane disaster. A Libyan civilian jet had in the last few days strayed over Israeli airspace. The Israeli Air Force, suspecting hostile intentions, shot it down, killing 108 passengers. Golda was forced to explain to Nixon why the Israelis had taken such action.

Nahum Goldmann, Nasser, and Golda

As prime minister, Golda had wanted, above all, to achieve a breakthrough with Egypt, the strongest and the most important of the Arab states. The most controversial of her attempts involved Nahum Goldmann, a man who at times had annoyed the Israelis but who had accomplished so much on behalf of world Jewry that he could not be ignored. As president of the World Jewish Congress, Goldmann had always been a thorn in Golda's side, eagerly giving unsolicited advice on almost any subject.

The Goldmann Affair, as the Israelis later called it, began in April, 1970, when the journalist Eric Rouleau of *Le Monde* called Goldmann at his Paris residence to inform him that an Egyptian officer, Colonel Ahmad Hamrouche, wished to meet him to present an important message.

Hamrouche, a leftist and a close friend of Nasser's, had participated in the ouster of King Farouk. When they met, Hamrouche told Goldmann, "Nasser wants you to come. You should, however, inform Golda Meir, not ask her permission, only inform her. It is true that Nasser has invited you as an individual [not a representative of Israel], but there will be a reception for you, and Nasser doesn't want Golda Meir to say it was all done behind her back."

According to Hamrouche, Nasser had three conditions for the meeting: 1. It must be held with Golda's knowledge (but not her approval). 2. Secrecy must be maintained, though Nasser would reserve the right to make his version of the meeting public. 3. Goldmann must come with concrete proposals.

A week later Goldmann rushed to the prime minister with the astonishing news. The president of Egypt appeared receptive to the idea of meeting someone who could represent Israel's position, if not Israel itself. Might this not be a significant breakthrough?

"I don't believe it," a skeptical Golda Meir shot back.

"If you don't believe it," Goldmann retorted, "give me your permission. You have no risk. If it's not true, I won't go." Goldmann himself harbored doubts about the Hamrouche message.

Golda told Goldmann that the matter would have to be put before the Israeli Cabinet. She had ignored this procedure for other peace feelers, but in this instance she felt it unwise to act on her own. Goldmann, after all, was not the best man to represent Israel's interests in such an encounter, although he was in a unique position. He held an Israeli passport and had a Jerusalem residence, but because he spent so little time in Israel he was considered an outsider.

By bringing the matter before the Cabinet Golda expected that she could easily abort the Goldmann mission. Goldmann, realizing the unfriendly reception his plan would likely receive from the full Cabinet, suggested that she bring the matter before her Kitchen Cabinet. When Golda returned with Israel's verdict on the proposed mission to Nasser, Goldmann discovered that the entire Cabinet had been called in and that it had not approved the idea.

Golda requested that Goldmann, "as a patriot," inform Nasser that he *personally* had rejected the invitation, and not indicate that the Cabinet had withheld its approval.

An incensed Goldmann refused. "If you ask me not to go," he said bitterly, "you must take the responsibility. I will inform Nasser and ask him to tell Hamrouche in Paris that the government here has asked me not to go."

And that is precisely what happened. The reaction in Israel was angry. Several political parties unsuccessfully introduced motions of no-confidence in the Knesset, and left-wing demonstrators carried placards in the streets, one of which read, "GOLDMANN TO CAIRO, GOLDA TO THE KITCHEN."

Not long thereafter, Aryeh Eliav, secretary-general of the Labor Party, received word that Nasser was willing to see him. Like Goldmann, Eliav held dovish views, which was certainly a major factor in Nasser's selection. Informing Golda Meir of the Nasser peace feeler, Eliav, only too aware of Goldmann's recent experience, wanted to be assured that he would travel to Cairo with the Israeli government's approval. Otherwise, he feared, his mission might be meaningless.

Golda was far more excited about Eliav's mission than she had been about Goldmann's. So as not to lose time by bringing the matter before the Cabinet, Golda granted him her personal approval. This, she told him, was sufficient. Unlike Goldmann, Eliav, to Golda, was a bona fide Israeli.

Eliav went to London and waited for word that he could come to Cairo. But while waiting, Nasser died and Eliav returned home.

From Nasser to Sadat

With Nasser dead, hope grew in Israel that his successor, Anwar Sadat, would be more responsive to peace talks. Golda doubted that the Egyptians would negotiate as long as thousands of Soviet advisers were on Egyptian soil. Nevertheless, she explored all possibilities.

Promising signs appeared to suggest that Egypt was modifying its attitudes. In early 1972 Rumania's deputy foreign minister visited Israel to inform the prime minister that the Rumanian president, Nicolai Ceausescu, had recently been in Egypt and while there had received a "most important message" from Sadat for Golda.

Golda was asked to visit Rumania. She could either travel to Bucharest in disguise or by official invitation. She selected the latter, thinking it undignified for an Israeli prime minister to travel incognito unless no other alternative existed. Ceausescu related that Sadat was now prepared to meet with an Israeli, perhaps even Golda Meir. In anticipation, Golda returned to Israel to await further developments. Nothing happened.

King Hussein and Peace

The only Arab leader who seemed genuinely interested in making contact with the Israelis was King Hussein of Jordan. And so Golda turned to him. Hussein had met secretly with the late Prime Minister Levi Eshkol. Now the king would have to decide whether to hold such meetings with Eshkol's successor. Ironically, Golda Meir and the rulers of Jordan had engaged in secret negotiations in the past. But the present king—Abdullah's grandson—had more pressing reasons for contact with Israel than reminiscing with Golda about her encounters with his grandfather.

Visit to the Jewish community. **At Sabbath Eve prayers in the Chorale Synagogue in Bucharest on May 5, 1972. Although not a habitual synagogue-goer, whenever on a journey Golda made it a point to frequent the local house of worship.**

In search of peace. **The prime minister with Rumanian President Nicolai Ceausescu during her official visit to Rumania in May, 1972. Golda was invited to Bucharest to talk with Ceausescu about a possible peace feeler extended to Golda by Egyptian President Anwar Sadat. Nothing resulted from the discussion, however.**

Reminder of Israel. **The prime minister is deeply moved as a teen-age choir sings "Jerusalem of Gold" at the Bucharest synagogue in May, 1972.**

Negotiating with the Israelis made sense to Hussein from several points of view. First, a peace agreement with the Jewish state could provide him with the insurance that he required to protect against an attack from Syria, his neighbor to the north and a constant rival. Second, it could help him reclaim territory Jordan lost to the Israelis in the Six Day War: the West Bank and East Jerusalem.

The talks had to be held secretly. In an interview with the New York *Times* magazine well after the talks had begun, Golda was asked to comment on Hussein's statement that secret contacts with Israel were beside the point because their positions were so far apart. "I agree. If our positions were identical, we could conclude a peace treaty by telephone. Not that we carry on telephone conversations."

The questioner then bluntly asked Golda whether she had met secretly with Hussein. Golda responded, somewhat irrelevantly, that she had met with his grandfather. The interviewer repeated the question. This time Golda craftily dodged the issue by spelling out Israel's position on the West Bank.

Golda Meets with Hussein

The first meeting between Golda Meir and King Hussein took place in Paris in the fall of 1970. Hussein had sent word that he was prepared to meet the prime minister while in Paris on an official visit. Golda contacted the Israeli ambassador, Walter Eytan, who then chose the most secretive locale he could think of: the apartment of a distant cousin, a woman who lived on the Rue Raynouard in Paris' Passy section. Eytan asked his cousin if she would make available her apartment for "a conference" lasting about four hours. The cousin agreed, and Golda went to the rendezvous undisguised.

That meeting in Paris was the first of ten secret meetings Golda Meir held with Jordan's monarch throughout her term as prime minister. On other occasions they met in London, twice they held their rendezvous in Tel Aviv, but most often they met near the Israel-Jordan border around the Israeli town of Eilat. The meetings were scheduled at times when the absences of the two leaders would be the least noticeable. The Israelis ruled out Sundays, for that was the day that the Cabinet held its weekly session.

At the outset of these meetings, Hussein tried to express to Golda his regrets about the past. "I've made a historic mistake," he told her softly in English. He was referring to Jordan's decision to attack Israel in the Six Day War, which resulted in Israel's capture of East Jerusalem and the entire West Bank, pushing the Jordanian Army eastward across the Jordan River. Golda sensed from the king's startling admission that bargaining with him might be possible. At least, the future seemed hopeful.

The two leaders respected each other. Hussein held Golda in esteem in view of her past sessions with his grandfather. He sensed that she was being honest with him. For her part, she considered Hussein wise and patriotic—a gentleman. He addressed her as "Your Excellency" or, more simply, "Mrs. Meir." Golda always called him "Your Majesty."

At times Golda met with Hussein alone, and at times in the company of other

Dado. The prime minister and Chief of Staff David "Dado" Elazar at Nahal Na'aran in the Jordan Valley on November 28, 1972. For the first time in a number of years, Israel's borders were quiet. Terrorism in the Jordan Valley had come to a halt. The nation began to look forward to an uninterrupted period of peace, but that would be abruptly broken in the coming year.

Portraits. Photographs taken during the prime minister's interview with the Israel Defense Forces' journal *Bemachaneh,* in honor of the State of Israel's twenty-fifth anniversary.

senior Israeli officials such as Moshe Dayan. Dayan, Eban, and Allon also met with the king separately. The king clearly wanted to cultivate these relationships, and he was generous with his gifts as well as his time. He gave Allon, of all things, an Uzi machine gun, and to Eban he gave a fountain pen which the foreign minister was to use when they would sign a peace treaty. But Hussein and Golda never felt comfortable enough with each other to exchange gifts.

A consensus in the Israeli government and, no less important, in the Labor Party, agreed that the Allon Plan (named after Yigal Allon) should be presented as a tentative proposal to Hussein at these secret encounters. This plan called for the return to Jordan of populous Arab communities on the West Bank, with Israel being assured of its security by a series of armed settlements along the Jordan River Valley, on land that Israel would continue to control. While the secret talks took place, eleven such settlements were already established, five of them military outposts.

Golda was confident that if the king could accept this idea, the seeds of a solution to the Palestinian problem might be planted. But, predictably, Hussein would not entertain anything short of the complete return of the land he had lost in the Six Day War, and this meant all the West Bank and East Jerusalem. Under the Allon Plan, Hussein would get back only part of his land, and not surprisingly, he rejected the proposal.

"The talks," said one Israeli official who participated in almost all of them, "never broke down. They just didn't produce any breakthrough. When the chips were down, Hussein demanded a return to the 1967 lines. He didn't want any changes in the borders. He rejected the Allon Plan. Sometimes he said he wouldn't accept our ideas, sometimes he said he *couldn't*."

For all their apparent futility, the conversations with Hussein lifted Golda's spirits. Here she was, talking to an Arab leader. She had always asked the Arabs to come to the bargaining table, and now one had done just that. Nonethless, the unbridgeable gap in their positions was a source of immense frustration to her. But the fact that Hussein wanted the talks to continue for so long was encouraging. "She felt," said another Israeli participant, "she was accomplishing something, something important, and dangerous."

The conversations with Hussein, the last of which was held on May 27, 1974, less than a month before the prime minister left office, were a factor in Golda Meir's increasingly hawkish attitude toward the West Bank—and toward the rest of the occupied territories. She now understood that the Arabs were saying in public what they really believed in private. They wanted Israel to return everything—all the territories, including Jerusalem. That was the price of peace. But that Golda was not prepared to do. And so, she took an even tougher line on the territories.

One intriguing development was Hussein's decision to refrain from directly attacking Israel in the Yom Kippur War of 1973. Admittedly, the fact that Israeli forces were lined up along the Jordan River must have been a convincing argument against entering the fighting against the Jewish state. But now, with these secret meetings a fact of life in the Israeli-Jordanian relationship, Hussein had much more incentive to stay out of the conflict. Hussein's conversations with Golda Meir led him to believe that one day it might be possible to reach a peace agreement with Israel, however far apart the parties were at the present time.

17

The Yom Kippur War

When war broke out on that tranquil Saturday afternoon in October, 1973, there was shock and pain. It was the Day of Atonement—Yom Kippur—the holiest day in the Jewish calendar.

On this day war was far from the minds of the Israelis. In May of 1973 the nation's twenty-fifth anniversary had been celebrated with a mammoth military parade through the streets of Jerusalem. Planes, tanks, and troops were on display that day, and the feeling among the general populace was that no Arab nation would dare attack so powerful a nation.

But 1973 also brought with it diplomatic stalemate and a steady ascendancy of the hawks in Israel's government. Israel was preparing for an election that fall, and it was expected that the Labor Party would have no trouble retaining power. In Arab minds the occupied territories, if not the root cause of the Arab-Israeli conflict, were now at the heart of the struggle. To the Israelis, however, these areas had come to be regarded as less and less expendable.

The Nation's security was linked to the vastness of the Golan; and Sinai made Israel safe from attack. Yitzhak Rabin, returning as Israel's ambassador to the United States in March of 1973, asserted that Golda Meir "has better boundaries than King David or King Solomon." From the rugged peak of Massada, overlooking the Dead Sea, Defense Minister Moshe Dayan, in April, 1973, recited his personal vision of "a new State of Israel with broad frontiers, strong and solid, with the authority of the Israel Government extending from the Jordan to the Suez Canal."

Like Dayan, Golda Meir believed in the supremacy of the Israel Defense Forces (IDF). She, too, was convinced of the necessity of keeping the occupied lands as a strategic buffer. Despite both American and Arab pressure to compromise, Israel would not consider relinquishing the new territories.

Arab Armies on the Move

The Arabs viewed matters quite differently. In late September of 1973 the Syrian and Egyptian armies were on the move, strengthening their front-line units and generally fraying the nerves of Israeli intelligence. Was war around the corner? The general Israeli appraisal was negative.

But after September 13, when the Israel Air Force downed thirteen Syrian

Hubris. As part of the celebration of Israel's twenty-fifth anniversary on May 7, 1973, improved Israeli Centurion tanks roll alongside the Old City walls of Jerusalem. The huge military parade through the Holy City was later regarded by many as a symbol of the excessive self-confidence Israel had felt in the early 1970s, a factor which had lulled the country into believing that the Arabs would never dare attack.

MIGS, a warlike atmosphere began to be felt. Syria was beginning to dig in at the front lines. Moshe Dayan, eager to issue a warning to the Syrians, toured the Golan Heights on September 26. He announced that 800 Syrian tanks and guns faced Israel across the northern frontier and the IDF was prepared for an Arab attack. The warning was designed to discourage the Syrians from opening fire, but in fact the Israelis were far from prepared. And even as Dayan was touring the Golan, word reached Israeli intelligence in Tel Aviv that Egypt was preparing for war.

The escalation of tensions did not keep Golda Meir from leaving for Strasbourg, France, to address the Council of Europe. Two days before her journey, on September 28, three armed Arab terrorists boarded a train carrying

Soviet Jewish immigrants to Vienna, from where they were to fly to Israel. Upon entering Austrian territory, the terrorists took five Jews and a customs man hostage. Although they demanded free passage to an Arab capital, Austria's chancellor, Bruno Kreisky, responded much more generously than anticipated. Rather than merely satisfy the terrorists' demand for free passage, he went even further and announced the closing of the Schonau Castle near Vienna, the way station where Soviet Jews rested and received briefings by Israeli officials before the final leg of their journey to Israel.

Golda, infuriated by Kreisky's action, sped from Strasbourg to Vienna to urge him to change his mind. She failed.

While in Europe, in a telephone conversation with Israel Galili on October 1, Golda first learned of the Arab troop concentrations on the Golan Heights. She informed him that she would return to Israel the next day, and she called for a meeting on the subject to be held two days later.

Not the best of friends. **Prime Minister Meir with Austrian Chancellor Bruno Kreisky during their Vienna meeting of October 2, 1973. Palestinian terrorists had raided a train carrying Russian Jewish immigrants to Austria. Five Jews and a customs man were taken hostage. Kreisky responded to the terrorists' demands not only by giving them safe passage out of Austria, but also by offering to close down the Soviet Jewish transit camp in Vienna, where Soviet Jews stayed before making the final journey to Israel. Golda tried unsuccessfully to convince Kreisky to change his mind about closing the camp. The meeting took place four days before the outbreak of the Yom Kippur War.**

The Israeli public paid little attention to what was taking place near the borders, but Israeli officials were clearly concerned about the troop movements in Syria. The head of the Syrian desk in the research department of Israeli military intelligence believed that the Syrians meant business. His counterpart in Egypt was more sanguine about the Egyptians. When the Syrian specialist conveyed his concern to his superiors, he was met with indifference. Only the northern front commander, Yitzhak Hofi, seemed to take him seriously.

On the Egyptian front war tension was felt more acutely. The Egyptian Army was clearly on the move, transferring boats and fording equipment. Officers on the Israeli side of the Suez Canal decided to put their soldiers on alert, although many preferred to believe that the Egyptians were engaged in nothing more than a military exercise. The Egyptians, after all, had mobilized their troops and engaged their field forces in warlike maneuvers often enough in recent years—and in the end no war had erupted.

Returning to Israel Tuesday evening, October 2, the prime minister was met at Lod International Airport by members of her government. In a secluded corner, with a few colleagues, she was told more specifically about the ominous reports. The situation was much more serious than Egypt's mobilization in May. Golda listened carefully and then said tersely, "We shall meet tomorrow and talk."

Wednesday, October 3, 1973

For two hours on Wednesday morning, October 3, 1973, the prime minister conferred with her Kitchen Cabinet, which on this occasion included additional military men. Present were Allon, Dayan, Galili, Elazar, and Brigadier Aryeh Shalev, the chief of intelligence research (the director of intelligence, Eli Zeira, was ill).

Shalev expressed doubt that the Arabs meant war. After presenting a picture of Arab troop deployment, he told Golda that unquestionably they could launch an attack but, he added quickly, the military had come to the conclusion that an offensive was unlikely—and certainly not imminent. The Arabs were deployed in defensive positions; there was no evidence that an attack was planned.

According to Golda's closest associates, the prime minister was bothered by something. "Tell me," she asked of the military men seated around the table, "is there anything, any weapons system that we don't have, that we could ask for right away from the United States?" Benjamin Peled, the Air Force chief, spoke up. "Well," he said thoughtfully, "we could ask for more Shrikes [air-to-ground missiles that hone in on SAM missile radars], but it wouldn't make such a difference."

Mostly to herself, Golda said fretfully: "This reminds me too much of 1967, when we were waiting, expecting." The generals tried to soothe her. At most the Arabs might stage a local action, they might attempt to overrun a particular fortification or two. But the army (IDF) would quickly repulse them. She had nothing to worry about.

The meeting adjourned, and Golda felt a bit better as a small group stayed behind to talk. She hoped there would be no need to go to war, she told them, that the problem would disappear. Jokingly, she added: "It would be good if we could send Assad [the Syrian president] to synagogue on Yom Kippur with Bruno Kreisky."

When everyone but Galili had left, Golda could no longer joke. "There's a contradiction," she told him worriedly, "between the signs on the ground and what the experts are saying."

Nobody else saw a contradiction. At the Cabinet meeting later that day no one brought up the subject of Arab troop deployments. Ze'ev Sharef, the minister of housing, had been visiting the Golan Heights that same day to inaugurate some housing projects built by his ministry. After the ceremonies he conferred with the northern front commander, Yitzhak Hofi, who told him about the unprecedented buildup of Syrian troops along the northern front. During the tour, Sharef was summoned back to Tel Aviv for the Cabinet meeting. The main discussion concerned Golda Meir's talk with Kreisky. Sharef did not mention the views expressed to him by General Hofi.

If there was tension within military circles, the top brass concealed it well. That same day Elazar was host to the press at a naval base. Newsmen predictably asked about Arab troop concentrations already reported in the foreign press. "I do not believe that the enemy would decide to take any irrational step," Elazar declared.

Some generals were less optimistic. One of them, Albert Mendler, was due to take over command of Israel's armored corps, the promotion to take effect on Sunday, October 7. When a visitor to his General Headquarters in the Sinai shouted congratulations to him, Mendler raised his hand: "Don't be in such a hurry to congratulate me," he said. "You never can tell with the Egyptians. Maybe by Sunday they will have changed my plans." Tragically, they did. On that Sunday, the second day of the war, he was killed, the only Israeli general to die in the fighting.

Thursday, October 4, 1973

On Thursday, October 4, Golda followed her normal routine. Simcha Dinitz, who in March, 1973 had replaced Rabin as the Israeli ambassador to the United States, was at his mother's home in Tel Aviv; he was in mourning for his father. Golda phoned Dinitz to apologize for not having been able to pay a condolence call, explaining that she was preoccupied with the war threat. "I'm not happy with the situation in the North or South," she said. "I've asked for an evaluation from intelligence."

That afternoon the prime minister did some electioneering at a kibbutz, where she rebuked Gahal, Menachem Begin's opposition party, for continually predicting that the Arabs were going to attack. "Not one bit of the black prophecies of Gahal have come true. Why don't the Gahal people have the courage to admit their error?" she demanded.

That evening the Israeli general staff convened to hear a report from Eli Zeira, chief of military intelligence. Zeira stated that the families of Soviet military advisers in Syria were packing to leave. Upon hearing the report, Elazar ordered, effective the next morning, that all active units be placed on maximum alert.

Friday, October 5, 1973

On Friday morning, a troubled group of military men met in Moshe Dayan's Tel Aviv office. The country was making final preparations for Yom Kippur, which would begin at sundown. Reports of Arab troop concentration on the border were continuing to flow in. Should the complicated mobilization apparatus be put into effect? Dayan wanted Golda's advice.

Dayan met with the prime minister immediately after the session in his office had concluded. Aerial photographs were spread before her. That there had been a military buildup in Egypt and Syria was obvious. "These are the artillery batteries," she was told. "Here are the missile bases. Here you can see the hundreds of camouflaged and dug-in tanks. Here are the general supply headquarters for the advanced enemy units."

Golda shook her head. That was her habit when the news was bad. "What does the army think?" she asked eagerly. "What does the general staff propose?"

No one talked about full mobilization. Instead, Elazar put forward the suggestion that the mobilization apparatus be placed on alert. He won quick agreement, and all leaves were cancelled. Anyone on his way home for the holiday was called back.

As the morning progressed, military reports continued to be grim: nothing had changed along the tense frontiers; the Arab buildup was continuing. Golda was alarmed. She rushed out of her office and shouted to Lou Kaddar, "Get all of the ministers that you can—today."

Not lacking nerve, Lou, seated at her desk, replied tartly, "What, on Friday? In the middle of the morning? Before Yom Kippur?"

Golda stood stone-faced. Her face fell, and Lou calmed down.

"When do you want them?"

"Any time they can come. Even if they come at different times—as soon as you reach them."

"I'm not sure I can get them all," Lou muttered.

Turning to reenter her office, Golda said, "Get as many as you can get."

Lou placed the calls, and within an hour ministers began to arrive. At Galili's initiative, Golda and Dayan received authority to mobilize all the reserves without first obtaining Cabinet approval.

By late morning, Golda had decided to alter her own plans for Yom Kippur. "The way things are," she explained to her advisers, "I think I won't go to my daughter Sarah at Revivim."

"Why not?" asked an aide. "If anything happens, we can send a helicopter for you."

Golda reiterated that she would stay in Tel Aviv.

Most Israelis, including many closest to the highest echelons of government, were unaware of what was transpiring. The wife of the president, Mrs. Nina Katzir, for example, phoned Golda's office that Friday morning after an article had

Keren Kayemet Archives

At Kibbutz Revivim. **It was this kibbutz, home of Golda's daughter, Sarah Rehabi, that Golda visited often. Revivim became Golda's second home. Left to right: Menachem, Sarah, Naomi (Sarah's daughter), Zechariah Rehabi (Sarah's husband), Shaul (Sarah and Zechariah's son), Amnon Meir, Golda, Danny Meir, Aya Meir, Gidi Meir.**

appeared in that day's *Ha'aretz,* which took Mrs. Katzir to task for her habit of spending money on hotels and trips abroad. Lou explained that the prime minister was busy, that she would be unable to come to the phone. Later, when told of the telephone call from the president's wife, Golda looked at Lou in amazement. How insignificant such things were at a time like this. But Mrs. Katzir, like most Israelis, was unaware of the gravity of the situation.

The fear of imminent war was fast taking hold of Golda. At 1:00 P.M. she informed Lou that she was going to pay Dinitz a condolence call. As the two were leaving the office, Eli Zeira, the chief of intelligence, approached and saluted the prime minister. "I'm glad I've got you here," he said rather cheerfully. "I've brought you a picture." It was a recent photograph of Golda taken by one of Zeira's colleagues.

Then, observing the dejected Lou, he said, "Don't be so depressed. Nothing is going to happen. There won't be a war." Golda stared at him, unable to understand the optimism.

Later, at Dinitz's mother's home, Golda told the ambassador gloomily, "I think you'll have to go back to Washington. I don't like the way things are developing." She instructed him to catch the first flight out on Saturday evening.

Golda's instincts told her that war was imminent. Her mind raced back to May, 1967—the eve of the Six Day War. She recalled soberly that the Arab press then was alive with reports that the Israelis were massing their troops against Syria. This was precisely what the Arab press was saying now. The coincidence unnerved her.

Yom Kippur Eve

It was late in the afternoon and most Israelis were at home or en route home to partake of their pre-fast meal. Most then made their way to the synagogue for the Kol Nidrei service.

Some of Golda's Cabinet ministers were in their synagogues, the prospect of war on their minds. Interior Minister Yosef Burg was in Jerusalem's Yeshurun Synagogue when a synagogue official whispered that a few men had just been called out to join their units.

Shlomo Hillel, the police minister, wasn't in the synagogue. He was at home listening to radio broadcasts from the Arab world. All at once he darted from his chair and placed a phone call to Shaul Rosolio, the police inspector-general. They talked intently about the best way to deploy the nation's 6,000-man police force if an emergency were to occur within the next few hours.

Ariel Sharon, only recently retired from the army, had hoped to spend a quiet Yom Kippur with his family on their sprawling farm in the center of the country. A military car arrived at his home and rushed him to army headquarters in Tel Aviv where he was urgently needed. Once there, he was shown the latest aerial photos of the Egyptian deployment. "It's war," he said ominously.

Golda remained at her Tel Aviv home that evening. Others, friends of Menachem's, sat outside in the garden and talked. The home of the prime minister and that of her son's family adjoined each other.

Golda doubted whether she would be able to fall asleep. She told no one of her anguish.

Zero Hour

A few minutes before 4:00 A.M. the phone rang in the Tel Aviv homes of three military men: Zeira, Lior, and Yeshayahu Raviv, Dayan's military secretary. The voice on the other line had the same message for all three: "INFORMATION HAS BEEN RECEIVED CONFIRMING THAT EGYPT AND SYRIA INTEND TO START A WAR TODAY. ZERO HOUR IS 1800!"

Lior hung up and immediately dialed Golda's number. He reported that it was now certain that there would be war. The attack would begin at 6:00 P.M. "Egypt and Syria will simultaneously begin the offensive from the North and from the South."

Golda rubbed her eyes, wishing that Lior would somehow hedge what he had just said. Or better still, deny it completely. She dressed as quickly as possible, ordering him to summon a meeting of Cabinet ministers for 8:00 A.M. Meanwhile, Raviv alerted Dayan and Elazar.

Elazar had read the war signals correctly that morning. He insisted to Dayan that the entire reserves be called up. Still worried that Israel might appear provocative for mobilizing, Dayan preferred a more limited call-up. He wanted two divisons, one for the North, one for the South. "I will suggest to Golda," he said to the chief of staff, "that we mobilize 50,000 men." Elazar asked that his own broader proposal be presented as well: the mobilization of 100,000 to 120,000 men. Dayan grudgingly agreed.

The crucial meeting to decide on mobilization began at 7:00 A.M. in the prime minister's Tel Aviv office. Among those present were the prime minister, Dayan, Elazar, Galili, and Zvi Zur, Dayan's assistant. Yigal Allon arrived in the middle of the session. Both proposals were placed before the group.

Dayan soon sensed that his view would not be accepted. "If you want to accept his [Elazar's] proposal, he said dramatically, "I will not prostrate myself on the road and I will not resign. But you might as well know that it is superfluous."

Golda was convinced that a substantial mobilization was necessary. "If war breaks out," she declared, "it's better that the world is angry with us and we be in a better position." It pained her to go counter to Dayan's wishes, but her decision was firm: 100,000 men would be called up immediately.

Reaching for one last straw in the hope of averting war, at 11:00 A.M. Golda summoned the American ambassador, Kenneth Keating, and said, "The Arabs think we are about to attack them." She asked Keating to contact the Egyptians, the Syrians, and the Soviets and to try to dispel any such notion. It would be wise, she added, for his message to also indicate that Israel was well aware of Arab war plans.

"Are you adamant about not firing the first shot?" the ambassador asked Golda.

"That is our decision," she responded. "Israel will not open fire. Moreover, Israel is not mobilizing fully, to prevent such an act [from] being interpreted as provocation." Golda and the other Israeli leaders did not believe Keating would meet with success.

Golda now turned her attention to a consideration of a preemptive air strike. According to the Air Force's Peled, the strike could begin as early as 1:00 P.M. It would be targeted only against Syria. Even at this late hour few thought Egypt would dare cross the Canal, and thus preemptive action seemed unwarranted.

For Golda Meir, whether to order an air strike would be the most agonizing decision she would face in the Yom Kippur War. As tempting as the idea of a strike was, something gnawed at her. She was fearful of how America would react. Her instincts told her that the United States might consider a preemptive strike good enough reason to refuse further military aid to Israel. Israel would look like a war-happy nation. She wanted the United States and the world to have a more positive image of Israel. "This time," she said, "it has to be crystal clear who began the war, so we won't have to go around the world convincing people our cause is just."

Golda was convinced that her actions were proper.

Shortly before noon Golda and Israel Galili were in private conversation. "Do you think they could have something to drink, tea, coffee?" Mike Arnon, the Cabinet secretary, asked Lou Kaddar. Mike had just stepped out of the room where the prime minister and Galili were conferring.

"Mike," asked Lou in return, "does Golda want it on Yom Kippur?"

In private the prime minister might decide to eat and drink freely on Yom Kippur, but Lou questioned whether she would want to do so publicly.

"We can't bring drinks into the room where Cabinet ministers are meeting on Yom Kippur," observed Lou.

Food proved difficult to obtain because of the holiday, but Lou managed to find some refreshments to satisfy Golda.

At the Cabinet meeting, which began at 12:00 noon, the Cabinet ministers learned of the prime minister's decision to mobilize some reserves. They also heard her reject the proposal for a preemptive strike. Significantly, no one raised an objection.

An hour later Golda asked Dinitz, who had been attending the meeting, to leave for the airport to catch an earlier flight to the United States. An Israel Aircraft Industries plane flew him to London, where he made a connection to the United States.

Shortly before 2:00 P.M. Ya'acov Shimshon Shapira, the justice minister, asked Moshe Dayan, "What will happen if war breaks out before 6:00 P.M.?" Dayan, taken aback, could only respond, "This is the most important question I've heard today."

Dayan had barely uttered these words when sirens were heard. Within minutes messengers from the high command came scurrying to the prime minister's office with a message for Israel Lior. At 1:55 P.M., looking ashen-faced, he walked into the meeting with the announcement that war had begun on both fronts simultaneously. No other details were available.

Members of the Cabinet were stunned, but Golda at first took the news calmly. Looking straight into the eyes of Shapira, seated opposite her, she said in English, "They'll be sorry for it."

Retiring to a private room, Golda spoke with Galili, Allon, and a few others. Mostly they filled time with silence and impatient waiting. Golda's worries increased as reports filtered in sporadically. For the first time reports of disorganization in Israel's armed forces were heard. There was talk of improvisation.

Later in the afternoon, General Rehavam Ze'evi (known to everyone as "Gandhi"), a special assistant to the chief of staff, appeared. He looked sad.

"What's happening from your point of view?" Golda asked him in a low voice.

"You'll excuse the phrase," he said in his usual outspoken manner, "but they got us with our pants down."

Golda Faces the Nation

Yom Kippur ended and Golda went on television to address a shocked nation. It was the most difficult speech she would ever make. Reports of large numbers of casualties had reached her. To tell the full truth now might demoralize the nation.

Nevertheless she had to say something. The nation had been waiting for words of hope from its leader.

Golda spoke from a prepared text, and as it often was when doing so, her style was stiff, unrelaxed. She barely looked up; her eyes were fixed on the paper in front of her.

"We are in no doubt," the prime minister told the waiting nation, "that we shall prevail. But we are also convinced that this renewal of Egyptian and Syrian aggression is an act of madness. We did our best to prevent the outbreak. We appealed to quarters with political influence to use it in order to frustrate this infamous move of the Egyptian and Syrian leaders.

"While there was still time we informed friendly countries of the confirmed information that we had of the plans for an offensive against Israel. We called on them to do their utmost to prevent war, but the Egyptian and Syrian attack has started."

For the first twenty-four hours of the war Golda pored over maps. As she continued to study them, in her Tel Aviv office so distant from the battlefields, she sensed the futility of what she was doing.

Dayan Faces Fire

In those opening hours of combat Moshe Dayan, the darling of the nation after the 1967 war, was anything but heroic or indestructible. Golda Meir too looked to him for guidance. But this Moshe Dayan was far different from the man who had answered the call in 1967. As the guns were fired that Saturday afternoon, Golda was shocked to see an immobilized, pessimistic, and despairing Dayan facing her.

The first day of war had left the defense minister disheartened, but he was determined to help Israel salvage what it could of the desperate situation. He proposed to Golda that Israel should abandon the Suez Canal line and organize along a new front further back in the Sinai. Recalling the situation later, he wrote: "We faced the danger of losing our strength and remaining without a force before we gained the desired military decision."

But his fears extended much further than that. He was expressing concern that the "Third Commonwealth" (a rarely used term for the State of Israel), might be destroyed.

After one conversation with Dayan, Golda closed the door behind him and wept openly. Lou Kaddar watched as the tears streamed down the prime minister's face.

"What's the matter?" she asked Golda.

"Dayan wants to talk about the conditions for surrender," she sobbed, brushing away her tears.

Did Dayan really use the word "surrender"? Lou Kaddar insists that Golda said he did, although many refuse to believe her.

Lou Kaddar's first reaction, upon hearing Golda mention that Dayan wanted to discuss surrender terms was that Moshe Dayan might consider surrender, but Golda never would. She would commit suicide first. Surrender the country? No, never, absolutely not.

Lou remained with Golda outside the door for what seemed a very long time, wondering about what the prime minister had just said. Then her mind turned to the unthinkable: she would get some pills from a physician friend, enough for herself and the prime minister. Golda might want to use them instead of surrendering to the Arabs. But after that fleeting moment, Lou relaxed. There seemed no hurry to take such drastic action.

A few days later Golda Meir confessed to Lou that she had thought it better to kill herself than to surrender.

"OK," Lou responded jokingly, "we'll do it together."

But the military situation was in fact never so bleak that such steps had to be considered. The Arabs were never that close to crushing the Israelis that conditions of surrender had to be seriously considered.

Golda was clearly saddened and horrified by what appeared to be the "disintegration" of Moshe Dayan. "The great Moshe Dayan," she proclaimed in a private conversation, "one day this way, one day that way." Yet she could not fire him in the middle of the war. That might give the impression that she was blaming him for all Israel's problems. Forcing Dayan to depart might also serve to discredit her.

Considerable pressure to dismiss Dayan was forthcoming, particularly from Ya'acov Shimshon Shapira, minister of justice. But like a mother reproaching a mischievous child, Golda scolded him for talking out of turn. "You can't say things like that about Dayan. The war isn't even over." When it became clear to Shapira that he was bringing little influence to bear, he tendered his resignation.

Dayan seemed perfectly willing to step down, but Golda would not hear of it. Instead, she turned to others for advice, especially David Elazar, the chief of staff. Running the war became his personal task—without direction from Dayan but with much interference. Golda sensed that under Elazar the war was in capable hands. He felt confident of the outcome, and he became a close adviser to the prime minister.

A Matter of Survival

In the first week of war Golda's spirits rose and sank, depending on the battlefield reports, but she always tried to present the bright side to the public and to those close to her. On the third day of the war, she phoned Clara in Bridgeport, Connecticut. They spoke for only ninety seconds because, as Clara said later, "We're both very mindful of the telephone rates." But in that minute and a half Golda let Clara feel her sense of confidence. "We've got everything under control," she assured her sister.

Clara repeated the prime minister's optimistic remarks to a Jewish Federation meeting covered by the press, which resulted in front-page stories proclaiming, at this early stage of the war, Israeli mastery on the battlefield.

Golda was encouraged to hear from Haim Bar-Lev, who at her request had traveled north to survey the front. "The situation is grave," he reported "but not desperate." Most heartening was the relatively brief time it took the Israeli forces to halt the Syrian advance through the Golan Heights.

Yom Kippur struggle. Israeli infantry, under air cover, move into the forward battle zone on the Golan Heights on October 8, 1973, the third day of the Yom Kippur War. In the opening hours of the war, Israel suffered reverses on both the Golan and Suez fronts. Eventually, Israeli forces were able to push back the Syrians and Egyptians and penetrate deep into enemy territory.

Dayan's pessimism persisted. On Tuesday, October 9, during an off-the-record briefing for Israel's newspaper editors, he gave a gloomy account of the IDF's efforts. The day before had been the worst for Israel on the southern front. Dayan informed the editors of his plans to appear on national television that evening.

Several of the editors were shocked, fearing that Dayan's gloom would lower morale. One of them approached Golda and suggested that the defense minister's appearance might be harmful.

She raised the issue with Dayan. "We are still in the thick of the fight," she said. "So there is no need to tell the people the whole story. The truth at this moment might change and not be the final truth."

The prime minister could not order Dayan to cancel the television appearance. She could only make a request. Dayan fulfilled that request.

That evening, in place of the regular military spokesman, Elazar dispatched Aharon Yariv to brief the press. With his blend of optimism and realism, Yariv offered a refreshingly calming voice at a time when one was most needed. Golda watched Yariv's television performance; in her mind she compared it with what Dayan's might have been. The next day she told Yariv, "I'm glad you're dealing with the information thing. Last night it was *aleph, aleph* [meaning, a superior performance]."

By this time, Elazar and Bar-Lev had become Golda's heroes. When she mentioned Dayan's name, it was with bitterness and sorrow: "You don't come to rely on a person who has lost his way."

The acceleration of American military aid was a major priority for Golda. Sometimes she acted like a desperate old woman, but she made no apologies. She phoned Willy Brandt one day to ask him if he would forego the anti-tank Tow missiles that the United States had earmarked for West Germany. The chancellor was very understanding, but Israel never received the missiles.

At 3 o'clock one morning, Golda phoned Simcha Dinitz to urge him to talk with Henry Kissinger about speeding up the airlift. "I can't wake him now," the ambassador replied. "I'll have to wait a few hours." This was not what Golda Meir, frustrated over the shortage of arms, wanted to hear.

"No, don't wait," she spoke into the phone. "Wake up Kissinger and tell him what I'm requesting. And tell him I said he'll sleep after the war as much as he wants."

Golda pressed her personal appeal for American arms against a battery of pressures. She had to battle an irritated ministry of defense, which maintained that acquiring arms was too technical a matter for the prime minister to handle.

With all the good will that Golda had built up with Richard Nixon, she was still not certain that he would meet his personal commitment to Israeli security. And so she turned to others in and out of the Administration for help.

In a phone call to her old friend George Meany, Golda pleaded that the labor leader talk to Nixon. She instructed Dinitz at one point to check whether she might travel to the United States incognito to press Israel's case. She feared that a public journey would seem an act of weakness. Ultimately, the trip was not required.

The actual reasons for the delay in the American airlift of arms and supplies to Israel are shrouded in controversy and mystery. According to Nixon's memoirs, Kissinger accepted the United States defense department view that Israel should be sent only three large cargo planes since sending more would lessen the chances of the United States becoming the peacemaker after the fighting. Kissinger did not want his country to appear to be too pro-Israel. Nixon did not agree. "Look, Henry," he said to his secretary of state, "we're gonna get just as much blame for sending three, if we send 30, or a hundred, or whatever we've got, so send everything that flies. The main thing is to make it work."

After Golda learned that Nixon had come to Israel's aid, she responded quickly. "Your decision," she wrote the president on October 12, "will have a great and beneficial influence on our fighting capability. I knew that in this hour of dire need for Israel, I could turn to you and count on your deep sympathy and understanding. We are fighting against heavy odds, but we are fully confident that we shall come out victorious. When we do, we will have you in mind."

Taking the Offensive

With the flow of American arms assured, Israel could take the offensive. For Israel time was running out.

Kissinger was pressing the Soviets for a ceasefire. A daring tactic was needed to throw the Egyptian war machine off balance. It was supplied by dusting off a

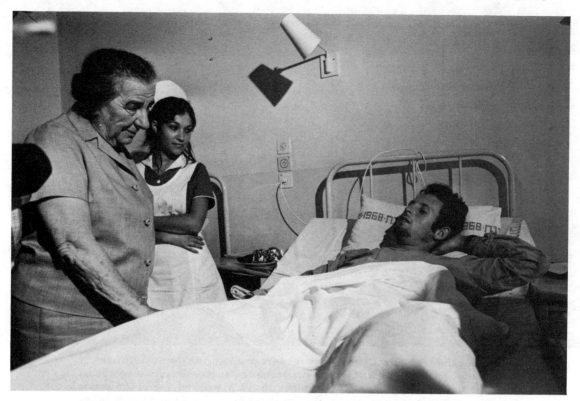

Caring for her "family." Golda is shown here with a wounded soldier on October 15, 1973. **What upset her most about the war was the mounting list of Israeli casualties.**

five-year-old plan for a sudden counterattack across the Suez Canal. The stratagem was double-edged: it would prevent Israeli troops from falling victim to a war of attrition, and it would take the battle to the Egyptian heartland, trapping the Egyptian troops on the Israeli side of the Suez Canal.

Proposed early in the war, the plan was shelved until it was felt sure that Israeli tanks could destroy the major fighting forces of the Egyptians in Sinai. While Dayan doubted the plan's wisdom, Haim Bar-Lev pushed it aggressively, telling Golda, "It's not simple, it's a risk, but it's worth it, because otherwise we're stuck."

By October 14, Bar-Lev was ready to put the plan into action. The tactic was actually Ariel Sharon's brainchild. Some years before he had devised it, bulldozing roads near the Canal and marking his intended site of embarkation with red bricks. Golda liked the idea, and at 5:00 P.M. on October 15 the first tanks under Sharon's command rolled out of Tasa toward the Canal. Golda and other Cabinet ministers spent a most anxious evening awaiting reports.

The crossing ran into unexpected problems. Four hours after it had begun only 200 paratroopers had actually started to cross the Canal. Heavy fighting with the Egyptian forces on the eastern bank of the Canal kept Sharon from sending his troops over the water quickly.

Hoping for word of success all that evening, Golda finally sent her weary

Crossing the Suez Canal. Israeli tank reinforcements cross the western bank of the Suez Canal after Israeli General Ariel Sharon's successful crossover. Sharon's thrust across the Canal on October 16, 1973, marked one of the major turning points in the war, leaving the Egyptians in the Sinai cut off from other forces.

ministers home at 6:00 A.M. By 9:00 A.M. on October 16 only thirty tanks and 2,000 men had reached the western bank.

The Egyptians could have easily put an end to the crossing had they understood Israel's strategy correctly. That they did not was fortunate for Israel. The strategy worked.

Israel took control of the western bank of the Suez, and Sharon became an instant hero. "Arik, King of Israel," his soldiers called him affectionately.

Golda relished the report she presented to the Knesset that day. Hers was the first official announcement that Israeli troops were operating across the Canal.

Golda was now satisfied that the war would be won.

Nine days later, the fighting was over. Israeli troops had advanced far into Syria and Egypt, leaving the nation with a feeling that once again the Arabs had not been able to defeat the State of Israel. The Arabs, recalling those first few hours of the war when their troops overran Israeli positions with ease, claimed victory despite their perilous situation on October 25th when a cease-fire was finally agreed upon.

Israel's victory was marred by her high casualties: 2,552 soldiers dead and another 3,000 wounded. Only in the 1948 War of Independence had more Israelis fallen.

The shock and pain caused by the war and its terrible consequences would be felt in the country for a long, long time.

18

Final Judgment

With the Yom Kippur War finally over, the public demanded a full-scale investigation into what had gone wrong. Why was Israel caught off guard? Why were there so many casualties?

The Agranat Commission

Although reluctant to meet the call for an investigation, Golda finally gave in to pressure. On November 18, 1973 a commission led by Dr. Shimon Agranat, the American-born president of the Israeli Supreme Court, was created.

The commission was well aware of Golda's fears: that the Israeli public would blame everyone connected with the government for its outbreak, not distinguishing between political and military leadership. Therefore, at the very outset the commission established a distinction between political and military leaders in determining where the responsibility lay for what went wrong. It also laid down one important criterion for judging political leaders: if a minister's advisers had been unanimous in a recommendation, and if that advice turned out to have been a mistake, that minister had to be judged not guilty. Accordingly, Golda Meir, confronted with a unanimous assessment from her advisers that there would be no war, was judged "innocent" by the commission.

Moshe Dayan was also exonerated. For him, the commission employed a corollary to the criterion by which it judged Golda. A minister could also be judged innocent if he had followed the advice of one of his advisers who had dissented from the consensus, and that adviser had been proven correct. When a northern front commander had expressed unhappiness with the Syrian troop buildup—in effect, offering a minority viewpoint that had eventually been proven correct—Dayan had thought it wise to call for reinforcements along the northern frontier. Thus the commission excused the defense minister.

Elazar, the chief of staff, was judged by a different standard. In the commission's view the only valid criterion for judging a military leader was to determine whether he had deployed his troops properly so as to defend against a surprise attack. Yitzhak Rabin, the chief of staff during the Six Day War, had been successful in this respect, but Elazar, six years later, had not. The commission recommended that Elazar be relieved of his post.

What impressed the commission members about Golda's appearances before

[247]

the body was her calmness and dignity. "Her own feelings were," recalled Yigael Yadin, a commission member, "that she was haunted by the fact that she wasn't aware of what was happening." While others who testified were eager to defend themselves and their actions, Golda was not. She accepted full responsibility for what had occurred.

Haim Laskov, another commission member, was impressed by Golda because "she carried the full burden. There was no attempt to shove responsibility onto someone else. She answered every one of our questions in dignity. There was no affectation. She was tired, smoking more than the normal rate. But you couldn't feel a change in the voice or anything. She answered questions steadily, clearly. She wasn't shaking or despondent. It was Golda at her toughest, not stooping. There was that incisive voice, that American drawl."

For the most part, the commission gave Golda good marks. In its interim report of April 2, 1974, it exonerated her with this statement:

> The commission is convinced that Prime Minister Meir acted fittingly during the critical days preceding the outbreak of the war . . . The prime minister used her authority properly and wisely when she ordered mobilization of the reserves on Saturday morning, despite the weighty political factors involved. This was an important act in the defense of the country.

Yet, in the unpublished part of the report, Golda Meir was blamed for not having been sufficiently aware on war's eve of what the Arab troop buildups might signify. She was also criticized for having kept fully informed only a small group within her Cabinet. The whole body should have been kept abreast of all developments, the commission maintained.

The conclusions reached by the Agranat Commission gave Golda little joy. She was deeply wounded by the verdict on Elazar. She refused to accept that only he bore the responsibility for prewar errors.

Early in April of 1974 a combination of forces were at work trying to discredit the commission's findings. Elements within the Labor Party and within the country at large were planning to unseat Golda and her government. The report of the Agranat Commission, particularly its exoneration of Dayan, made Golda's opponents angry. And this, naturally, upset Golda. She tried to follow a course that would keep her in office because she wanted desperately to repair the damage that had been done to her reputation.

The Elections

Because of the war, the national elections, which had been scheduled for October, were postponed to December 31, 1973. On November 28 the Labor Party Central Committee approved the original prewar list of candidates by a vote of 256-107, with 30 abstentions. But at a second meeting a week later Golda asked the party for a vote of confidence through a secret ballot. She wanted anyone who so wished to have the opportunity to propose another candidate for prime minister. No one did.

The meeting of the committee lasted into the evening. Speaking last, Golda staunchly defended Moshe Dayan. If she were to succeed in repairing the harm that had been done to her and to her Government's reputation over the war, she had to begin by making sure that her prewar Cabinet remained intact. This meant, first and foremost, to resist demands that her minister of defense, Dayan, be held responsible for many of the prewar errors, and be fired. She argued that under Israeli law all government officials were collectively responsible for all actions. The message was clear: Dayan should not be made into a scapegoat. A vote was taken, resounding in a triumph for Golda, 293-33 with 17 abstentions.

On election eve Golda was the first of the Labor Party leaders to arrive at party headquarters in Tel Aviv. Tension was high. Each leader realized that the war was an imponderable that might bring defeat to Labor. They sat together in a conference room, sipping glasses of hot tea, watching television for hopeful signs. The mood lightened when it became clear that Labor would win despite the war.

On the Golan Heights. **Golda rarely left her office in Tel Aviv during the Yom Kippur War. This photograph, taken with Israeli troops on November 21, 1973, marks one of the first times she traveled to see troops at the time of the fighting.**

More than likely, it was aided considerably by the voters' awareness that Israelis and Arabs would soon be meeting at the planned Geneva Peace Conference.

Golda Vents Her Fury

Accepting responsibility for the war did not keep Golda from lashing out at others. She was bitter, deeply disappointed that some of her Cabinet associates, especially Dayan and Eban, allowed her to be blamed for the war without acknowledging their own blunders. She was also terribly resentful that some Israelis felt the need to continually remind her of her guilt. Furthermore, she was irate at some of Israel's supposed allies. Friends in peace, a number of West European nations had proven that Arab oil was more important to them than Israeli friendship. Israel's calls for help during the war had in many cases gone unheeded.

Golda Meir was particularly angry at Helmut Schmidt, the West German Social Democrat leader, whom she met at a postwar Socialist International Conference in London. Schmidt had been lecturing her on the Western need for Arab oil.

Talking with the troops. General Yitzhak Hofi, then northern front commander, and Moshe Dayan, minister of defense, listen to the prime minister on the Golan Heights on November 21, 1973.

"Oil," he said, "is not only important for Western affluence, it is vitally important to Socialist stability and political stability in Europe. Without sufficient oil," he continued, "there would be unreasonably high unemployment in Western Europe, and this might induce some of these democracies to turn to Fascism or Communism."

In her fury, Golda replied: "I wish you well, and I want you to prosper and to be stable, but not at our expense. If you want to do it at our expense, you will go with us."

Schmidt was shaken. He wanted to make sure he understood the prime minister accurately.

"Do you mean the [atomic] bomb?" he asked.

"I didn't say so," Golda replied tartly. "You said so."

Golda's Guilt Complex

It would have been easier for Golda Meir to blame others rather than accept the blame herself. She was determined, however, to face herself honestly. After the war she stood before an audience in Jerusalem and explained that "in these hands, I held the reports. My military advisers didn't regard them as important. And who am I, a woman without any military experience, that I should disagree with them? But I should have seen, I should have understood."

Guilt continued to plague her. A hundred times and more, she said publicly and privately in the months after the war that she was a changed woman—obviously for the worse.

She could not explain precisely what she meant, yet it was easy enough to figure out.

The war had been Golda Meir's greatest failure, a setback she never could have imagined possible. It had come at the twilight of her life, a life in which she had participated in nearly every major event connected with the founding and building of the State of Israel. Whatever glory she had won might now be lost.

Dayan's Exit

In an attempt to salvage something of her reputation, the prime minister worked feverishly to save her government from collapse. She knew that if Dayan were to be forced out, she might be next. She therefore decided to fight to keep Moshe Dayan from being forced to resign as defense minister.

The Dayan matter came to the fore in February of 1974. During the behind-closed-doors session, a colonel on the Israeli liaison team with the United Nations rose to assail the entire government, Dayan in particular, for the outbreak of the war. He called for the minister of defense's resignation. Enraged at the accusations, Dayan demanded that the officer be ejected from the meeting.

Yossi Sarid, a dovish Knesset member who belonged to the Labor Party, raised a Parliamentary Question in which Dayan was asked to explain his actions. Dayan strenuously objected.

Within five minutes Minister of Finance Pinchas Sapir phoned Sarid, his protégé. Sapir informed Sarid that Golda Meir and a few ministers were with him at Golda's home. Sapir continued quietly, "We have heard the question you put, and I urge you to retract it.

Sarid was stunned, mystified. Why would Golda want to protect Dayan from embarrassment? Why would Sapir, Dayan's most persistent critic, want the matter dropped?

"I'm sorry," said Sarid, holding his ground, "no chance." Sarid was furious with Dayan and the military for their prewar misjudgments. If necessary, he would fight the battle alone. Sapir could not budge him.

A few minutes later Sapir called again. "You don't know what you're doing," the minister said, this time with anger in his voice. "Golda just said if you don't take the question off, she'll resign. Tonight."

Sarid was not about to be bluffed. "So she'll resign. I'm not taking it off." And the Parliamentary Question held firm.

Confronted with Sarid's stubborness, the prime minister ordered military censors to keep the whole affair from finding its way into the Israeli press, but it was too late. When Dayan announced, one week later, that he would not be part of Golda's new government, he indicated that this incident was the main reason for his decision.

Kissinger's Shuttle Diplomacy

The weeks following the Yom Kippur War were a time of intense diplomatic maneuvering. The term "shuttle diplomacy" came into popular usage as a direct result of the intense activity of U.S. Secretary of State Henry Kissinger. Kissinger was determined to end the Arab-Israeli conflict; and of all of Golda Meir's dealings with foreign statesmen, by far the most complicated and significant were those she had with Kissinger.

Over a period of seven months after the war, Golda Meir, Henry Kissinger, Anwar Sadat, and Hafez Assad became the principals in a drama that eventually produced two major agreements: the Israeli-Egyptian Separation of Forces accord of January, 1974, and the Israeli-Syrian Separation of Forces accord of May, 1974. Many third parties had tried but failed to shake the Arabs and Israelis out of their deadlock. Only Kissinger proved to have the ability, the will, the energy, and the imagination to succeed.

Kissinger the Jew

A professor and a German Jew, Kissinger was automatically suspect in Golda's mind. She disliked intellectuals and German Jews with equal intensity. The great unknown at the outset had to do with his Jewishness: would it benefit or harm Israel? Golda assumed that it would help.

On occasion Kissinger himself reinforced Golda's belief. One day, after returning from Syria, he arrived at the prime minister's office late in the evening. "This morning," he declared in his low voice, "I looked through my hotel window at the Old City [of Jerusalem] and thought how my father would have been happy." Golda knew that Kissinger had been reared in an Orthodox Jewish home

Diplomatic success. The shuttle over, Dr. Kissinger appears at a farewell party at the prime minister's office in Jerusalem. Just ended was the thirty-five-day shuttle between Israel and Syria, culminating in the Israel-Syria Separation of Forces agreement for the Golan Heights front. That agreement marked an end to the war of attrition between the two countries.

and that his relatives had been victims of the Holocaust. But knowing that Henry was not a practicing Jew, she was particularly impressed by his emotional words.

Henry and Golda

The relationship between Kissinger and Golda Meir was most unusual and most complex. It was a mixture of adoration, admiration, and exasperation. "I loved Golda Meir," Kissinger said on the day she died, "because of her strength, her warmth, her humanity, her sense of humor . . . " Then he added, "She was sort of the earth-mother of elemental strength, wariness, and profundity."

Golda could never lavish such praise on anyone, Henry Kissinger included. She did defend him forcefully against those Israelis who argued that he was too pro-Arab. "I had bitter arguments with him, very bitter," she said. "Israel's statesmen will have tough arguments with him, more than once and on more than one subject. But to arrive at a conclusion that he is ready to abandon Israel and sell us out to the Arabs—this is groundless and will remain groundless and incorrect."

But the prime minister did criticize him, sometimes ever so gently, for tilting too strongly toward the Arabs. During the January, 1974 negotiations between Israel and Egypt, Kissinger complained to Golda that "when I reach Cairo, Sadat hugs and kisses me. But when I come here everyone attacks me." Golda responded, "If I were an Egyptian, I would kiss you also."

Golda once asked Kissinger how his Jewishness affected his welcome in Saudi Arabia, the most extreme anti-Jewish state in the region. Kissinger explained that the king had once said to him, "I treat you as a human being, not a Jew." To this Golda responded, "You know, Mr. Secretary, some of your best friends are human beings."

Kissinger respected Golda for her convictions, and he was often moved by them. "Her craggy face," he wrote in the first volume of his memoirs, "bore witness to the destiny of a people who had come to know too well the potentialities

Meeting in Washington. **The prime minister, Simcha Dinitz (right), and Henry Kissinger (then Nixon's national security adviser) in Washington in February, 1973.**

New prime minister. Prime Minister-designate Rabin and Israel Galili, minister without portfolio, toast outgoing Prime Minister Golda Meir on June 4, 1974. Golda resigned in April but remained in office as head of a caretaker government while the Labor party chose her successor. Golda felt both sadness and relief at leaving high office.

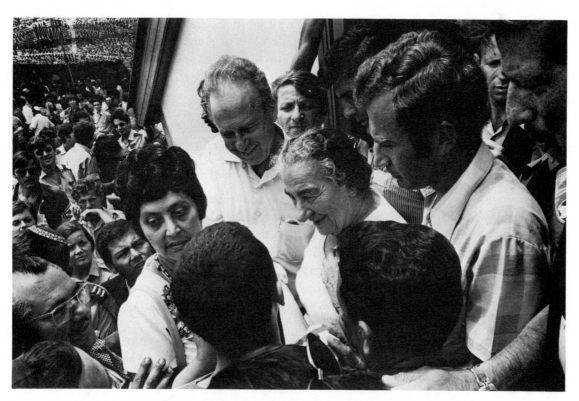

They're back! On June 6, 1974, Golda and Rabin visit with Israeli POWs repatriated from Syria. The Israeli POWs' return was part of the agreement worked out by Kissinger during his shuttle between Israel and Syria.

of man's inhumanity. Her occasionally sarcastic exterior never obscured a compassion that felt the death of every Israeli soldier as the loss of a member of her family."

He was moved by her strong emotions as well. Recalling the day he handed her the list of Israeli prisoners held in Syria after the Yom Kippur War, Kissinger said, "It was the first time, the only time, I saw her burst into tears."

Sometimes Kissinger was infuriated by Golda, for often he found himself attempting to navigate between the demands and viewpoints of two worlds. Golda Meir was willing to see matters only as they affected the State of Israel. As a result, clashes were inevitable. One such instance occurred in May, 1974, when Kissinger, the master of *Realpolitik*, was on a collision course with Golda Meir, defender of a Jewish nation. Kissinger was trying to arrange a separation of forces accord between Syria and Israel. The key town of Kuneitra on the Golan Heights was at issue.

Kissinger: "It's necessary to give back Kuneitra, plus a bit of the areas west of the pre-October line. We need a line that's negotiable, or the negotiations will collapse very soon. Israel should understand the Syrians' perception. You're sitting on their territory."

Golda Meir (her voice angry): "We didn't just get up one day in 1967 after all the shelling from the Heights and decide to take Golan away from them. In October [1973] we had 800 killed and 2,000 wounded in Golan alone—in a war they started. They say this is their territory. Eight hundred boys gave their lives for an attack the Syrians started. Assad lost the war—and now we have to pay for it because Assad says it's his territory."

Kissinger: "Each side has its own definition of justice. Remember what this is all about—to keep the negotiating process alive, to prevent another round of hostilities which would benefit the Soviet Union and increase pressure on you, on us, and on Sadat to rejoin the battle . . . "

Moshe Dayan: "Maybe we could divide Kuneitra."

Kissinger: "It won't work."

Golda Meir: "There's a Cabinet meeting tomorrow—we must ask for authority to propose a new line. We'll have a big fight in the Knesset and with our people who live in Golan."

Israel returned Kuneitra to the Syrians, and in time the two sides reached an understanding that led to the Kissinger-styled accord of May, 1974—yet not without pain and frustration on all sides.

But Golda proved more than a match for Kissinger. At times she overpowered him by the sheer force of her personality. Hafez Assad said later that "one of the weaknesses I discovered in Dr. Kissinger was his special love of that woman. It struck me as strange that this university professor and secretary of state was unable to conceal such a furious affection."

Kissinger himself had to admit that Golda Meir had handled him superbly. "To me," he wrote in his memoirs, "she acted as a benevolent aunt toward an especially favored nephew, so that even to admit the possibility of disagreement was a challenge to family hierarchy producing emotional outrage. It was usually calculated."

Henry Kissinger made more progress in establishing movement toward peace than any other mediator in the long, violent history of the area. But to accomplish this, it seemed to Golda, he had to foster American relations with an Arab world that was pointedly tilted against Israel.

Nevertheless, when she left office in the spring of 1974, guns were silent on both major fronts for the first time since October 6, 1973.

Golda forgave Kissinger for the hardships he had imposed upon her during the arduous negotiations of the past year. She forgave him because he had helped to bring the shooting to a halt. She forgave him because he encouraged the Arabs to take the first, grudging steps toward an accommodation with the State of Israel. But in the back of her mind there always persisted the thought that Kissinger did not care enough about Israeli interests.

Golda was also distressed that too often Kissinger insisted on blaming Israel for the deadlock in the conflict. He continued to do so even a year later, in March, 1975, when Israel, under Prime Minister Yitzhak Rabin, refused to bend to Kissinger's wishes that Israel accept a second Israel-Egypt disengagement agreement. Kissinger then paid a courtesy call on Golda Meir, by then almost a year in retirement. "I shall not blame you," he promised her. And yet he did.

No sooner did Kissinger's homeward-bound plane leave Israel than he began spinning a tale of Israeli intransigence which had prevented him from making sufficient progress. "I don't understand him," Golda complained to Mordechai Gazit, her former aide, after learning that "a senior American official" had blamed Israel for the failure of those 1975 talks.

Thus Golda regarded Kissinger with affection and suspicion all at once. Kissinger returned the feeling. In public, the two were the picture of harmony, but behind closed doors Golda and Kissinger acted towards one another with toughness and guile, both zealous diplomats protecting their own interests first. But always, there was genuine mutual respect.

19

Resignation and Retirement

It was the Yom Kippur War that brought about Golda Meir's political downfall. She was wounded by the voices of bitterness and resentment that continued to be heard, but she was determined not to be forced from power. Were she to leave office too soon, history might not treat her generously.

It was an uphill struggle. To accomplish her immediate goal—to bring the wars of attrition on the northern and southern fronts to an end and to create conditions for a stable future—she could not permit the growing chorus of public protest to affect her.

Pressure Mounts

The protests began in early 1974. They had started among the soldiers who were returning slowly from the various war fronts beginning in November and December of 1973.

Most of the soldiers were anguish-ridden. Their minds were filled with memories of friends lost or injured in battle. Hadn't many of the casualties been unnecessary? they asked.

The protest movement was organized by a young captain, Motti Ashkenazi, the commanding officer of "Budapest," the northernmost stronghold on the Suez Canal and the only one near the Canal not to have fallen to the Egyptians. At first the main target of the movement was Moshe Dayan. During Ashkenazi's one-man demonstrations outside the prime minister's office in Jerusalem, the captain called for the defense minister's resignation.

Gradually the protests expanded. Public outrage on such a broad scale had never before been witnessed in Israel. Rallies attracted hundreds, then thousands. Eventually the focus switched from Moshe Dayan to Golda Meir's entire government.

Golda could not abide the protesters' effrontery at accusing her government of having caused the war. Nor could she respect them as the authentic voice of the broad population of Israel. She especially detested their tactics of taking to the streets. "I don't think they use sensible methods," she said. "For instance, they picket Labor Party headquarters day and night. They want us to do this and not otherwise. Fine, but I told them: 'Where do we confront each other? Where can I confront you?'

Happy moment. **On November 16, 1973, the prime minister meets with the families of Israeli prisoners of war who returned from Egyptian captivity. Egypt released 238 Israeli POWs and Israel returned 8,000 Egyptian POWs as part of the November 7th six-part agreement arranging for a final cease-fire between Israeli and Egyptian troops after the Yom Kippur War.**

"'You give your opinion, I'll give mine, and then there will be a democratic decision.' But they say: 'No, we want to influence from outside,' I cannot accept that way. Why should anyone, no matter what fine things he has done, be entitled to bring pressure on me to change my mind? That I don't accept."

Golda Meir did not accept pressure from the outside. But she was forced to confront the rising dissent within the Labor Party itself. If the voices in the street could not sway her, the arguments of party stalwarts and veterans like Aryeh Eliav and Yitzhak Ben-Aharon could and did. When someone as close to her as Chaim Gvati, the minister of agriculture and a longtime Labor Party acquaintance, publicly said that the country had lost its confidence in Golda's government, the prime minister listened.

Golda listened and she was moved to action. She believed that the Labor Party had a right to determine the role she should play in the movement. In December, 1973, the Labor Party had made it clear that it wanted her to remain as prime minister, but in February, 1974, when Golda tried to form a new government, the growing opposition to her government, principally directed against Dayan, made it difficult for her to contend with the warring political factions.

Golda's last Cabinet. On March 10, 1974, Golda appeared with her new Cabinet after taking two months to form a coalition. She was not to remain in office for long. The following month she resigned, having served just over five years as prime minister.

When Dayan had decided not to be a part of Golda's new government, her task became unbearable. She tried to dissuade Dayan from declining the post, but to no avail. At a party meeting on March 3, Yitzhak Rabin was to replace Dayan as minister of defense. But rather than form a new government without Moshe Dayan, Golda resigned.

Delegations rushed to her home, urging her to retract the statement. A central committee meeting two days later appealed to her—and to Dayan—to return to the fold.

Finally, Dayan concluded that he was better off inside the government. He gave as the "reason" for his change of heart the threat by Syria to renew the war on the Golan front.

"I could not have received a nicer present," she told Dayan when she heard the news of his intended return. One week later, Golda presented a new government, with Dayan as defense minister.

"The End of the Road"

By April the mood of the country had changed. The nation was not in sympathy with the report of the Agranat Commission, which declared Dayan innocent of wrongdoing. And by early April Dayan became the focus of an intense and bitter struggle within the party. If Dayan were not fired as minister of defense, one wing of the party, the former Ahdut Avoda faction, would stage a rebellion. On the other hand, if Dayan were to be forced out, his own former Rafi wing threatened to stage a walkout. In either case Golda would not be able to form a strong government. The party had sent Golda a clear signal. There no longer was room for her at the top.

On April 10, 1974, before stunned members of the Labor Party Knesset faction and Leadership Bureau meeting in the Knesset, she announced, with a sense of relief, that she was resigning.

"I have come to the end of the road," she said to a hushed audience. "It is beyond my strength to continue carrying the burden."

This time no one tried to convince her otherwise. This time her beloved Labor Party agreed that she had made the right decision. And this time she acted with dispatch so that resignation would lead to retirement. But Golda Meir let it be known very quickly that her interest in the political life of Israel would not cease. "I'm not going to enter a nunnery," she said. "I'll be in Israel and in the party and I'll take an interest in everything that happens."

Golda took one more decisive step: she gave up her Knesset seat. Now, by law, she would not be able to become prime minister again, not until she were to be returned to the Knesset at a future election, a remote prospect, indeed.

Finding a Successor

With Golda's resignation in hand, the party was under no obligation to call for new elections so long as it could provide a new candidate who could form a government. Golda's first choice was Pinchas Sapir, but he did not want the job. The prime ministership, he thought, was a worthless prize.

With Sapir out of the running, the party would choose one of two men from the "younger" generation. One was Shimon Peres, age 50, a founder of Rafi. Golda disliked him. The other was Yitzhak Rabin, age 52, of Mapai. He enjoyed only lukewarm relations with Golda. By any measure Rabin should have had Golda's strong backing. She had pledged to herself to keep Peres from becoming prime minister. And she had always considered Rabin intelligent, of good pioneering stock. Golda had known and admired Rabin's mother, Rosa Cohen, one of the early pioneers from Russia.

Yet, Golda stopped short of endorsing Rabin at the crucial moment. Surprisingly, she adopted a posture of neutrality. Some observers speculated that her withholding of support reflected her disappointment in him when, as ambassador to Washington, he seemed to usurp her role as she tried to orchestrate Israeli relations with the United States. She had found him too often brash as well as too opinionated. While these old grievances played a part in Golda's decision to withhold her endorsement of Rabin, it was clear that she still hoped that Sapir would reconsider and seek the office.

When it was certain that Sapir would not alter his position, Golda let it be known privately, never publicly, that Rabin was her candidate. However, she left the final decision to Sapir. She was confident that the finance minister, aware of her dislike for Peres, would choose Rabin as the party's nominee.

Golda was correct. And with the party's kingmaker supporting him, Rabin was virtually assured of the nomination. On April 22, 1974, by a vote of 298 to 254, Rabin was selected to assume leadership of the party and to form a new government.

Facing Retirement

Golda hoped to lead a simple, leisurely life after retirement. She had once said to her daughter, Sarah, that upon retirement she wanted to devote her time to the study of the Hebrew language, the Bible, and Hebrew literature. Sarah would be her teacher. But Golda would soon discover that many demands would be placed on her and she would never really have the free time she hoped for.

Golda also discovered that as a former prime minister she was entitled to an office, a monthly pension, a telephone, a car, a driver, a personal bodyguard, and a guard for her house. Her life would not be a simple one.

"A car and a driver?" she said to Lou Kaddar in amazement on the first day of retirement. "Why should I need that? There are buses and taxis. Or my son will take me." Before long, however, Golda understood that her schedule would be too hectic, her life too complex to do without a driver.

In answer to a question from Lou concerning how to deal with those wishing to contact the former prime minister, Golda said, "Give them my telephone number." But when Golda saw how frequently the phone rang, she had a change of mind. And despite the fact that the telephone number was unpublished, it became necessary for her to change the number three times.

With the pressures of public office lifted, Golda turned her thoughts to preparing her memoirs. It would provide her with an opportunity to reflect on the broad sweep of Jewish life, its triumphs and defeats. Through it she would be able to show that there was considerably more to her career than the tragedy of the Yom Kippur War, the accounts of which had been distorted, she believed, by the press.

To Golda, the attacks of the press were like poisoned arrows aiming to destroy her image. When one reporter, in discussing the Yom Kippur War, was especially critical of her behavior, the prime minister demanded of the newspaper's editor: "What does he [the reporter] want? I've already resigned. Does he want me to *die* too? I'll soon deliver on that."

Golda's image around the world had grown to legendary proportions after the guns of the October war were silenced. She was acclaimed both in the United States and Western Europe as one of the most admired women in the world. The Dutch voted their own queen first in popularity and Golda second. The British, in December, 1973, skipped over their own queen (who was first in the two previous years) to vote Golda the woman they most admired. She achieved the same popularity in the United States.

Abroad, the war had made Golda Meir into a kind of superwoman, a woman with an image of invincibility, courage, guts. At home, however, her image had become distorted. In her memoirs, Golda was determined to remind the public of the accomplishments of her career.

Memoirs and a Broadway Play

Golda actually began work on her memoirs in the summer of 1973, but the war intervened and the project was set aside. Now that she decided to begin work on her memoirs once again, she picked Rinna Samuels to assist her. Rinna had impeccable credentials as a ghostwriter but she had a political background that might have seemed inappropriate for someone assisting in the preparation of Golda's memoirs.

Rinna Samuels was the daughter of a man who in the 1930s had been second-in-command to Vladimir Jabotinsky, Menachem Begin's mentor. Begin had long been Golda's political adversary, and some thought this would influence the objectivity of the ghostwriter's presentation. But Golda believed in Rinna's loyalty; to Golda loyalty was all that counted.

Indeed, Rinna's loyalty was beyond suspicion. So concerned was Rinna that someone might some day discover that Golda herself had not written the memoirs that she destroyed the original handwritten manuscript. She also refused to have her name appear in the book (*My Life*, 1975).

Ironically, the memoirs turned Golda Meir, the austere Socialist, into a wealthy woman. The lady who had once taken in school laundry back in the 1920s to make ends meet, the lady who as prime minister at times found herself in the embarrassing situation of being overdrawn at the bank, was now a woman of means.

"You must be a rich woman now," someone said to Golda in a New York hotel lobby in January of 1976, a few months after the publication of her memoirs.

"To tell you the truth," answered Golda, "I never asked." The acquisition of money had not changed Golda Meir.

Golda took much interest in a Broadway play, *Golda,* that was based on her memoirs. It was neither a critical success nor a source of much satisfaction to Golda. Although Golda had approval of playwright William Gibson's script, she was shocked in rehearsals to find that the actress chosen to play her, Anne Bancroft, was developing a characterization she considered distasteful. Instead of de-emphasizing the image created by her handling of the Yom Kippur War, Bancroft was portraying Golda as an old, ineffective woman unable to control her government.

Golda was not really interested in writing memoirs or overseeing a Broadway production of her life. Politics had been her life, and although she was now, in 1974, 76 years old, she wanted to continue to play a role in the affairs of the country she loved.

The Elder Statesman

Although political figures such as Yitzhak Rabin and Shimon Peres might have wished otherwise, in retirement Golda Meir continued to involve herself in affairs of state. The prestige she enjoyed enabled her to influence government policy. Unbeknownst to the public, she was extremely active behind the scenes.

Laboring under great strain to form a new government, Yitzhak Rabin, the new prime minister, reached out to the tiny Civil Rights Party headed by former Labor Party member Shulamit Aloni. Golda had long been scornful of Aloni's backbiting. She was horrified that Rabin would have the audacity to make his government dependent on Aloni for its survival.

Rabin, however, was more concerned about forming a workable Cabinet. When Golda realized that her effort to keep Shulamit Aloni out of Rabin's government had failed, she stalked out of a meeting of Labor Party leaders. Before departing, she told her close friend Chaim Gvati, "Don't you understand? They don't want to see us anymore."

On one occasion Golda learned that Rabin had yielded on the issue of the Christian Arab villagers of Birim and Ikrit. During the 1948 War of Independence a few hundred Christian Arabs had been temporarily evacuated by the Israeli Army with an explicit promise that they would be returned once the fighting was over. The promise was never kept. Despite villagers' petitions to Golda's government in 1972, she refused to repatriate them, fearful that their return would become a precedent for other Arabs.

When Golda realized that Rabin planned to reverse her longstanding decision, she acted promptly. It happened that Shmuel Toledano, Rabin's assistant for Arab affairs, had decided that the time was ripe to press the villagers' cause. The new prime minister had given some indication that he would be more sympathetic than his predecessors.

"Let's do Birim and Ikrit and be finished with it," Toledano urged Rabin a number of times in 1974 and 1975.

One day, after another Toledano attempt to convince the prime minister to permit the villagers to return to their homes, Rabin turned to him sharply: "I got a call from Golda. Leave it." And they did.

Golda was active on other political fronts as well. When Peres challenged Rabin for the prime ministership in February, 1977, Golda pleaded with Peres to withdraw for the sake of party unity. He refused and Rabin went on to win the nomination fight by a bare margin.

Rabin's downfall in April, 1977, resulting from the revelation that he had an illegal overseas bank account, upset Golda terribly. Rabin's political demise meant, in essence, the automatic ascendancy of Peres to the prime ministership. Elections were scheduled for May 17, and Golda assumed, as did most of the nation, that Labor would again triumph.

During the final eighteen months of her life, the changing political scene brought a good deal of sadness to Golda Meir. In the May, 1977 elections the voters finally turned out the Labor Party and installed a new party, the Likud Party, for the first time in the nation's history. Menachem Begin's rise to power seemed to be an expression of the electorate's desire to rid itself of ineffective, less than honest leaders. Golda understood this, but she was infuriated nonetheless. When Begin and his Likud Party selected Moshe Dayan as foreign minister and Dayan agreed to serve, she was further infuriated. In fact, so upset was Golda at Dayan for having abandoned Labor and for having joined the Begin camp that she, Golda, vowed to have no further contact with the man who had been her defense minister.

Dayan, for his part, could not understand Golda's sudden coolness. They had always been cordial toward one another.

One Saturday afternoon in the summer of 1977, Dayan phoned Golda to ask if he could visit her for a cup of coffee and some conversation, as they had done so often in the past. She put him off, stating accurately that she was expecting a visit from family.

A few months later Dayan again made his request, and again Golda Meir begged off, giving the same reason. Dayan never phoned her again.

The Sadat Saga

Golda could never have imagined that Egyptian President Anwar Sadat would ever agree to visit Jerusalem, as he did in November 1977. She did not believe the Arabs really wanted peace with Israel, nor did she believe that they would be willing to have direct negotiations with Israel. She had, after all, spent much time during her prime ministership trying to establish a relationship with Sadat, and here, Begin, being in office only five months was able to bring Sadat to Jerusalem.

Golda could not believe that Sadat was sincere. She was also resentful of Begin. She had invested so much energy to establish peace and Begin was reaping the benefits.

Sadat himself acknowledged regret over not having been able to negotiate

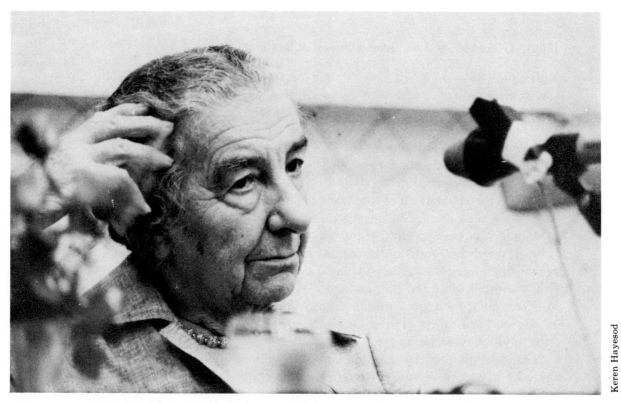

Ascent to power. Just a few months before a political revolution of sorts had occurred in Israel: the coming to power of Menachem Begin. Golda had always thought Begin, with his hard-line policies, would lead Israel to the brink of war once he assumed the prime ministership. But in November, 1977, Sadat's visit to Jerusalem made peace with Egypt suddenly possible, and Begin became a different politician.

with Golda Meir. In a *New York Times* interview (January, 1977) he was quoted as saying that he had "wanted to deal with her, although she was Israel's biggest hawk. She wasn't scared to face anyone when she was convinced." And again, in an interview with *Time* magazine shortly after his Jerusalem visit, Sadat insisted that he preferred to deal with the "Old Lady. She has guts, really."

Golda believed that Sadat's visit to Jerusalem was the act of a master politician, that he was successful in hoodwinking Menachem Begin and the entire Israeli nation. Her deep mistrust of the Arabs did not permit her to become excited about Sadat's seeming change of heart.

Golda was visiting the United States when Sadat announced plans to visit Israel. It would be almost unthinkable for her to be away while Sadat was in Israel, yet the opening of the Broadway play *Golda* was scheduled for mid-November, and Golda wanted to attend that as well.

"You must go home," urged Simcha Dinitz, who was also in New York.

"Why?" she asked. "I'm not a member of the government. I'm just a simple citizen. Nobody will miss me."

Disagreeing, Dinitz suggested, "History will miss you if you don't go." Golda agreed, but before leaving for Israel she told playwright William Gibson, "Sadat will come and make a beautiful impression, and leave us looking bad." Then she added, "It's very dangerous for us."

Back in Jerusalem, witnessing the joyful spirit that gripped the city, Golda said, "What's all this Messianic euphoria! When General [Aharon] Yariv went to Kilometer 101 [for post-Yom Kippur War disengagement talks with Egypt], people were also talking as though the Egyptian officers coming to talk to him were the Messiah. I said then, 'I've got one Messiah, and when he comes he's not going to stop at Kilometer 101 or otherwise qualify his coming.'"

Jihan Sadat, the Egyptian president's wife, gave her husband some advice before he departed for Israel. She suggested that he mind his manners, particularly with Golda Meir.

As Anwar Sadat's airplane was about to touch Israeli soil, onlookers at the airport saw an unusual sight: on the receiving line waiting to greet the Egyptian leader stood ex-Prime Minister Golda Meir. As Sadat neared Golda, she asked him, "Why didn't you tell me when I was prime minister that you wanted to come to Jerusalem? I would have had you here in a moment."

Somewhat irrelevantly, Sadat answered, "But I didn't ask you to resign."

Returning from the airport, Golda reported to friends that her brief encounter with the Egyptian leader had been friendly. "He's not as ugly as I thought," she observed jokingly.

A question arose about that first confrontation between Golda and Anwar Sadat. Did he place a kiss on her cheek? "No," said Sadat, "but I would not have been ashamed if I did." When Golda was asked, she replied, "Not on your life. It was the fellow [an Israeli Arab] next to me [whom Sadat] kissed."

The hard-line taken by Sadat in his speech before the Knesset, the highlight of the visit, left Golda disturbed. Sadat had come across as sincerely interested in opening a new chapter in relations with the State of Israel. Could he be trusted?

she asked herself. And if he could be, would the commitments made by him be honored by his successors?

Greeting the "Old Lady." President Anwar Sadat of Egypt greets Golda upon his arrival at Ben-Gurion Airport near Tel Aviv on November 19, 1977. Next to Golda is Chief of Staff Mordechai Gur and Yitzhak Rabin. Golda seriously doubted Sadat's sincerity about wanting peace with Israel. She died less than four months before the signing of the Israel-Egypt Peace Treaty in March, 1979.

On the day following Sadat's Knesset speech, the Egyptian leader met with political leaders. The affair was carried live on Israeli television and beamed around the world. Golda's banter with Sadat ranked as one of the memorable moments of the Egyptian president's visit.

Golda rose to the occasion with a touch of grand theater. She chided Sadat for calling her the "Old Lady" and praised him for *zechut rishonim*, "the privilege of being the first," inasmuch as he was the first Arab leader to come to Israel and say, "Let us have peace."

She spoke eloquently about Israeli mothers and Egyptian mothers who would benefit from his initiative. "Of course we all must realize," she continued, "that the path to peace may be a little bit difficult, but not as difficult as the path to war."

Israel, she assured Sadat, who was seated next to her and was listening intently, was prepared for territorial compromise, but on condition that its new borders would "give us security."

She ended with a plea: "Let us at least conclude one thing, the beginning that you have made, with such courage and with such hope for peace—let us decide one thing—it must go on, face-to-face between us and between you so that even an old lady like I am will live to see the day . . . You always called me an old lady . . . "

At this point, Sadat burst into laughter and offered, "Yes, I did call you an old lady!"

Famous meeting. **Sadat and Golda during their meeting in the Knesset on November 21, 1977. Shimon Peres is seated next to Sadat. It was at this encounter that Golda joked with the Egyptian leader over his referring to her as the "Old Lady." Golda urged Sadat to follow up his visit with further efforts to bring about peace between their two countries.**

"We will live to see the day," Golda continued, "whoever signs on the part of Israel, I want to see that day of peace between you and us, of peace between all our neighbors and us."

But Golda was haunted by the feeling that the Sadat visit was more performance than serious business. When asked for a reaction to the suggestion that Sadat and Begin be nominated for the next Nobel Peace Prize, she turned the question around and replied, "I don't know about the Nobel Prize, but they certainly deserve an Oscar."

Normalization. Dr. Eliahu Ben-Eliassar (left), the new Israeli ambassador to Egypt, meets Sa'ad Mortada, the new Egyptian ambassador to Israel, at Ben-Gurion Airport near Tel Aviv on February 24, 1980. The two men were on their way to take up their posts when they met quite by chance. The exchange of ambassadors was one of the first concrete illustrations of the normalization that was to take place between Israel and Egypt as part of the peace treaty the two countries signed in March, 1979.

Clarifying the Record

Watching the peace process unfold, Golda was deeply hurt by the criticism that she had missed opportunities for peace dating back to 1971. It wounded her when she heard critics allege that with a little more resourcefulness and flexibility on her part Sadat might have visited Israel much sooner.

She wanted to set the record straight. How could she accomplish this? At first Golda thought that Israel Galili, her closest political adviser, could write an article for the Israeli press. However, Golda soon realized that Galili, although a master of the written word and adept at articulating policy, would not capture the attention of the press sufficiently. She therefore quietly abandoned the idea.

But Golda persisted. She decided that she herself would face her critics and present the facts. If she could bring the proper evidence to light, she was convinced that her critics would be disarmed and silenced. There was one sticking point: so much of what Golda wanted to reveal was classified information.

Golda's mind was reeling with thoughts that had been brewing for years. But now, with Sadat's visit over, Golda believed it was time for her to act. Begin was taking too much credit for a peace process that had begun in her time; that was in fact her idea. Rather than being praised, Golda was now being blamed for having erected obstacles to peace.

Golda began to consider making her ideas known through a press conference. She knew that she might be the victim of backlash, however. She was in retirement, after all, and the country might find her assessment of history less than relevant. Despite her continued prestige in Israel and around the world, her charges might be construed as the carping of an old, sickly lady.

Golda would have to take that risk. She could not permit history to be distorted by either Mr. Begin or his associates.

What Golda Meir had set for herself was not an easy task. Before a press conference could be called, much work would have to be done. Documents would have to be located and studied; dates and events would have to be reviewed and verified; former aides would have to be asked to track down all pertinent material. Although the task would be large, there was no doubt in Golda Meir's mind that she could do it. Her wound was too deep to go untended.

Golda was determined to disprove the charge that as far back as 1971 she had not taken advantage of peace overtures that had been made. She would show the Egyptians to be deceitful, cagey, unworthy of trust. The truth could be found in the documents of that time. They would expose the Egyptian pledges to engage in sincere negotiations as a sham. Armed with the documents, she would be able to prove beyond a doubt that had Israel begun negotiations at that time, it would have been at a distinct disadvantage.

The preparations for the press conference did not go smoothly. For one thing, Menachem Begin's permission was required to search out the necessary documents. The prime minister was slow in granting the necessary approval. Furthermore, 1978 took its toll on Golda physically. She was frequently in pain, frequently hospitalized. Making arrangements for the press conference required a great deal of energy, energy that she did not have to spare. The deadly cancer was slowly taking her life.

Few people knew of Golda's planned press conference. Among them were Israel Galili and Eli Mizrachi, who had been the director of Golda's bureau during the prime minister's term of office. Golda asked Mizrachi to gather all necessary documents. Yonah, Golda's nephew, also knew about the plan. His shrewdness and perceptiveness had always been admired by his aunt. Among family members, excepting her children, Golda relied more for counsel on Yonah than anyone else.

Some time after Golda Meir entered Hadassah Hospital in Jerusalem for the last time, on October 19, 1978, she, Galili, and Mizrachi held a bedside chat in which they discussed the press conference. Upon leaving, Galili and Mizrachi agreed that as long as Golda remained in the hospital, little could be done.

Time was fast running out. To Yonah, it became increasingly evident that Golda was dying. He placed a telephone call to Galili, asking him to arrange for the press conference promptly, even if it had to be held at her bedside. Although theoretically in agreement with Yonah's idea, Galili felt that to hold a press

Carol Gootter

In 1976, private citizen Golda Meir acknowledges the good wishes of the Israeli public.

conference under the circumstances would not only be insensitive but unwise. It was agreed to leave the decision to Golda.

The decision would never be made. On Friday, December 8, at 4:30 P.M., Golda Meir died. Her fifteen-year bout with cancer was at an end.

The doctors revealed to a shocked public that Golda had been suffering from a malignant lymphoma that four months earlier had spread to her bones. Finally, her liver was affected, which resulted in jaundice.

To the very end Golda's mind was sharp, her curiosity about politics and people not stilled. Of all her fears, one of the most persistent had been that one day she would enter the dark world of senility, just as her mother and her sister Sheyna had. To Golda, physical handicaps were not degrading, but to lose one's capacity to think was inconceivable.

Golda Meir, the uncrowned queen of Israel, was lucid to the very end.

Index